AUTO

BODY

COLLISION

SHANNON

AUTO
BODY
COLLISION

SHANNON
EBNER

A U T O

Y　C O

I O N

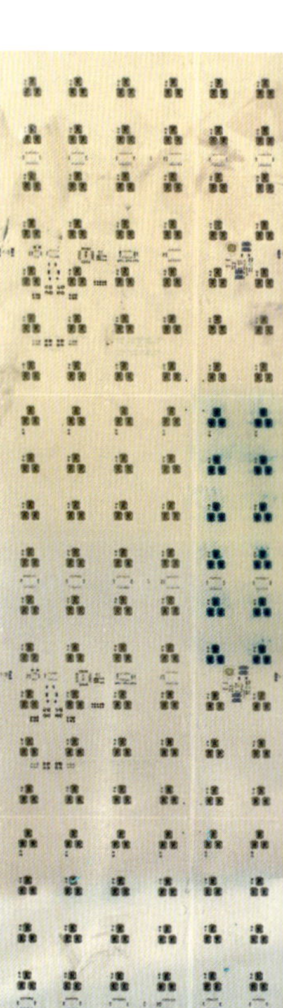

BOD
LLIS

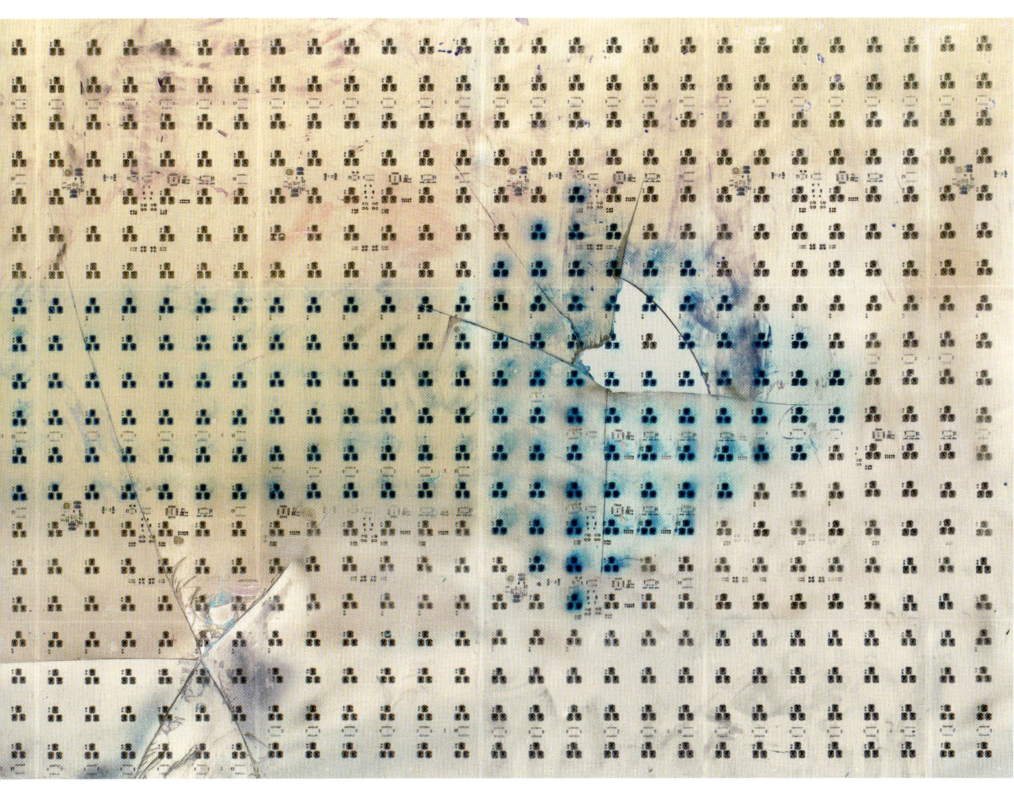

A M E R
S T O
L L I S

I C A '

P C O

I O N

STAN OVID

D E P R

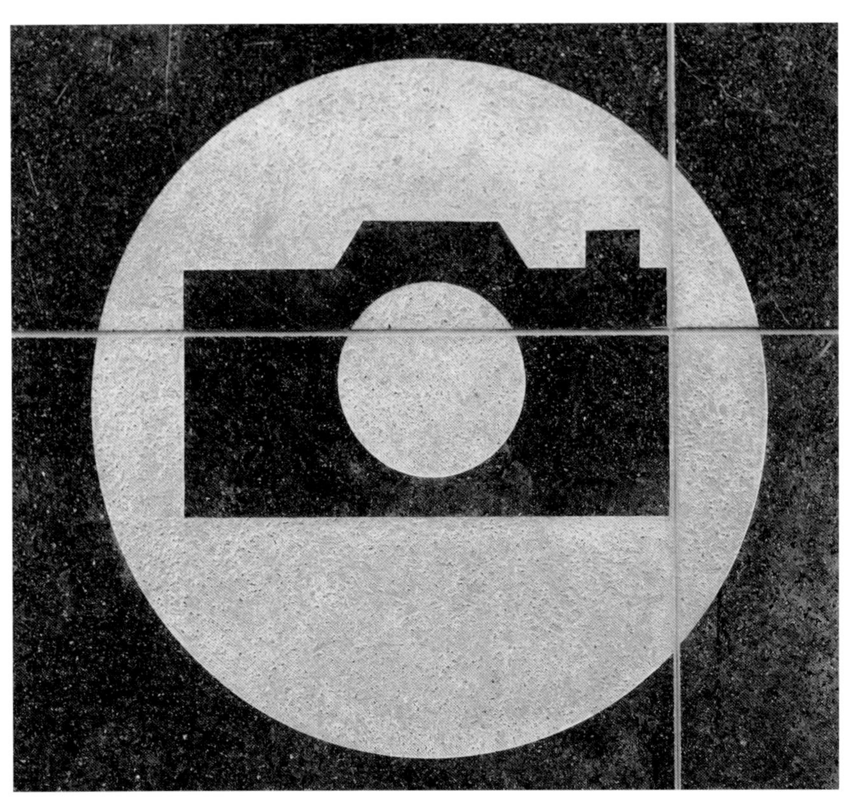

C O L L

N   R E

I S I O

P A I R

A S T

R A

A T O R

E N E R

ARTE

RADI

ATOR

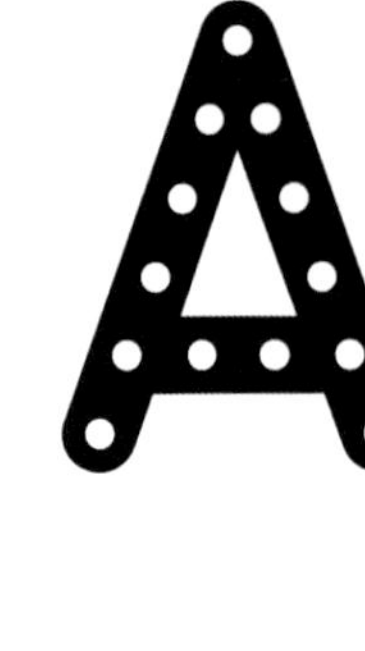 A L 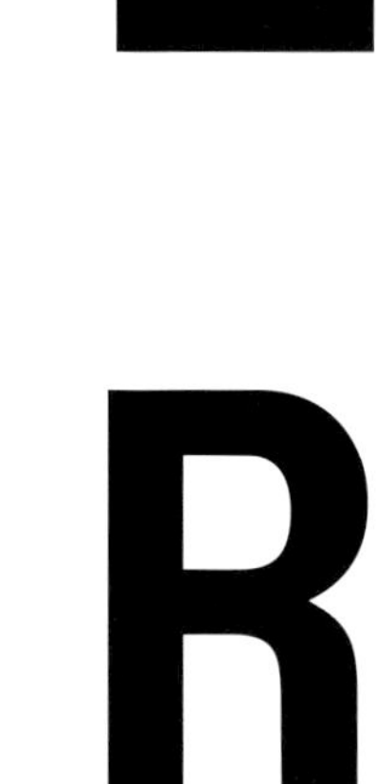

A T O R

O M P U

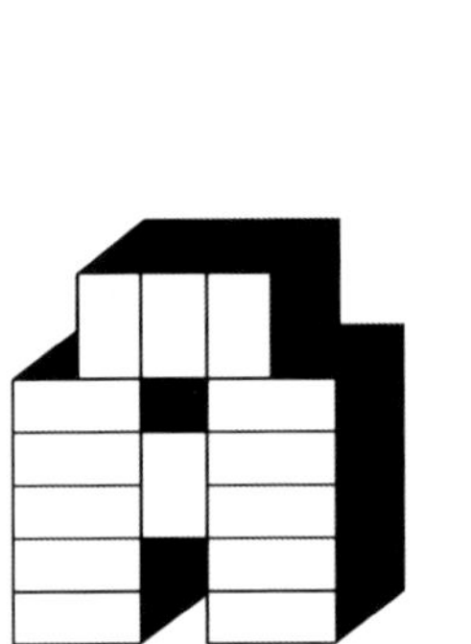 C E

TERN

C

TER

NTER

A O I

A B R

A S H

A C H

L

AKE

OCK

ANGE

A

T R

I

S S I

D I A

I S

A N S M

O N

G N O S

A S O

Ā I

T I O N

O N D I

C I A L

N J E C

C

T I O N

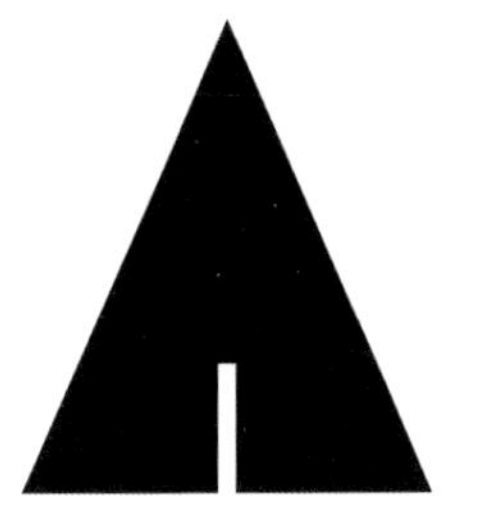

S E

L F

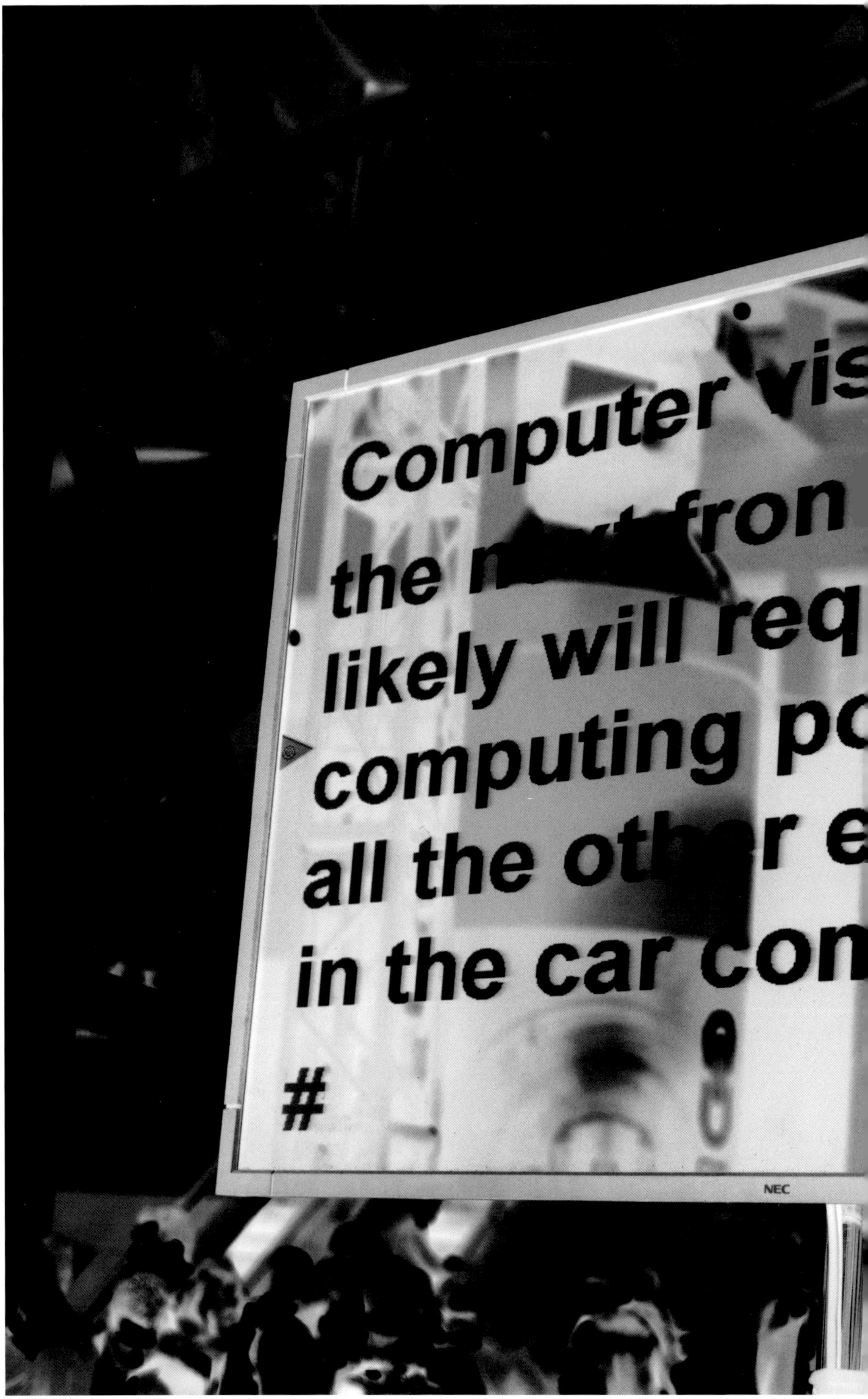

Computer vis
the n   fron
likely will req
computing po
all the oth r e
in the car con

#

NEC

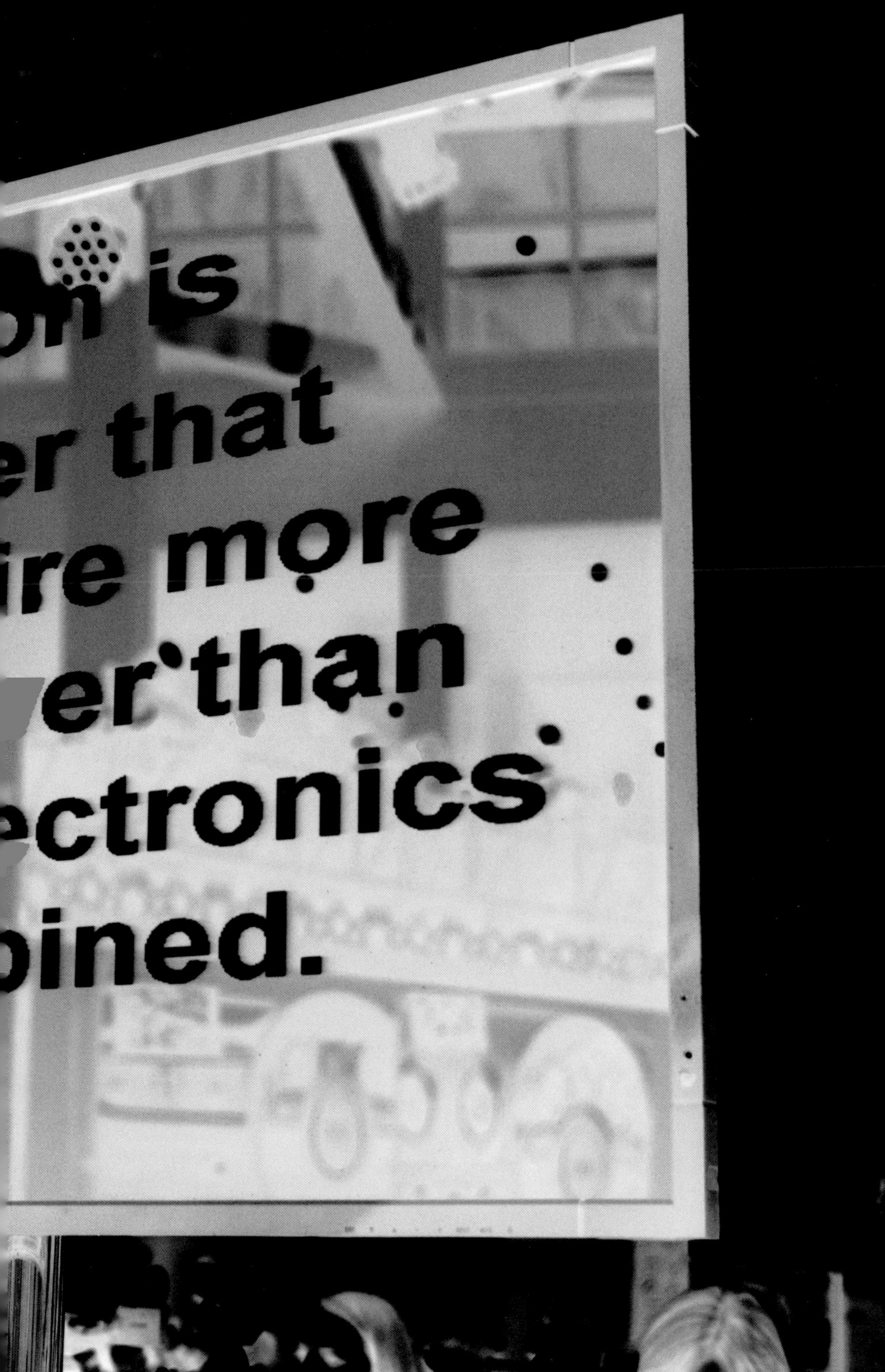
on is
er that
ire more
er than
ectronics
bined.

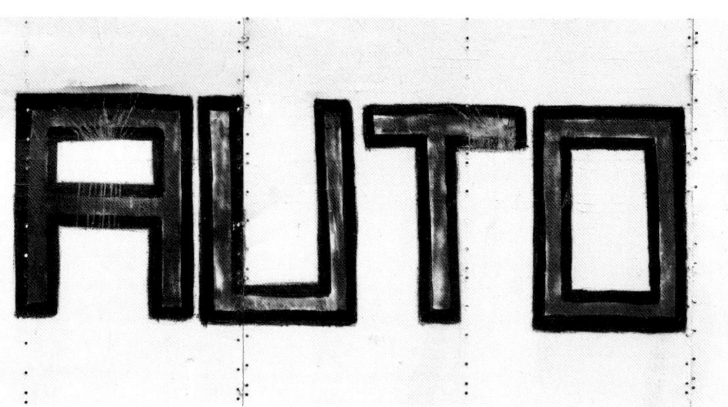
AUTO
MOTIVE

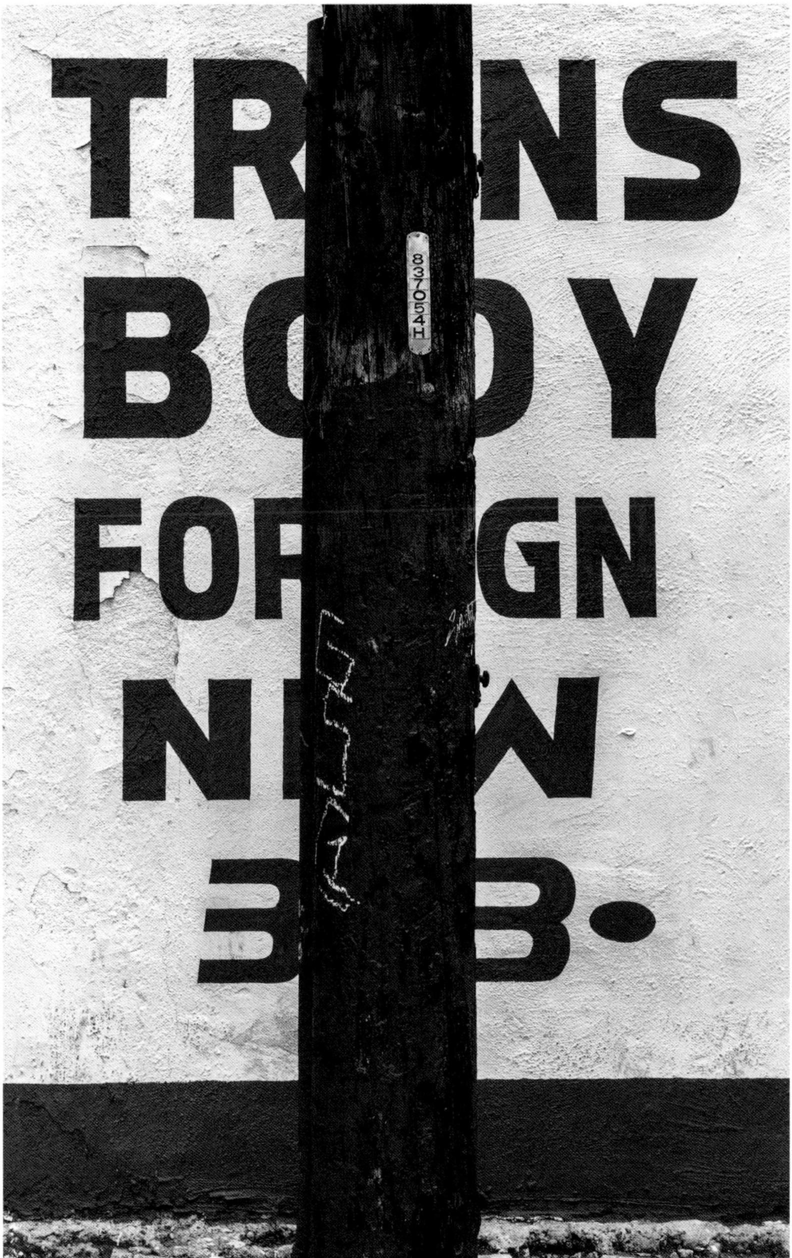
TR NS
BO Y
FOR GN
N W
3 B.
837054H

C L A I

A N D L

M S   H

I N G

E L E C

S C O P

T R O
E

F R E E

L I S I

O N S U

T S

COL
ON L
O N C
LTAN

N E T W

H A V E

E   D A

ORK

SOM

MAGE

T R A I

T E C H

A N S

NED
NICI

SETS

EVER

DEL

F O R

Y   M O

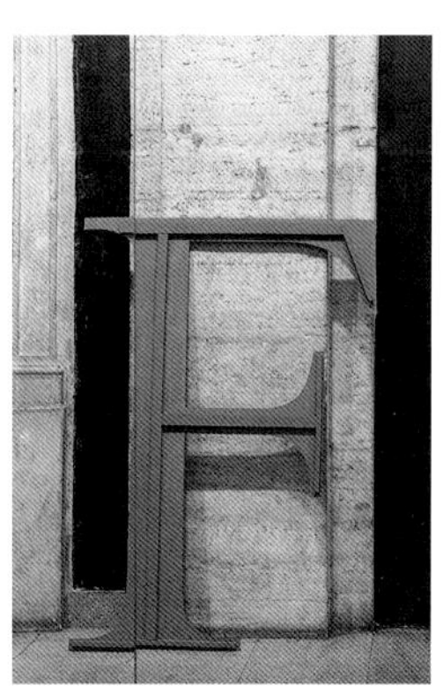
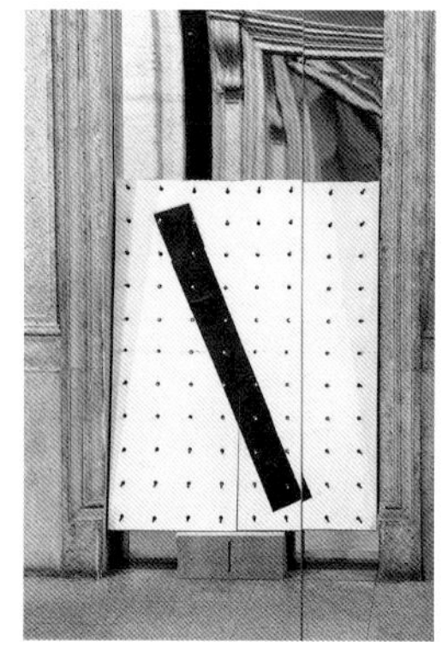
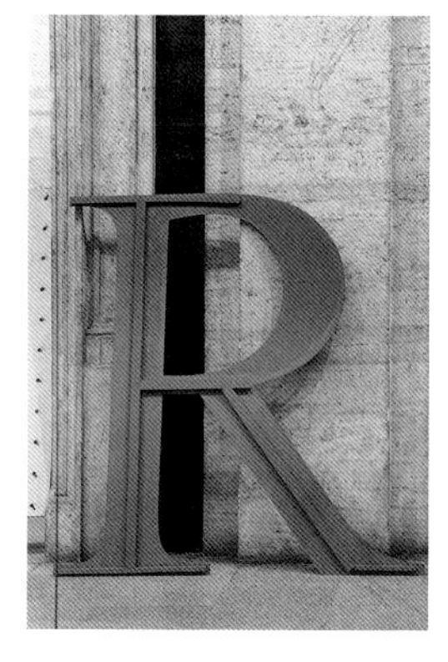
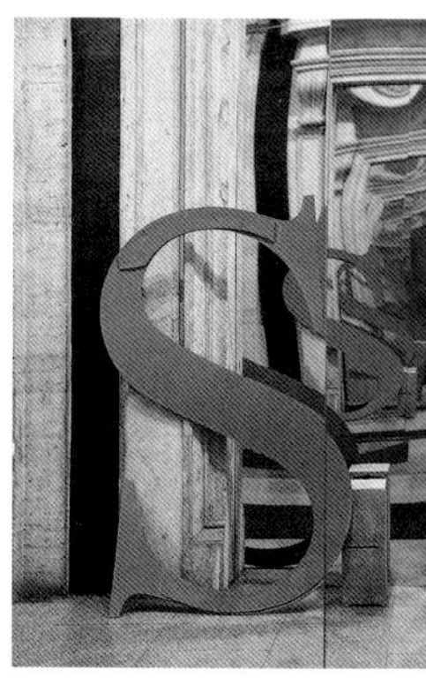
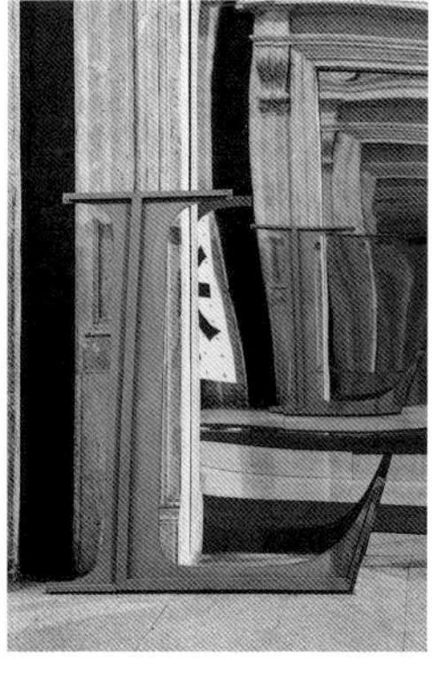
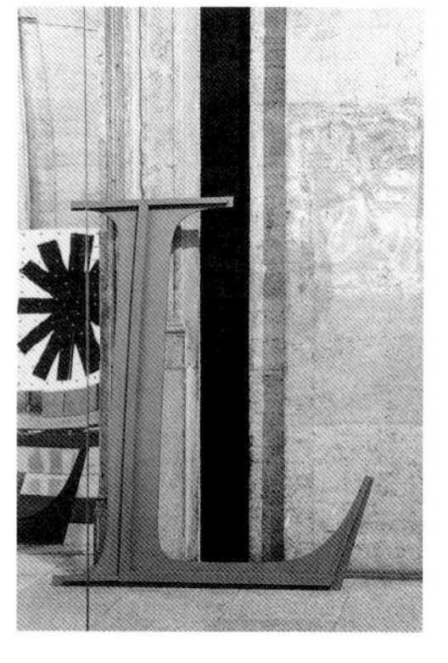
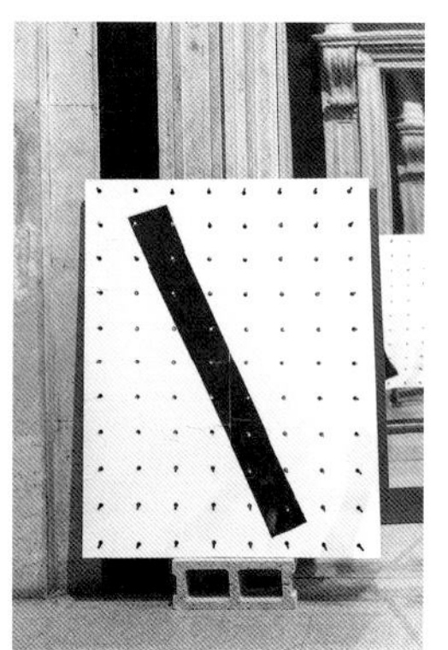
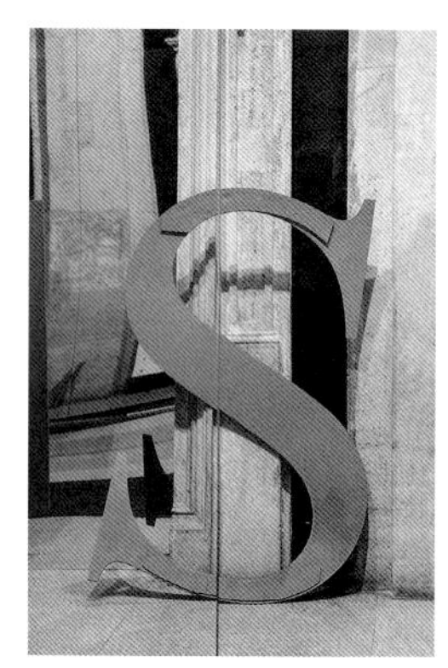
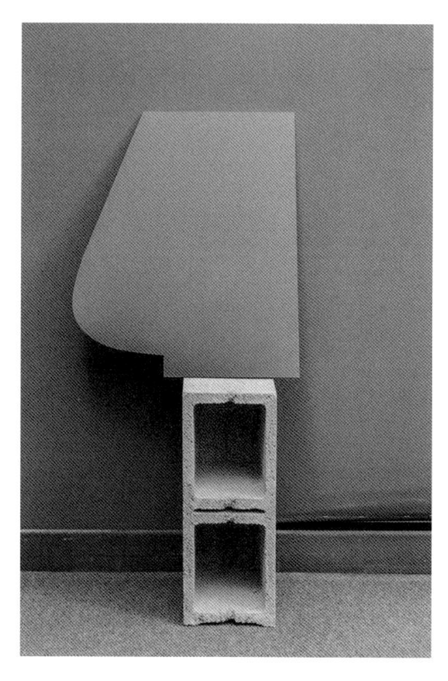

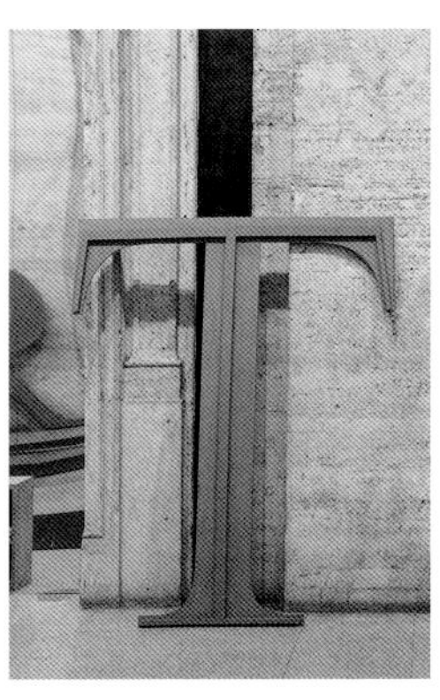
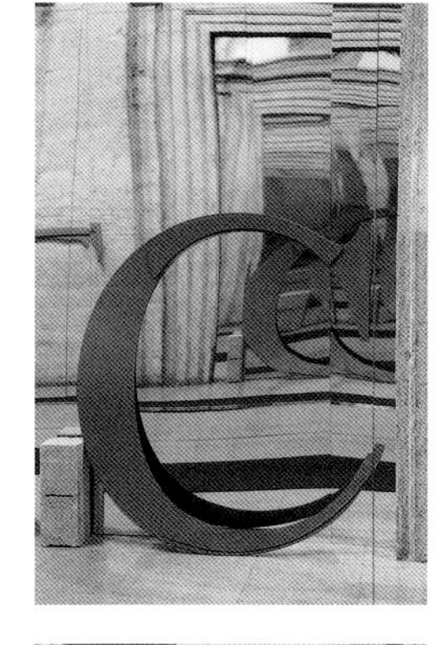
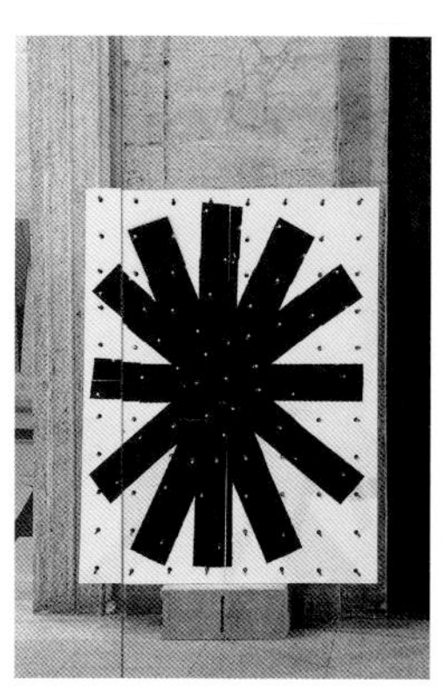
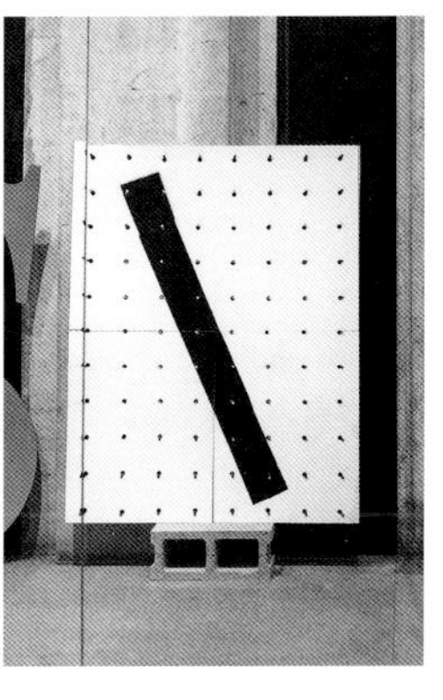
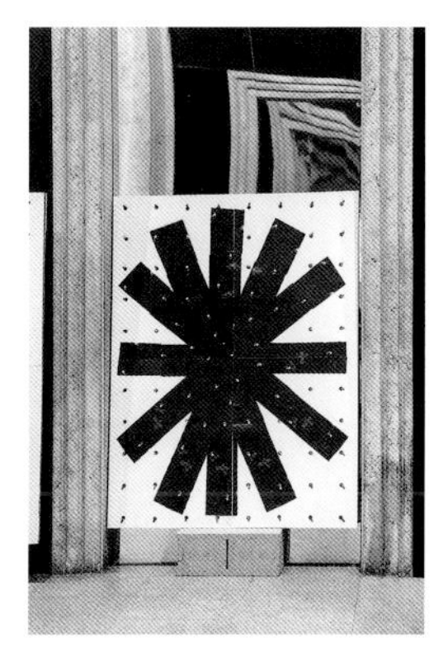
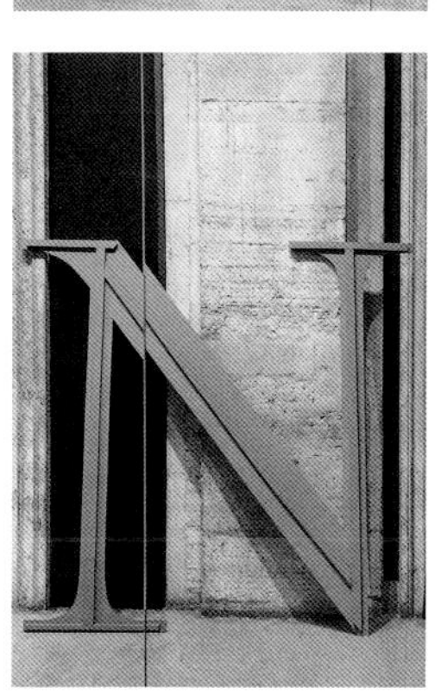
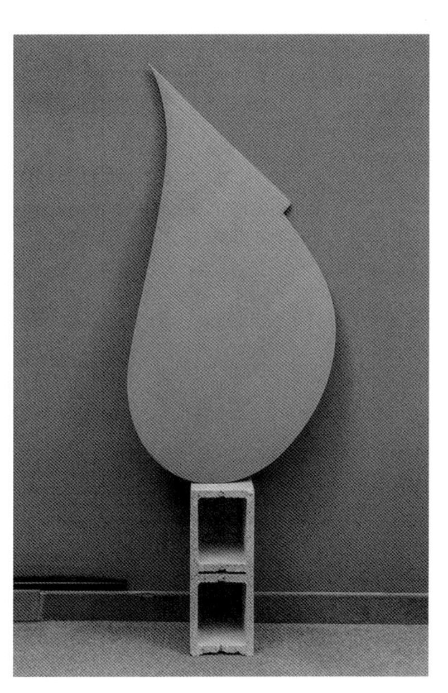
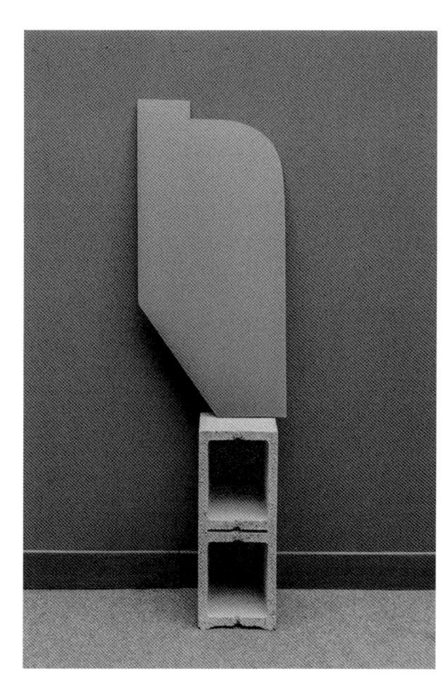

LARG

AME

IGHT

G

E F R

S T R A

E N I N

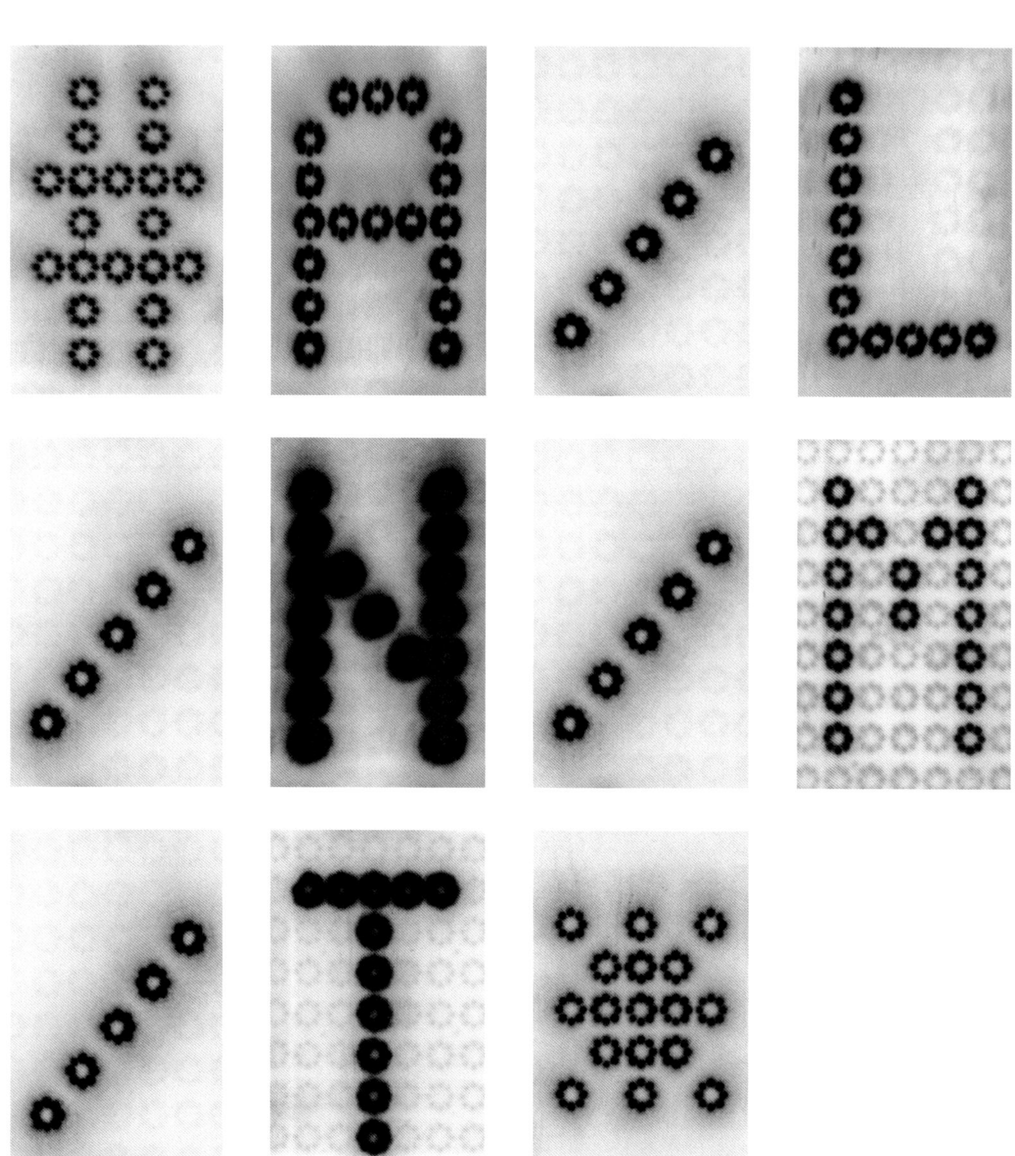

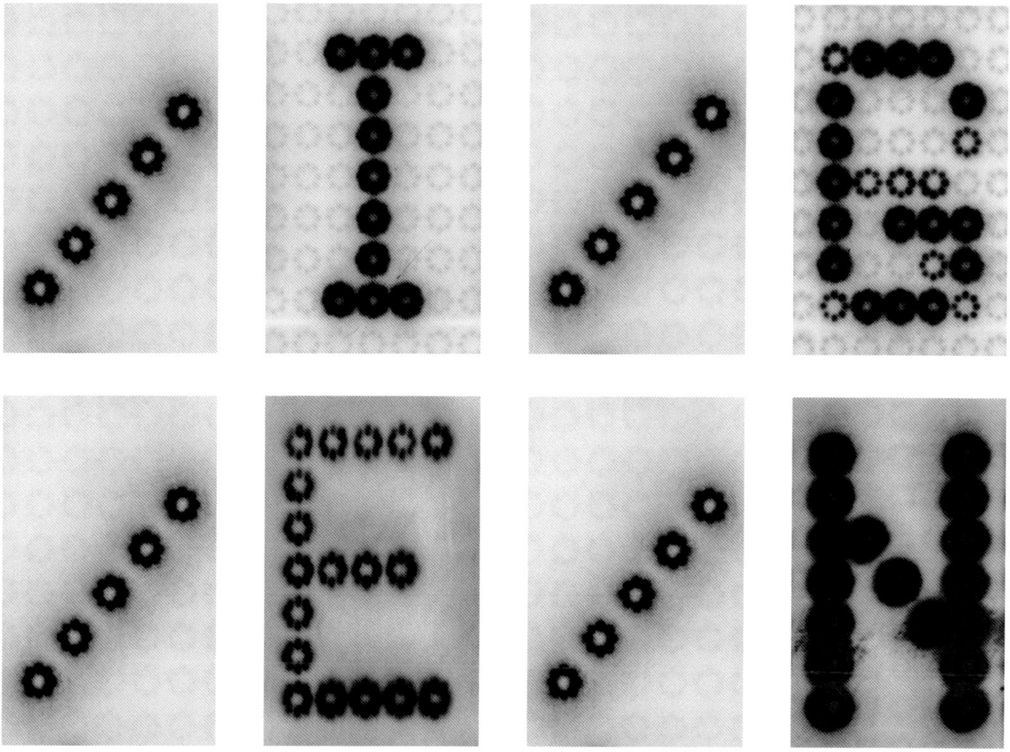

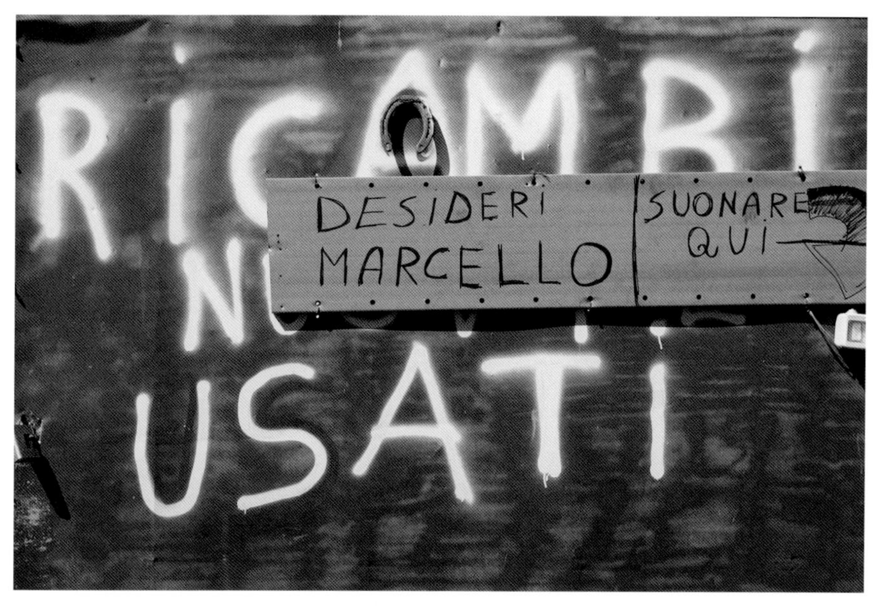

RICAMBI
N
USATI
DESIDERI
MARCELLO
SUONARE
QUI

S P E E

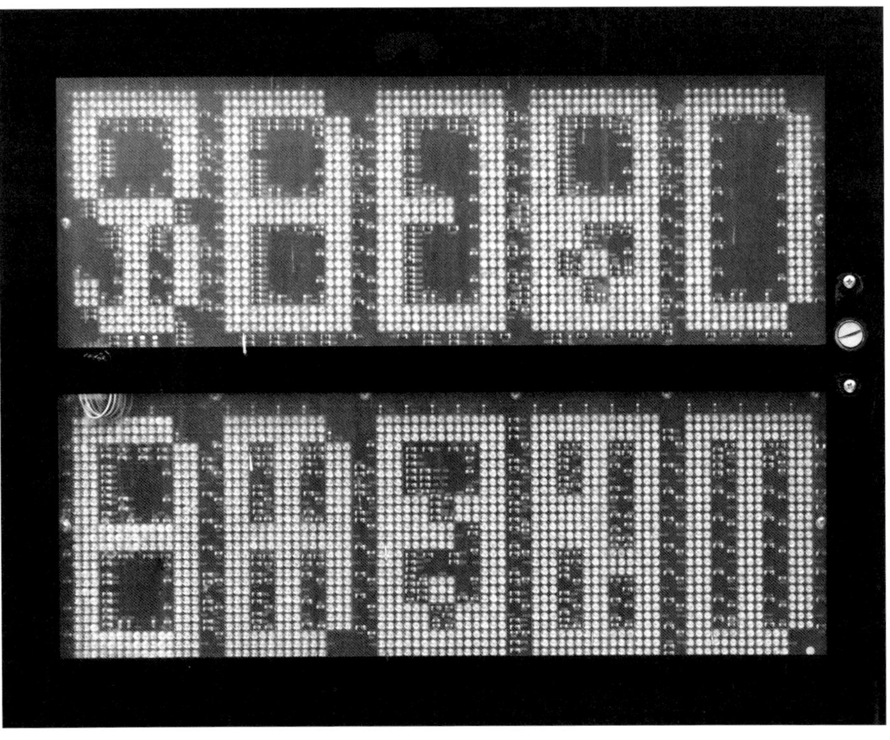

D

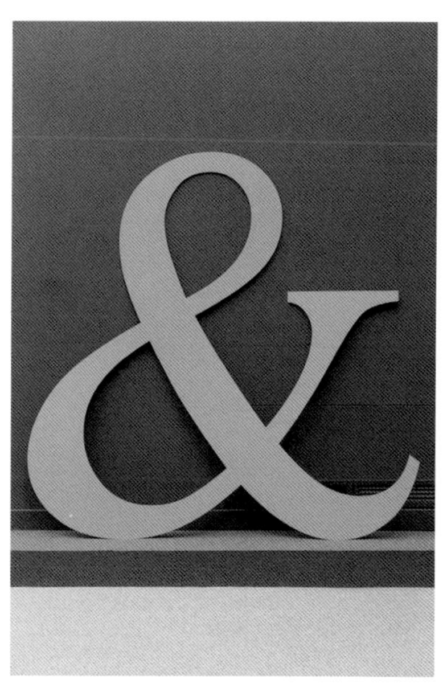

S U S P
O N

E N S I

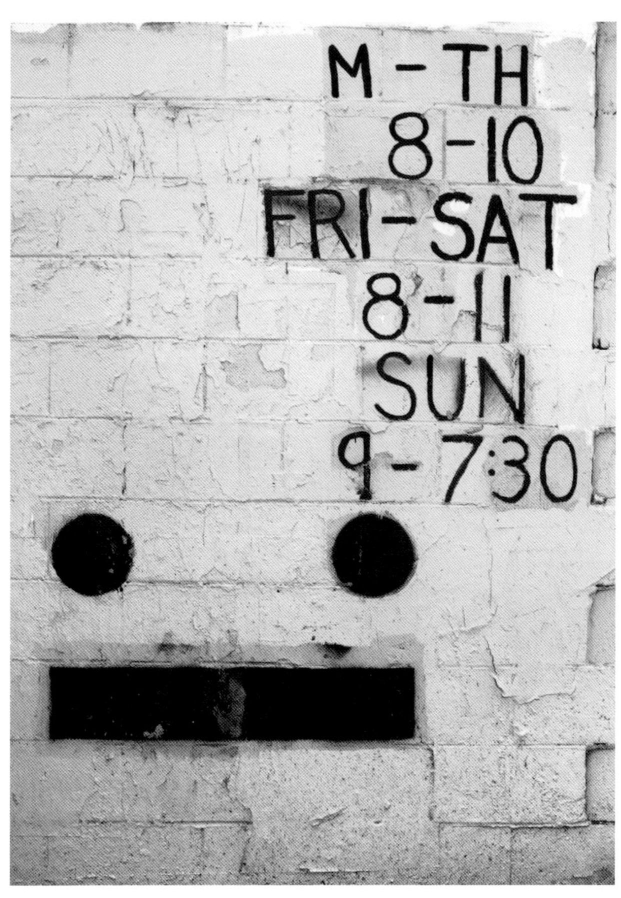

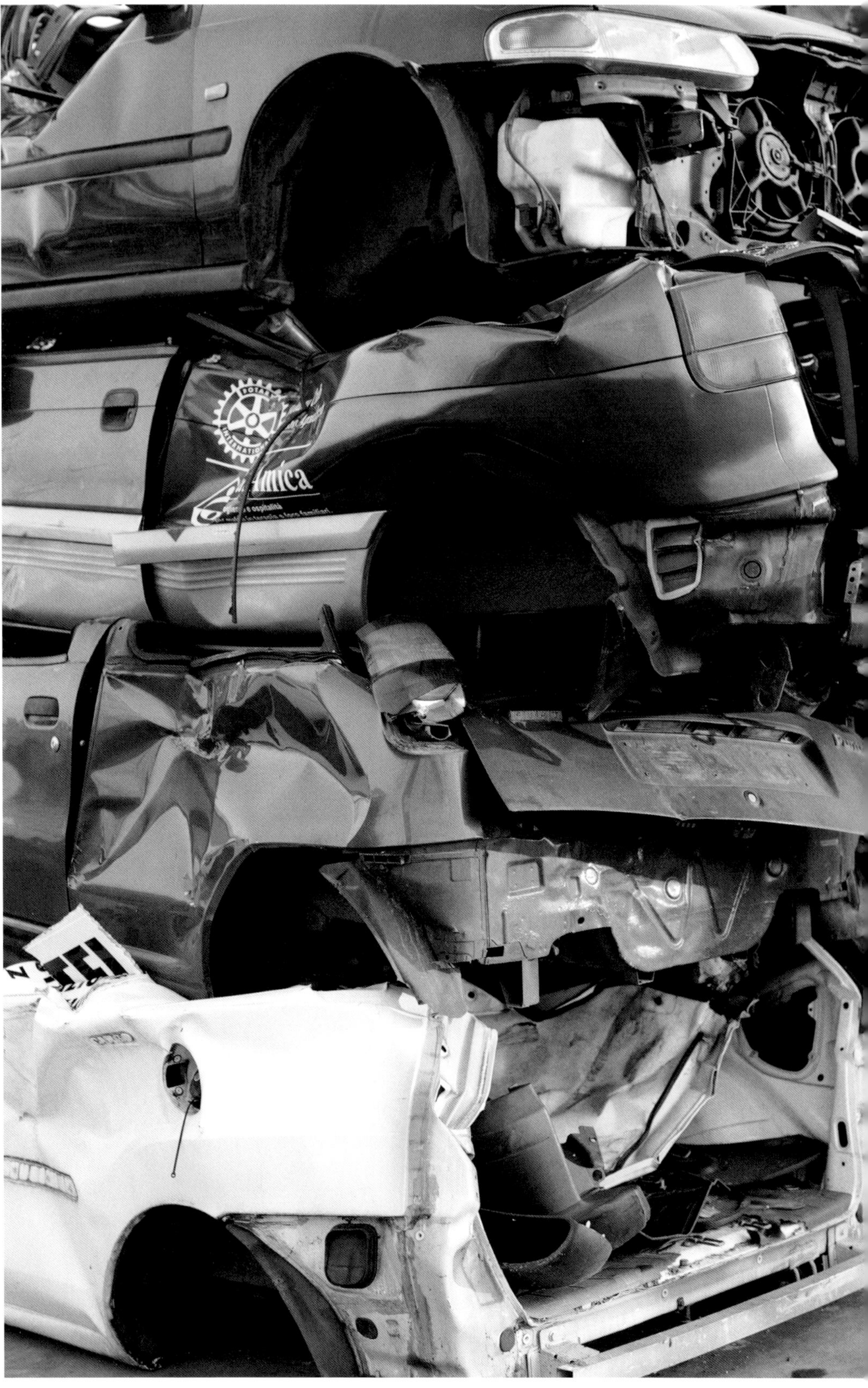

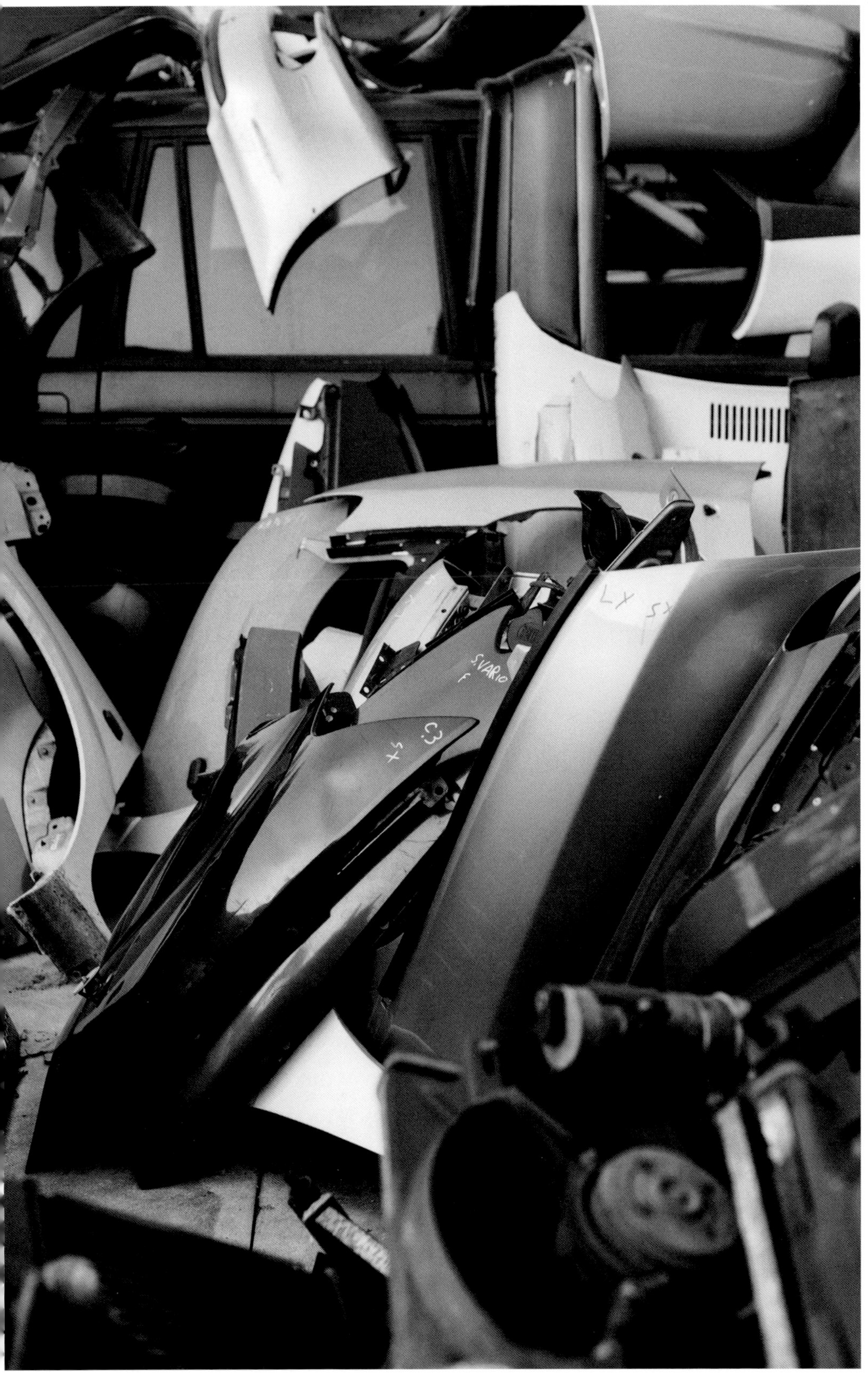

LY
SVARIO
F
C3

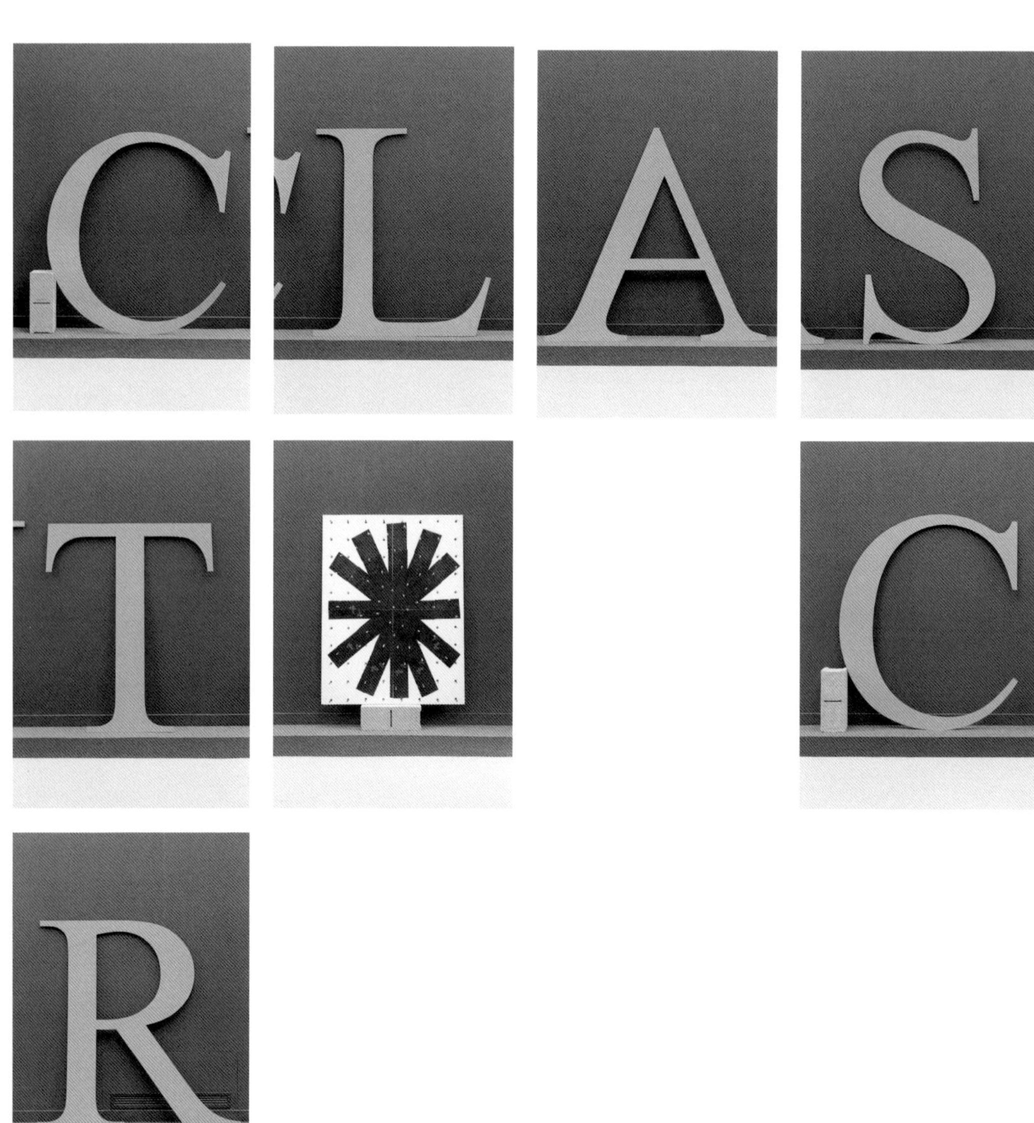

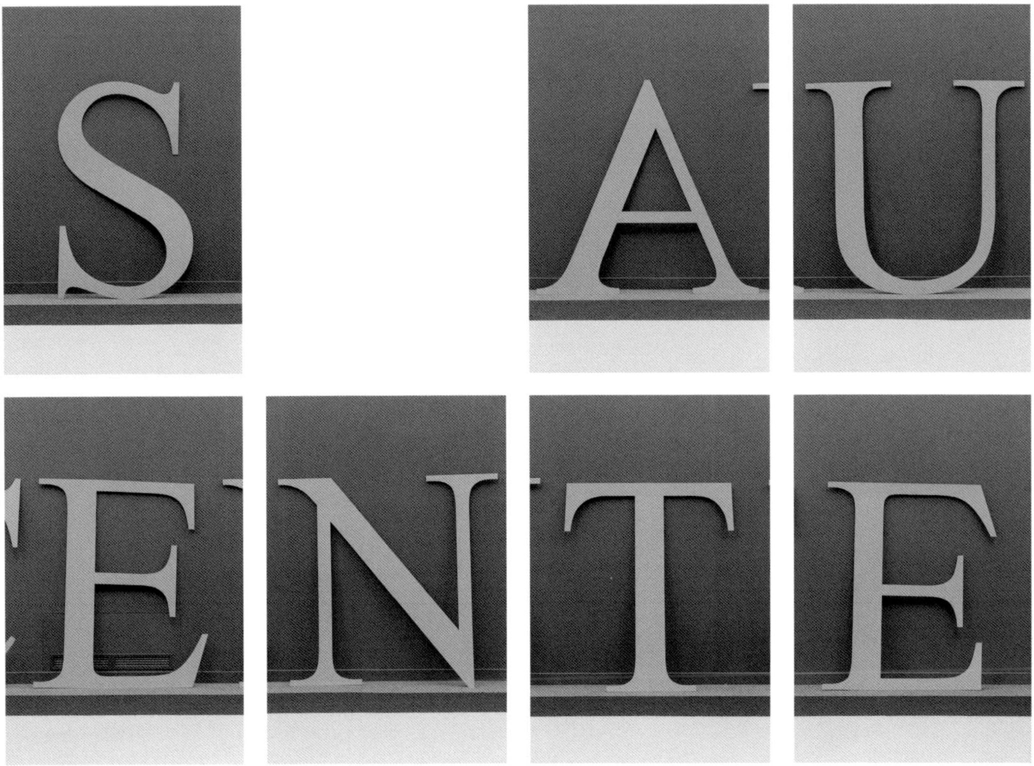

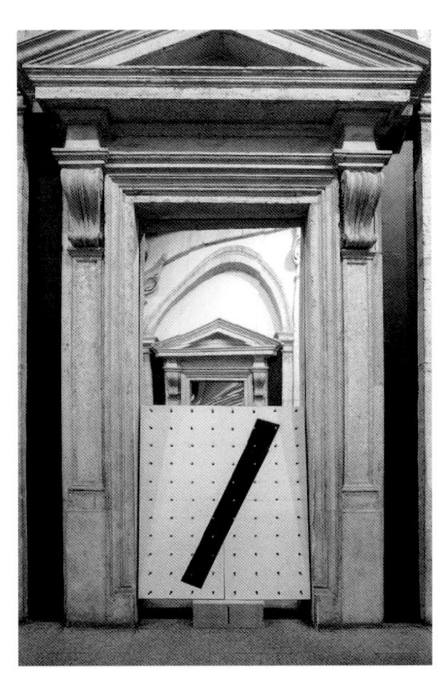

P E R F

A C C I

S

O R M

D E N T

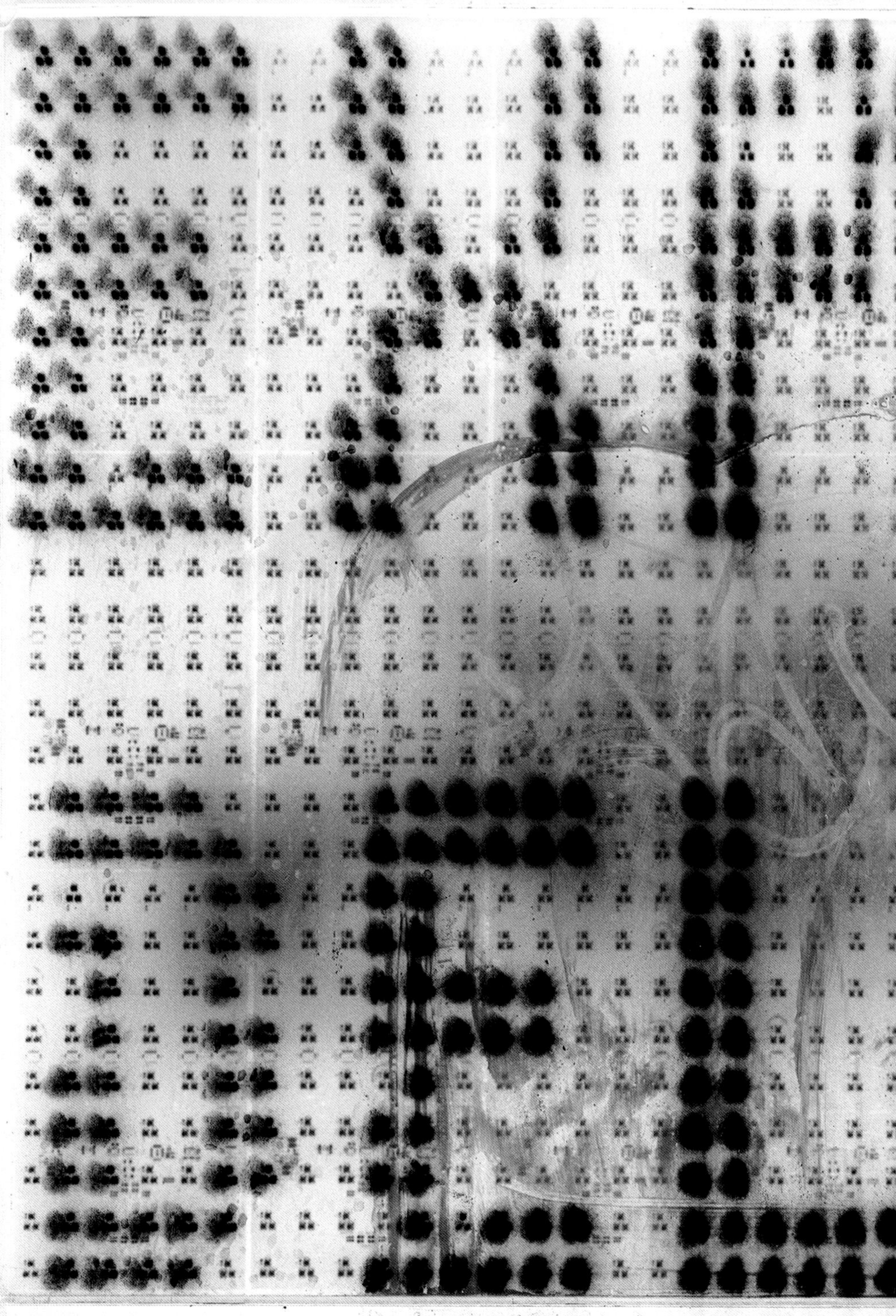

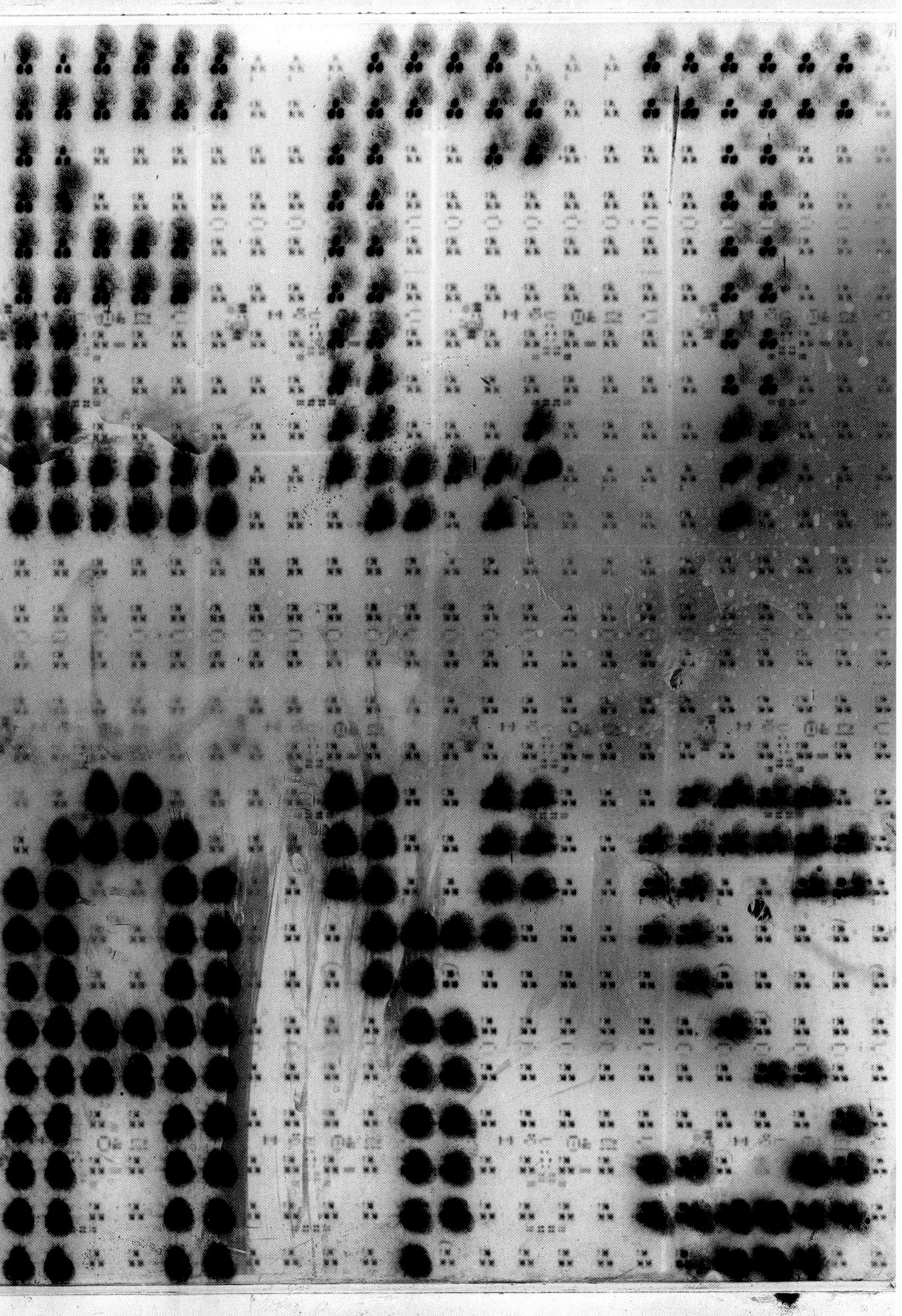

H A P P

N D

E N   A

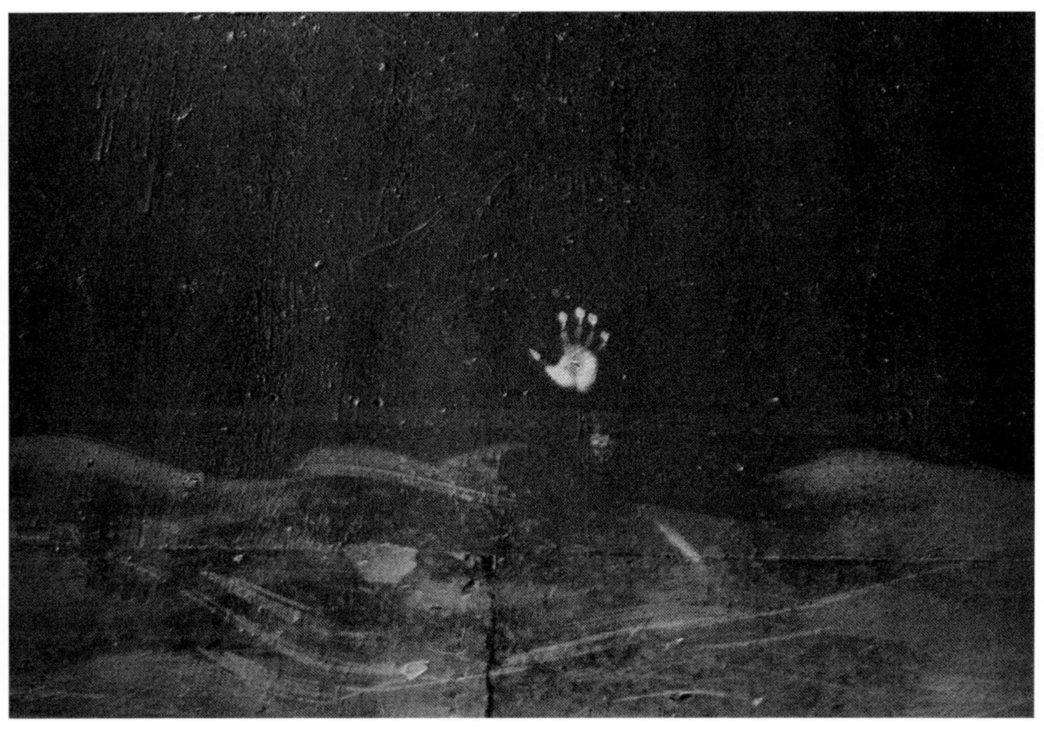

DELI

EXO

REPA

C A T E

T I C

I R S

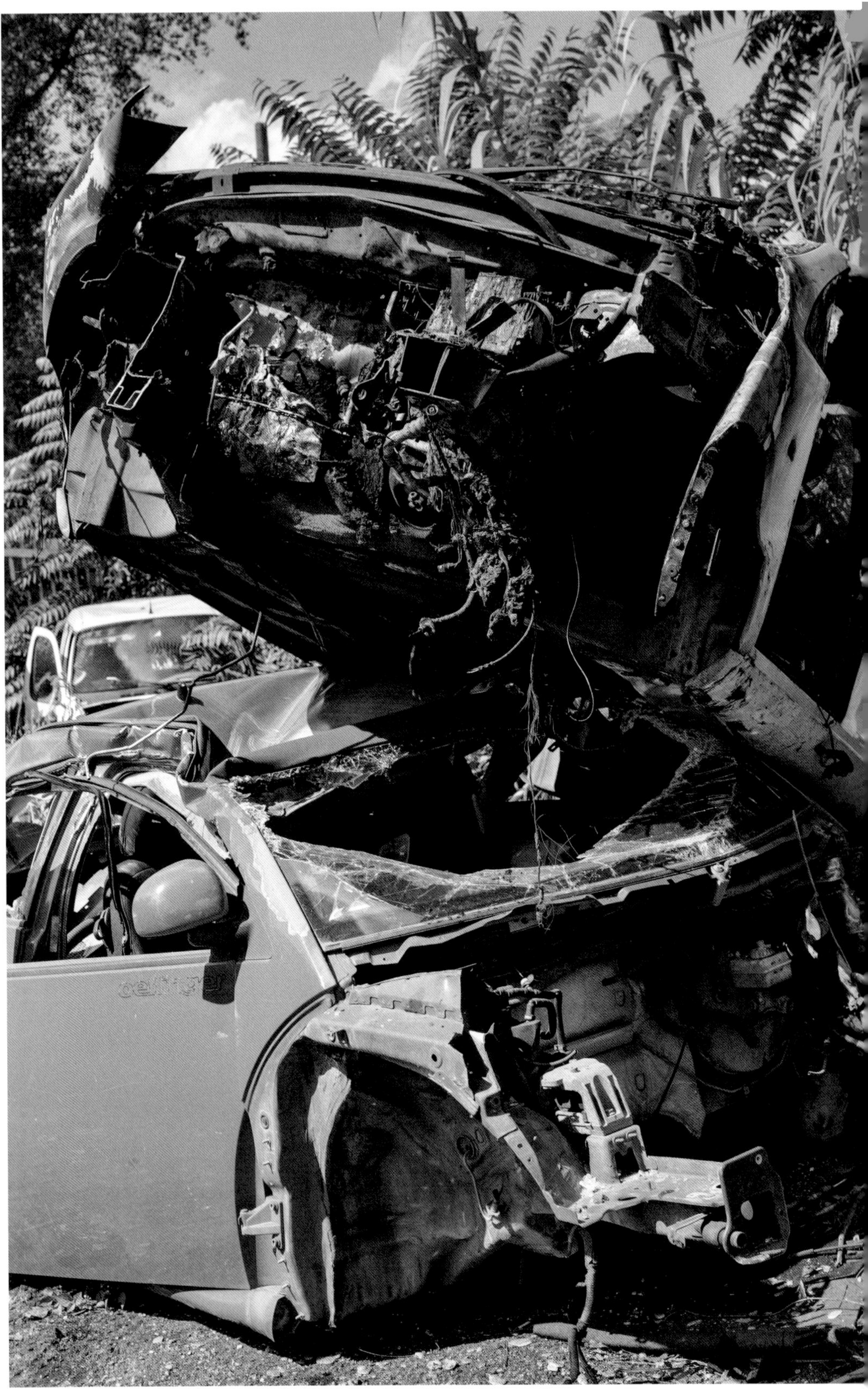

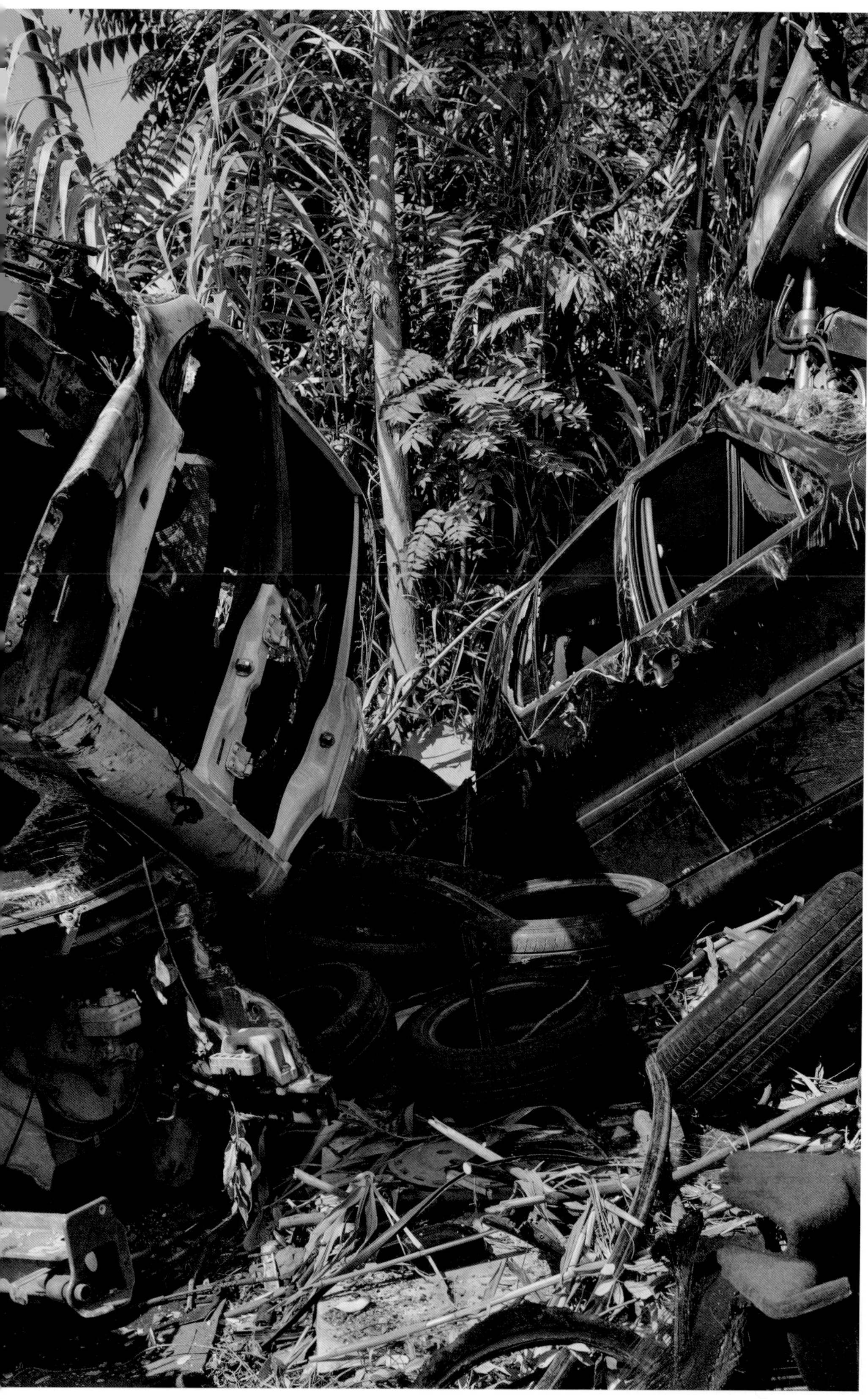

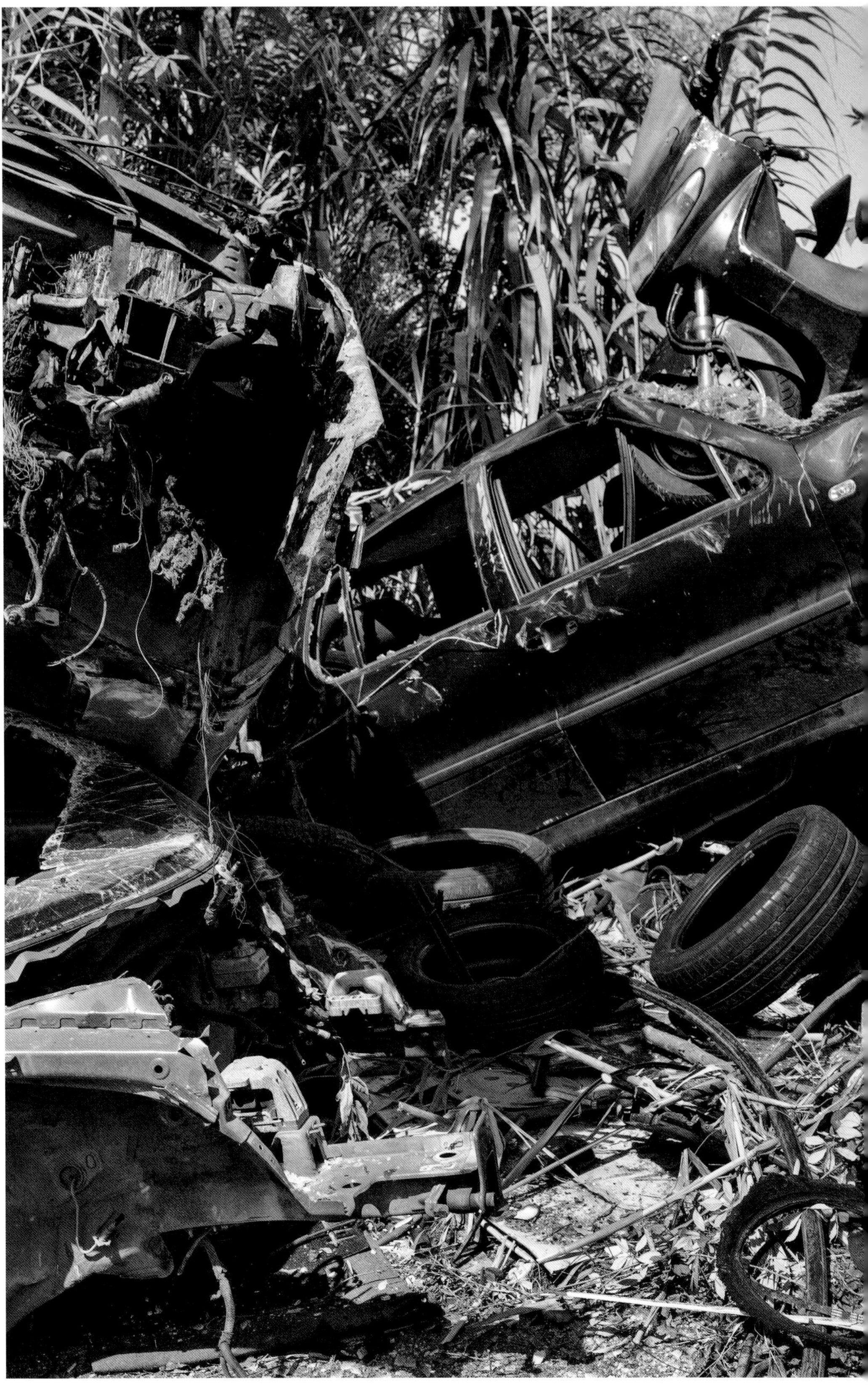

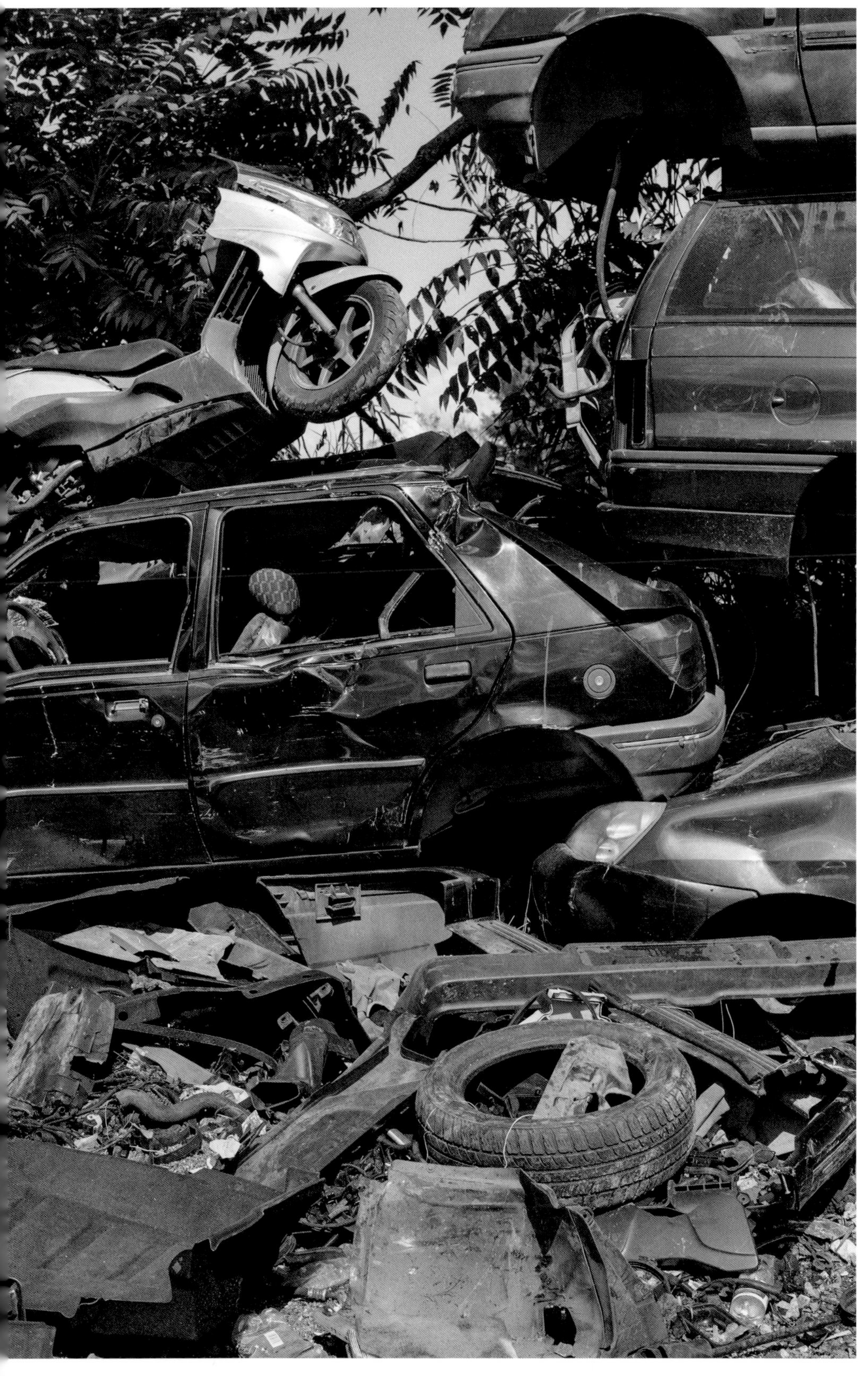

AUTO

AUTO AUTO

AUTO ALIGNMENT

AUTO ALTERNATOR

AUTO AXEL

AUTO CARBURETOR

AUTO CATALYTIC

AUTO EXHAUST

AUTO IDLE

AUTO INSTRUMENTATION

AUTO INTELLIGENCE

AUTO LUBE

AUTO MESSAGING

AUTO RADIATOR

AUTO RECALL

AUTO SHOCK

AUTO STROKE

AUTO SUSPENSION

AUTO TELEMATIC

AUTO TIMING

AUTO TORQUE

AUTO TRANSMISSION

AUTO VALVE

AUTO WHEEL

AUTO WIDTH

AUTO ZEV

L O S

E   C O

I O N

P R I C

L L I S

AN A

OF

L

RRAY

SKIL

I S   W

H E Y

A C C I

S

HY   T

ARE

DENT

F A U L

U R   O

T Y O
W N

G I F T

A N D S

E D   H

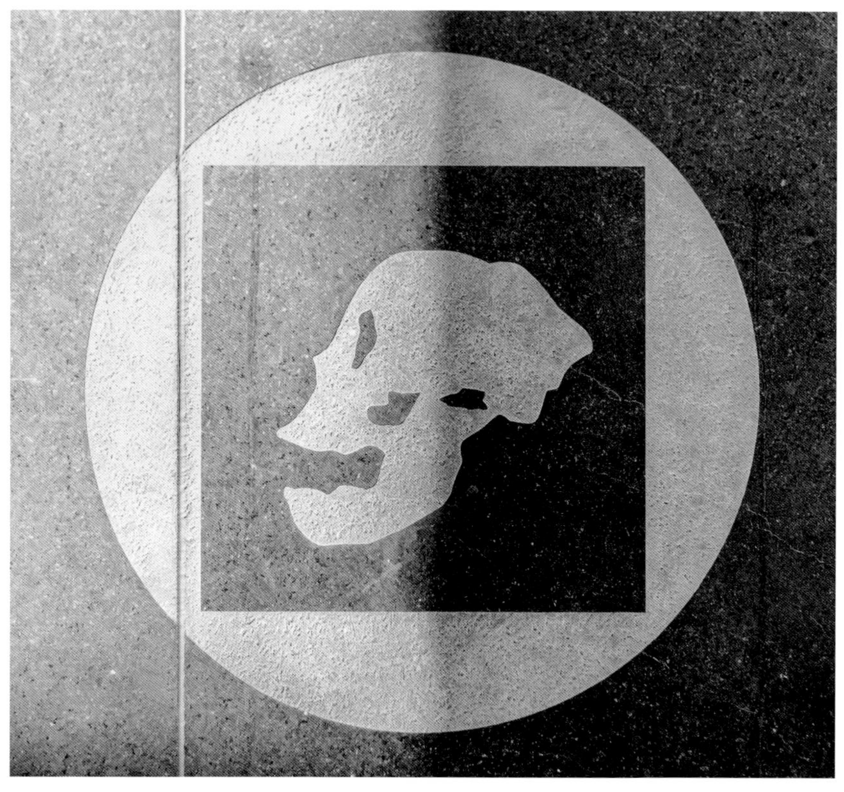

PROP
ET O
OLS

E R   S

F   T   O

MODE
OOLS

R N   T

T O   H

T E C H

A N S

E L P

N I C I

O N T

F T TH

N E

O P O

E L I

C O L L

N AU

S TER

ISIO
TOMA

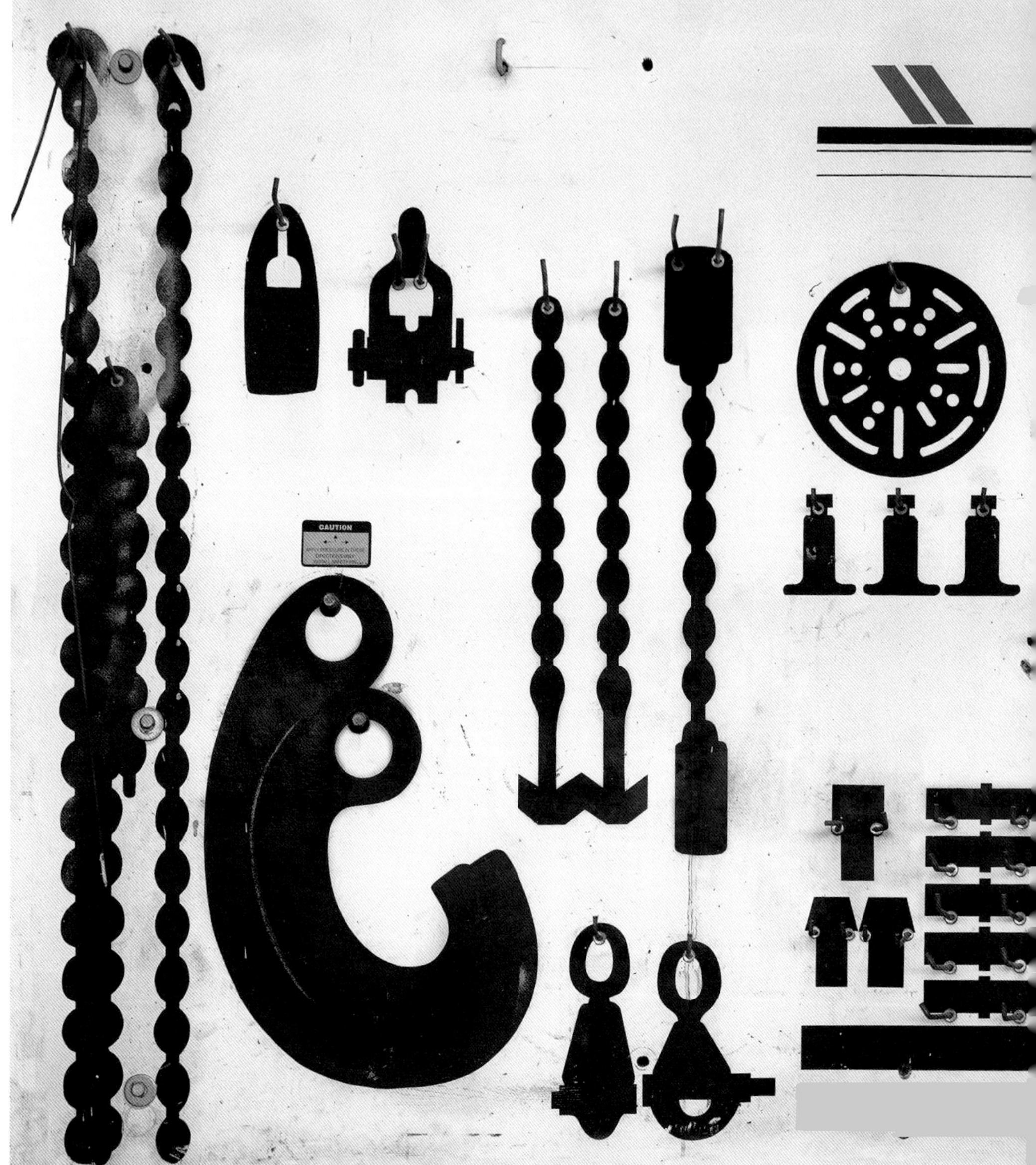

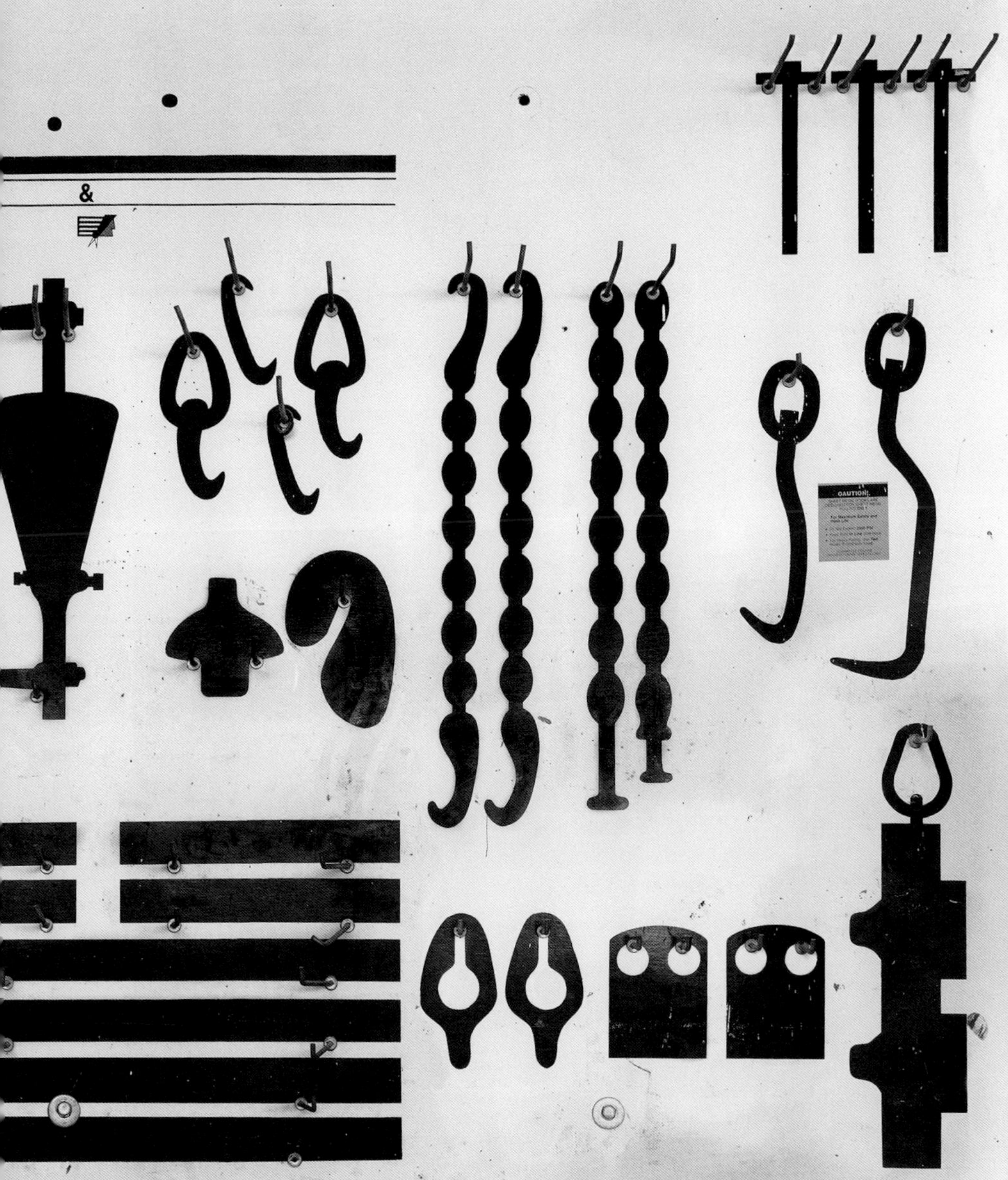

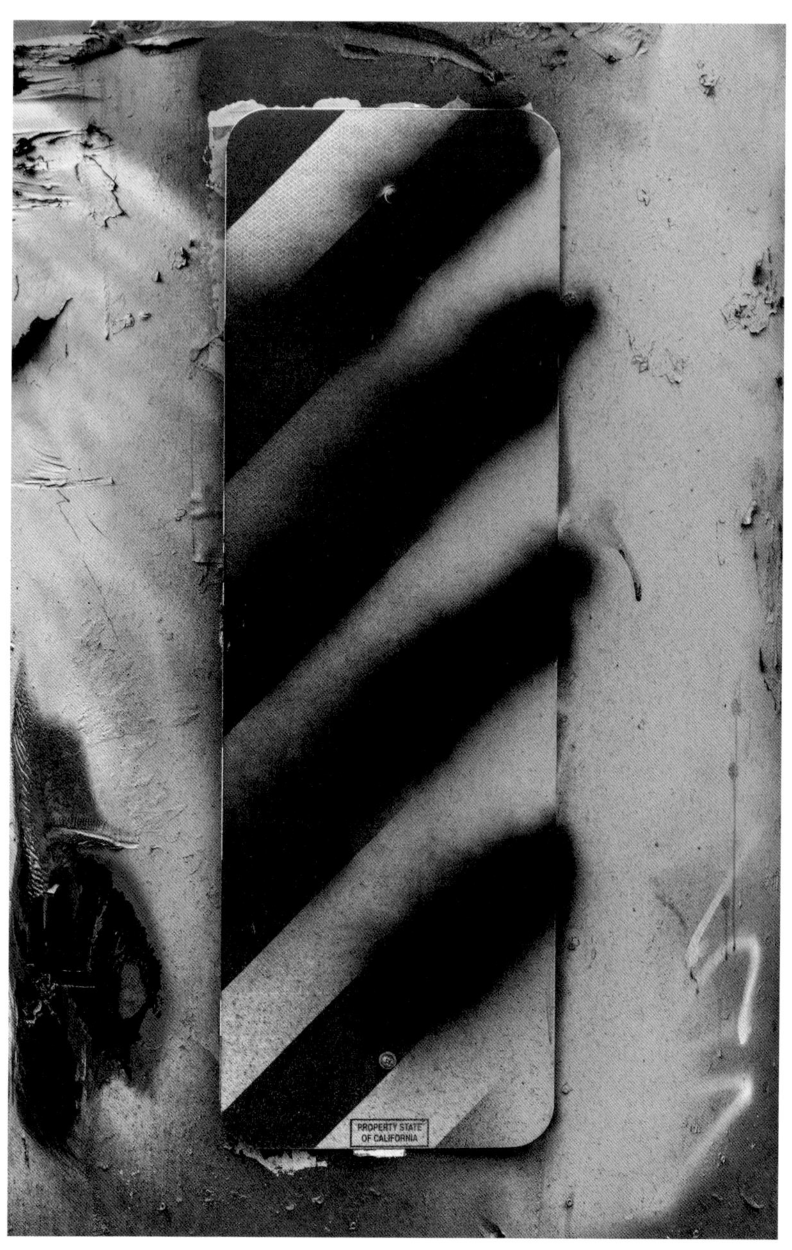

PROPERTY STATE
OF CALIFORNIA

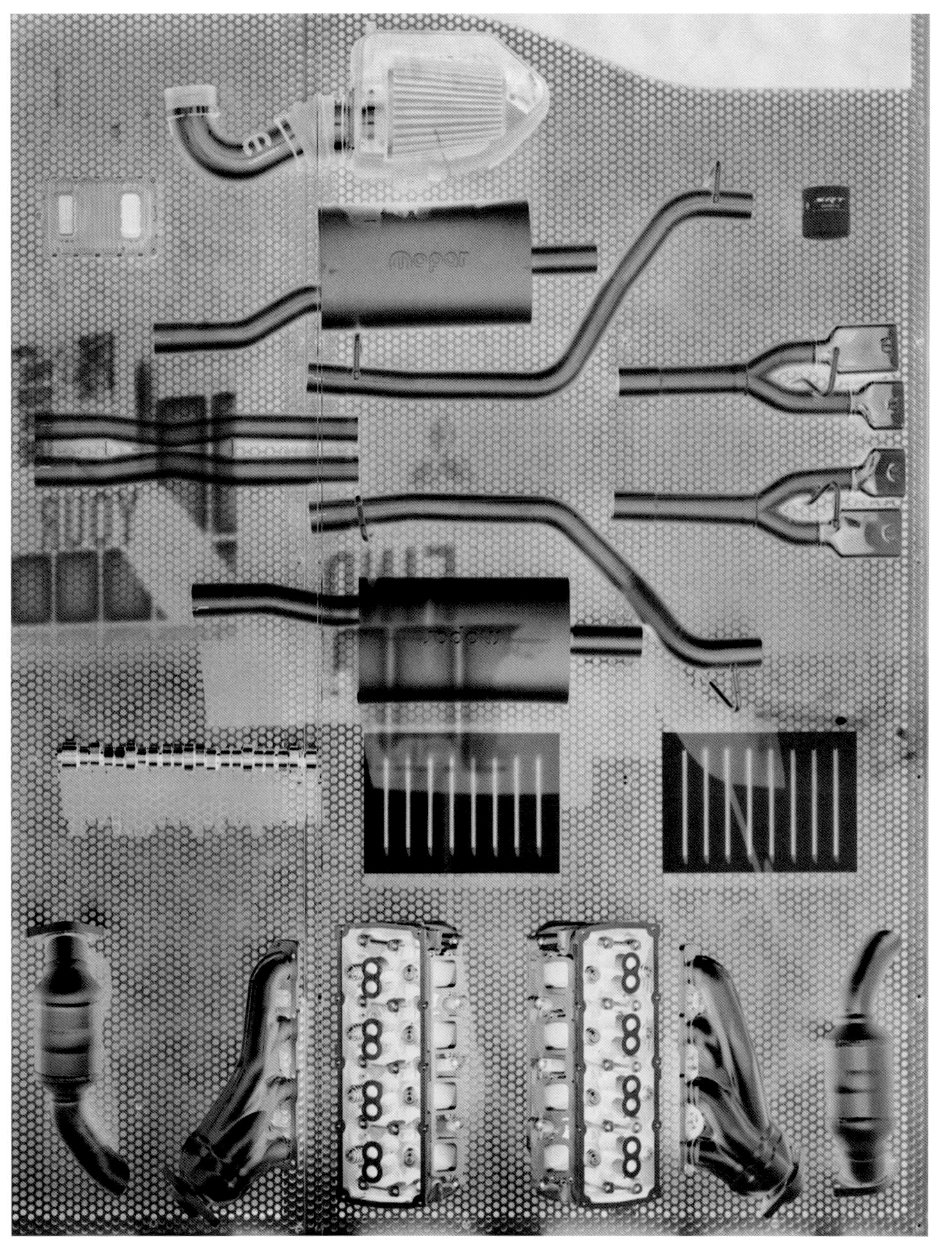

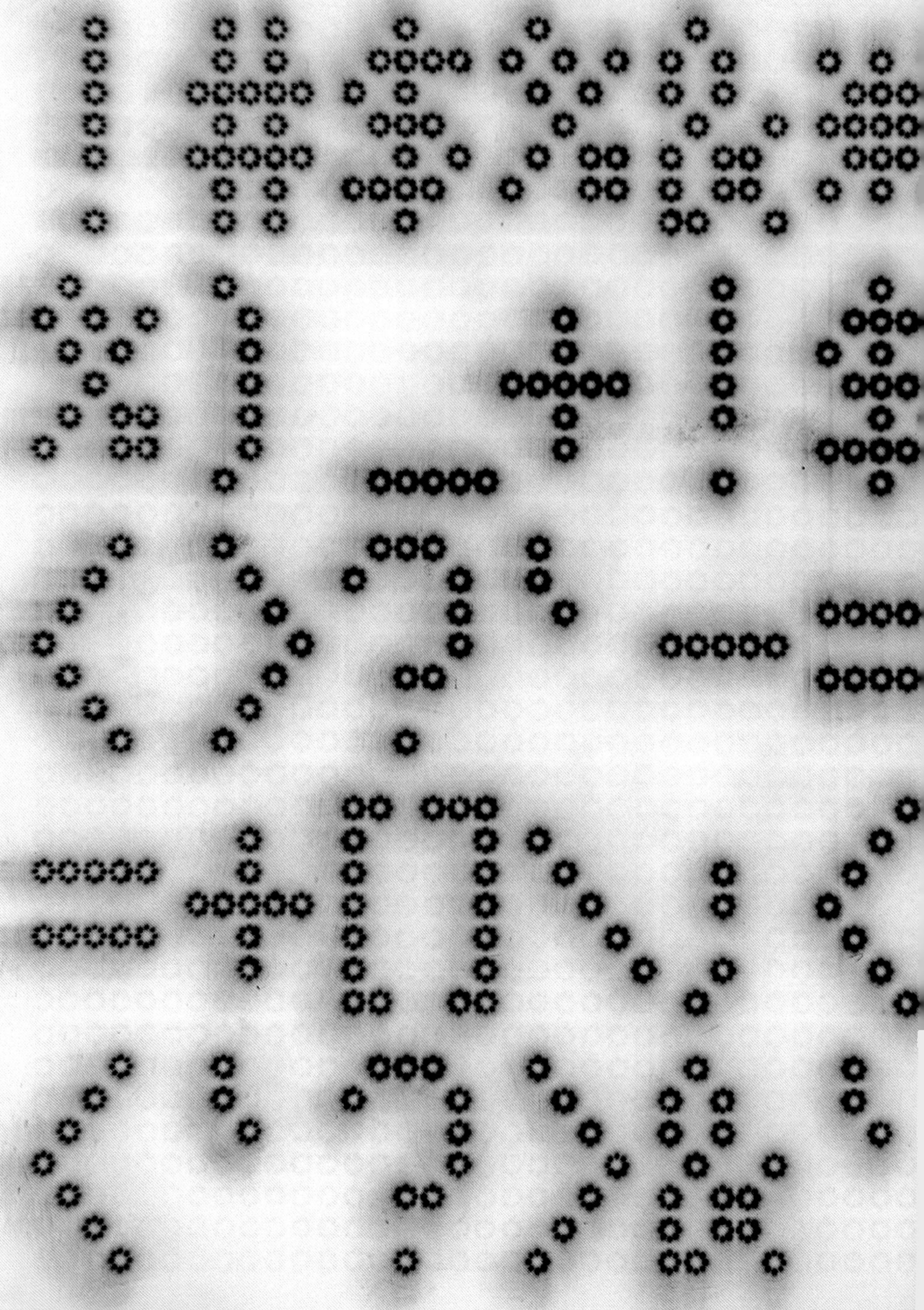

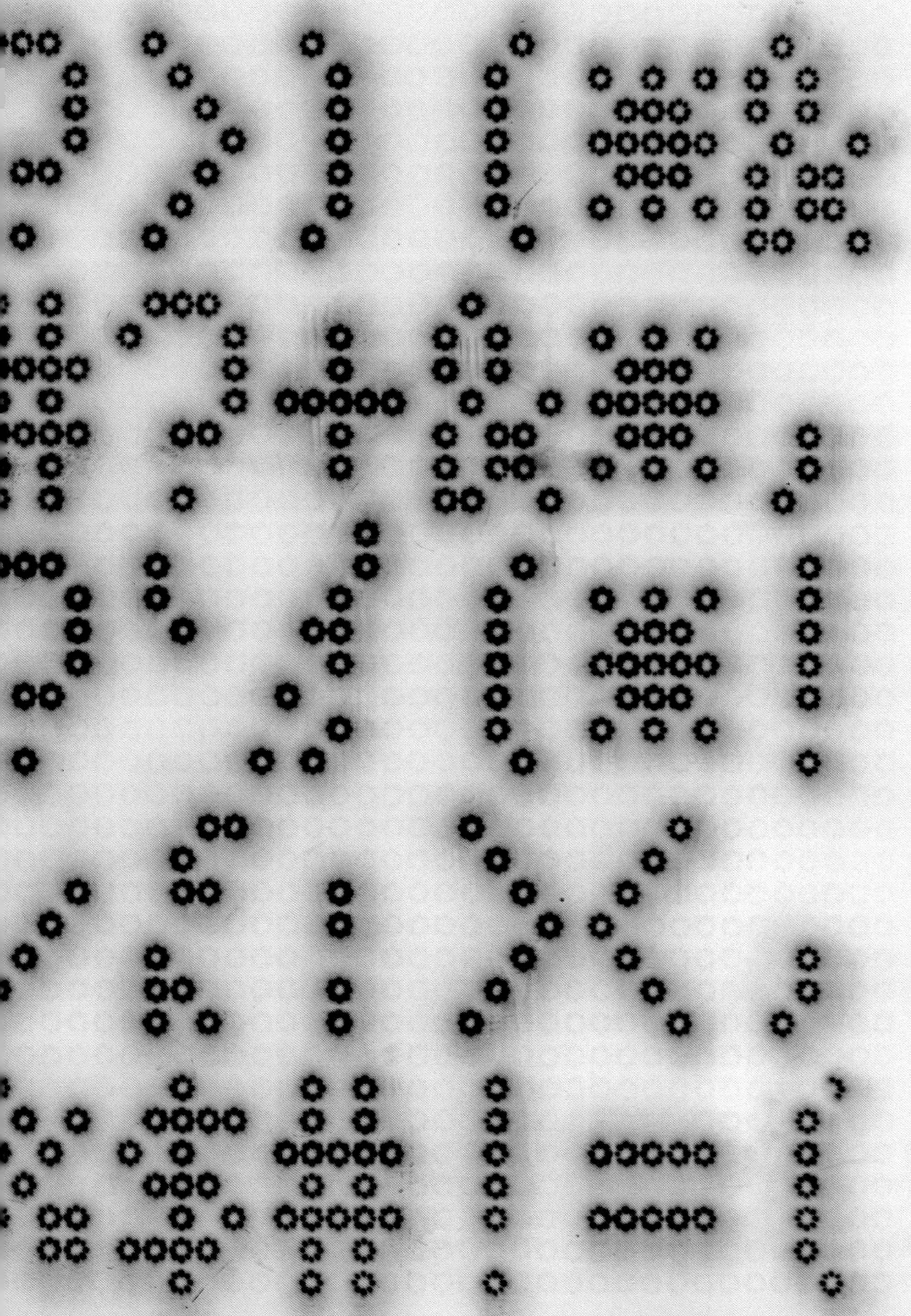

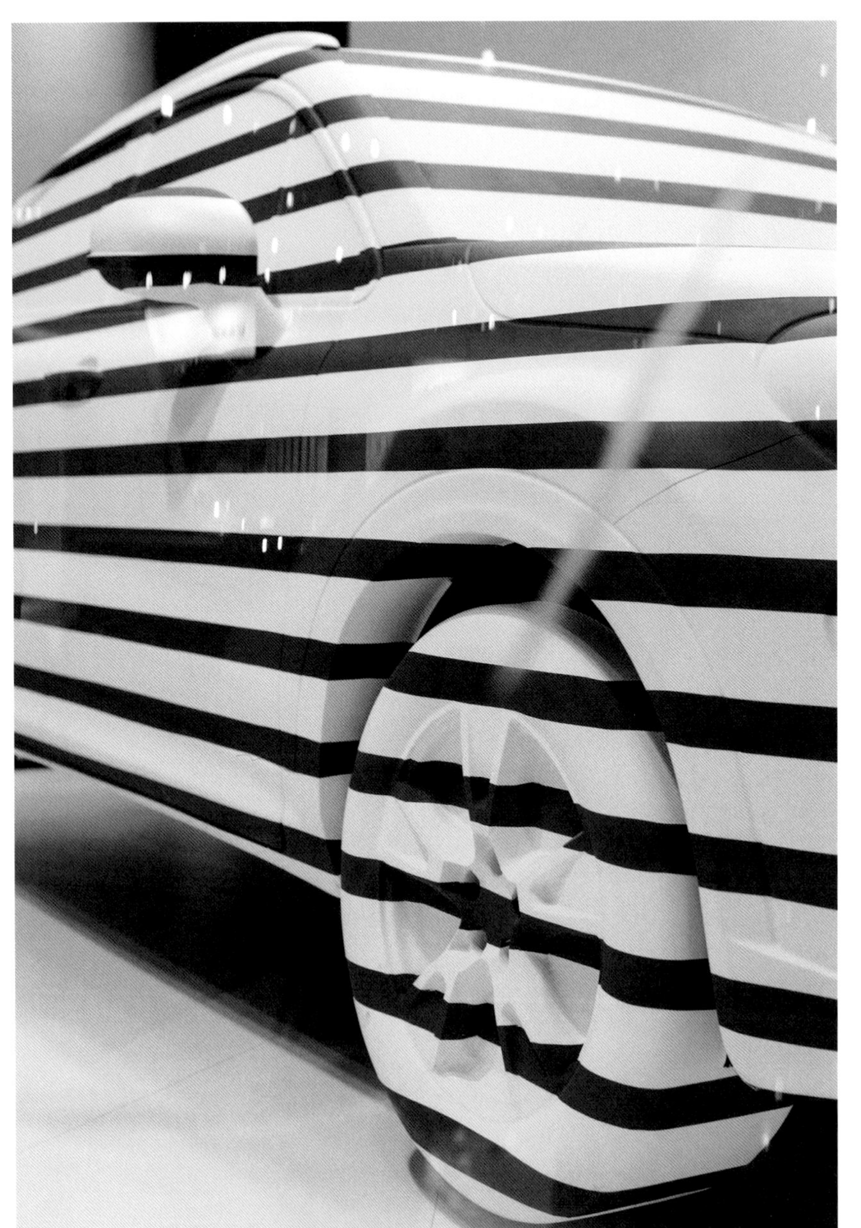

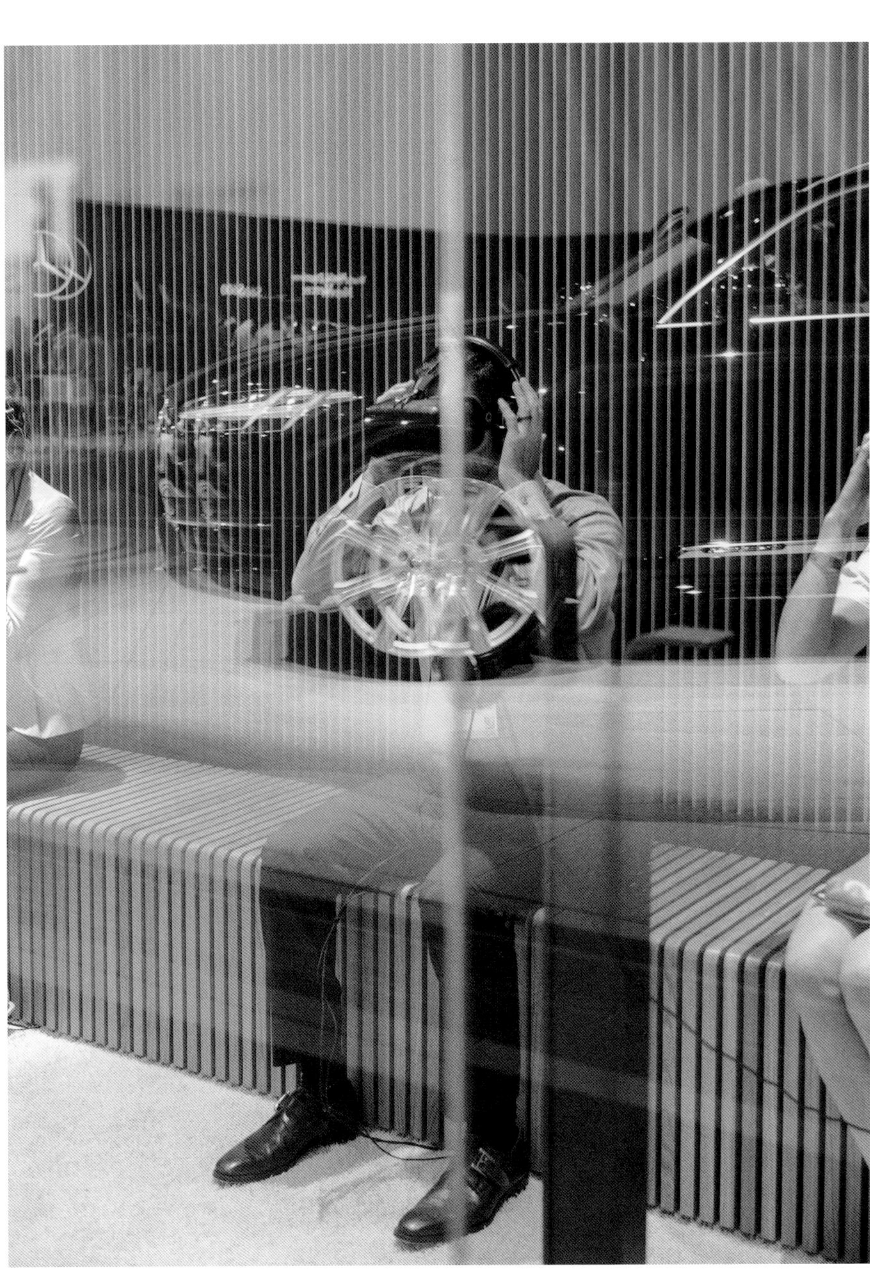

S U P E

T O   C

S I O N

R AU

OLLI

I NC

A M E R

C O L

O N   I

I C A N

L I S I

N C

P E O P

O L L I

S H O

C

L E   C

S I O N

P   I N

B E L L

L E   C

S I O N

E I S

OLLI

GLOBAL COLLISION CENTER

BLU AUTOMOTIVE

DYNAMIC COLLISION CENTER

MOTORAMA INC

A-1 COLLISION

A Z COLLISION INC

UNITECH AUTO COLLISION INC

CANDY'S AUTO BODY

ATLAS COLLISION INC

COLLISION CONNECTION 12 INC

DICK'S AUTO BODY

DETOX MIND & BODY

STAR COLLISION

ROYAL COLLISION INC

SKY COLLISION

AIRPORT COLLISION

MASTER BODY & COLLISION

LEGEND COLLISION

RITE COLLISION

HI-TECH COLLISION GROUP

H & M FLASH COLLISION

JOSEPH COLLISION

DANNY'S COLLISION

LARRY'S COLLISION

GENDELS COLLISION GARAGE

LOS PRICE COLLISION

MATRIX AUTOBODY

DIAMONDS AUTO COLLISION

COLLISION ZONE

NEW ZAY ENT & COLLISION INC

KINGS OF CUSTOMS COLLISION

METRO CAR COLLISION CENTER

PRINCE COLLISION

USA COLLISION & REPAIR

ALTER COLLISION

A NU COLLISION

DE TECH AUTO COLLISION

COLLISION PRO TECH

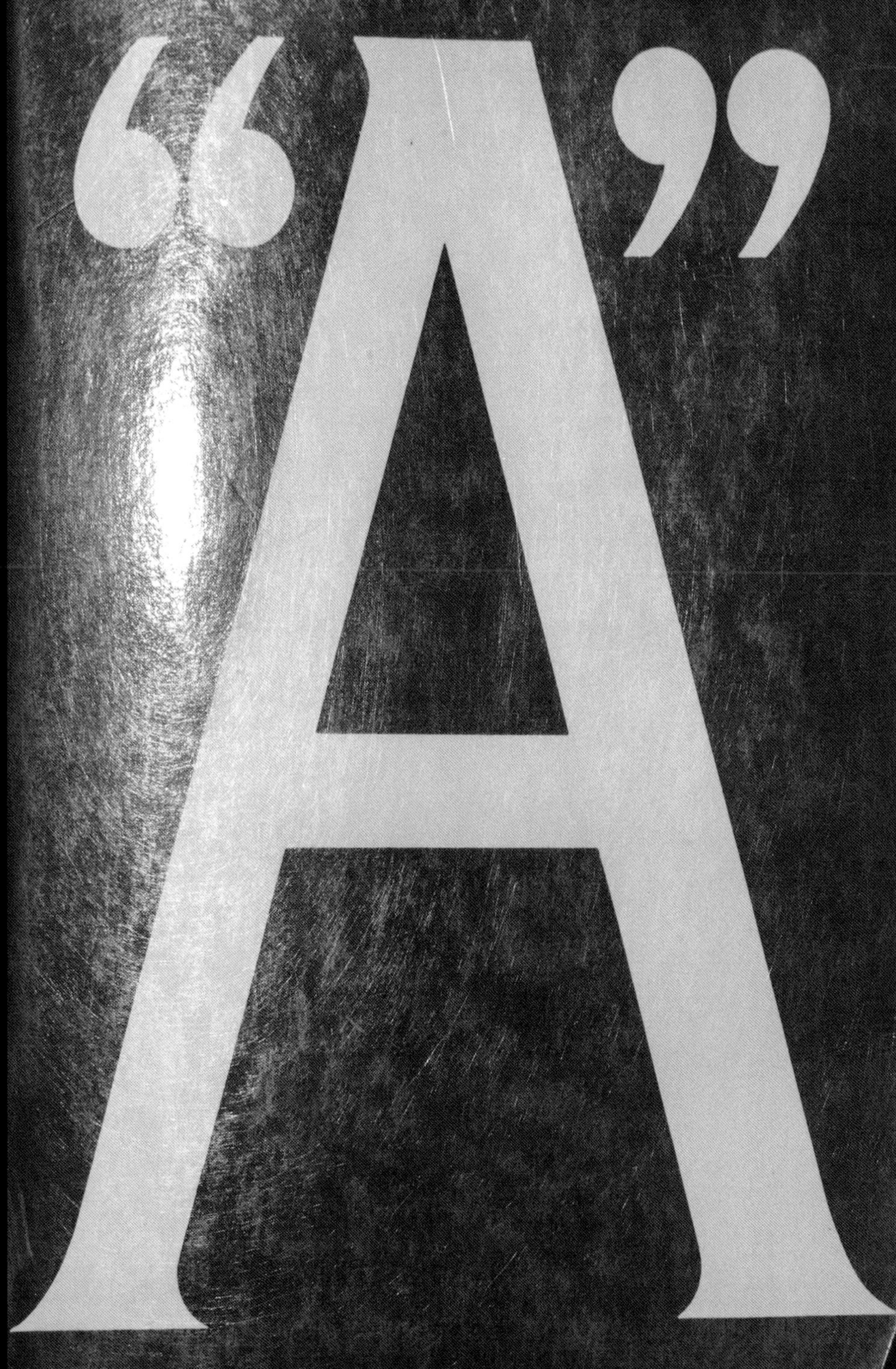

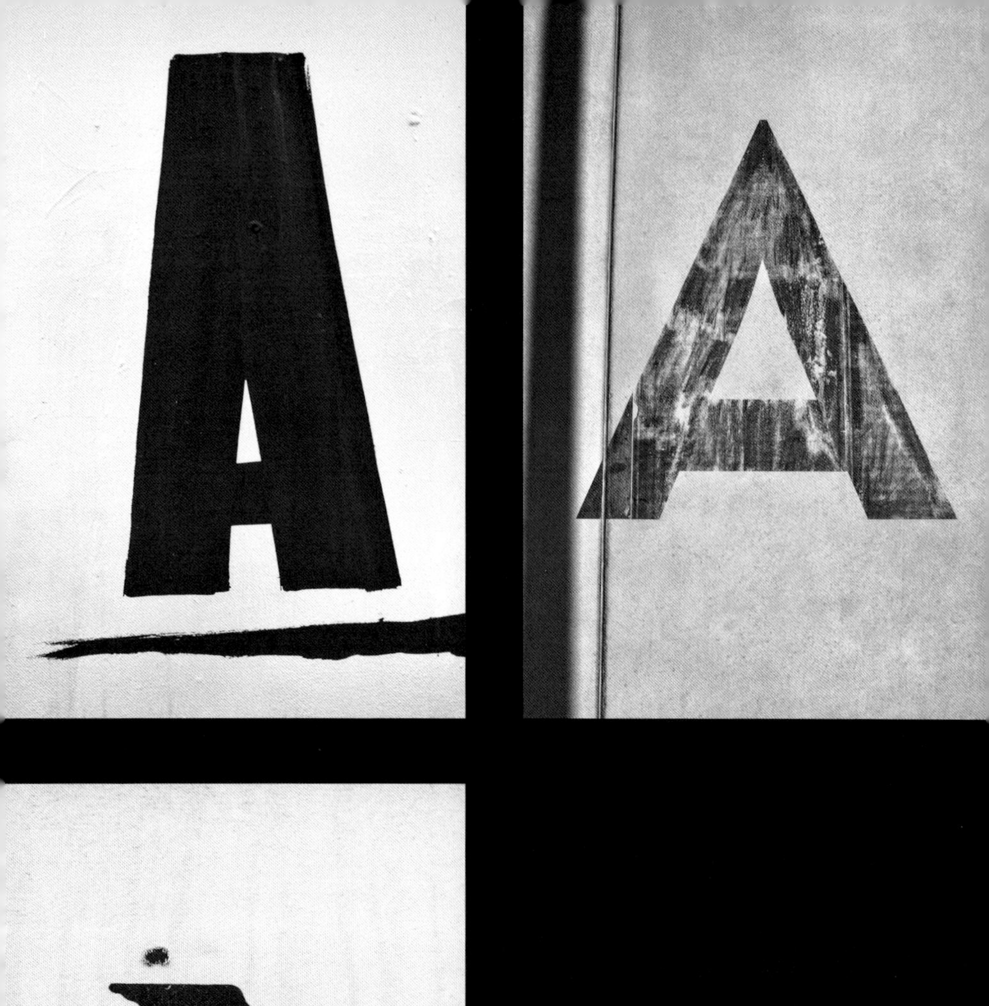

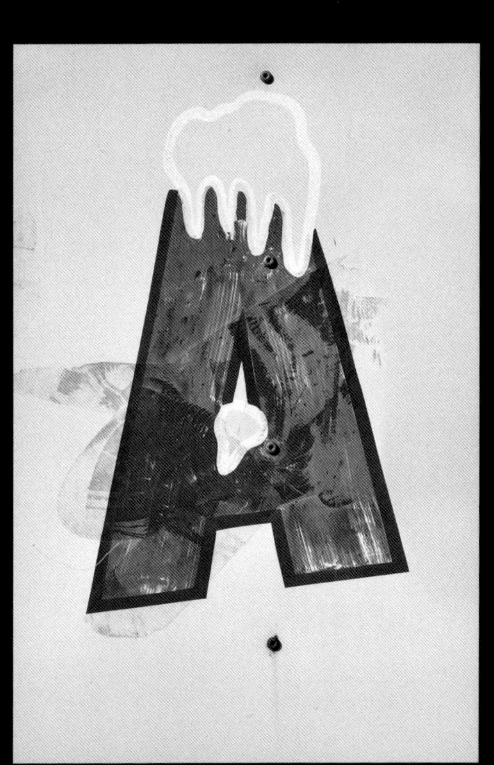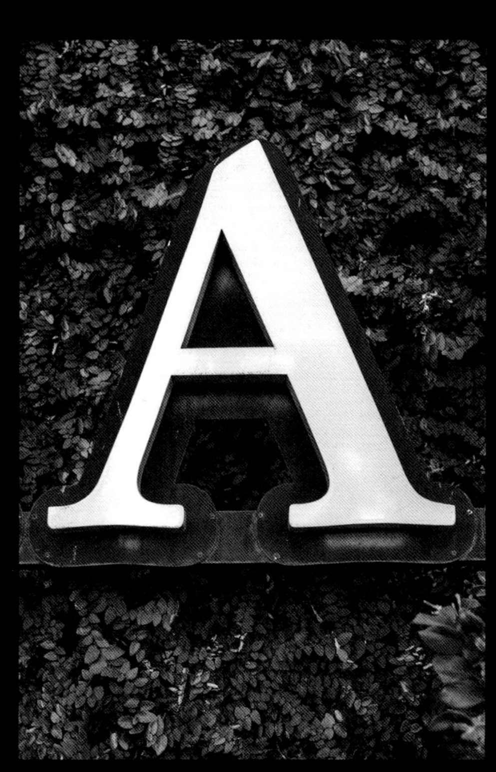

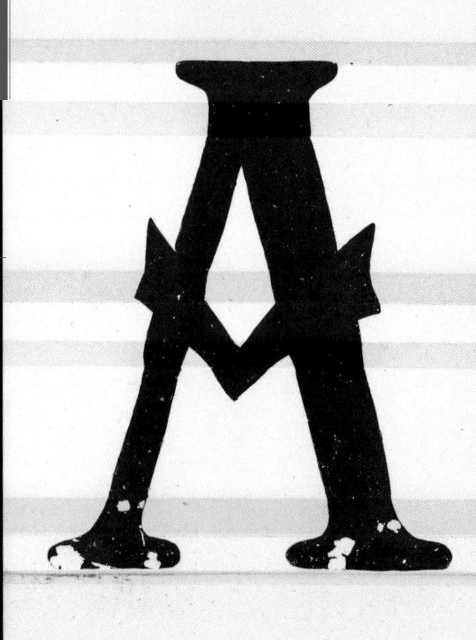

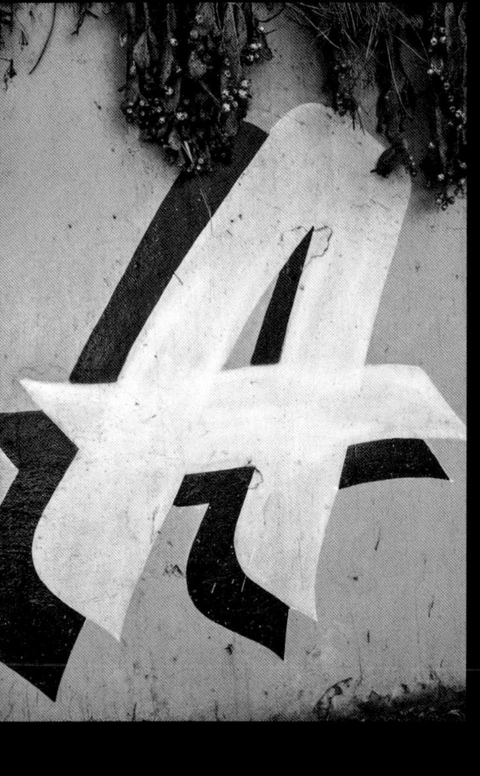
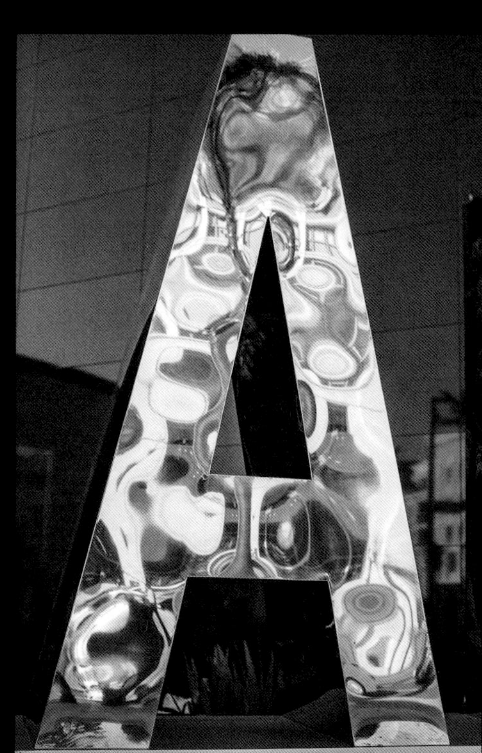

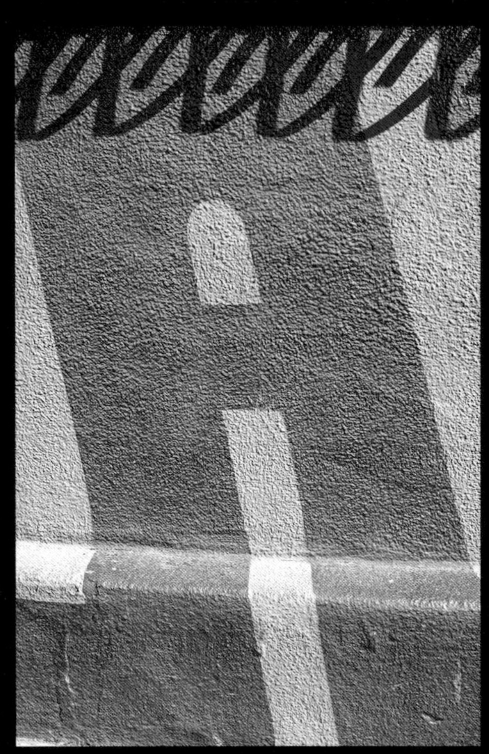

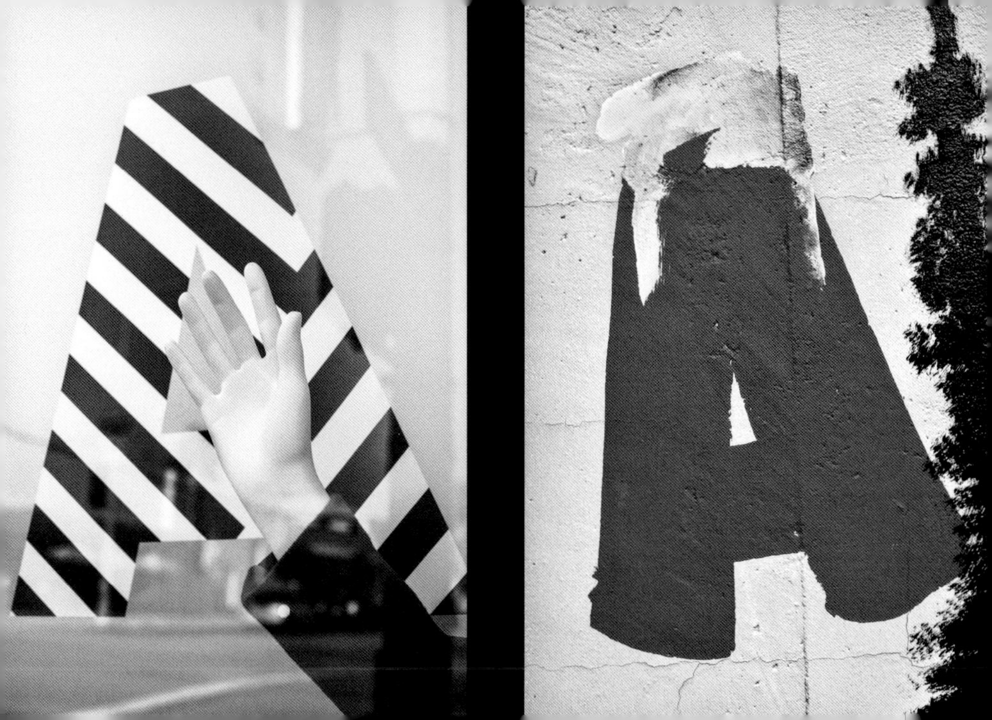

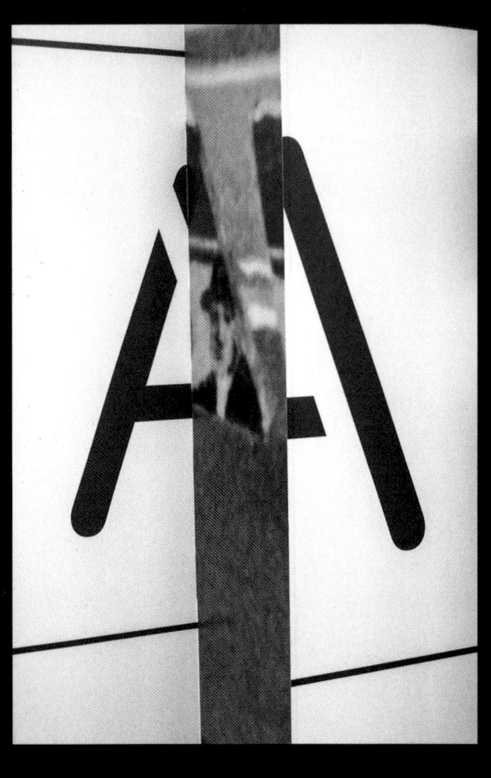
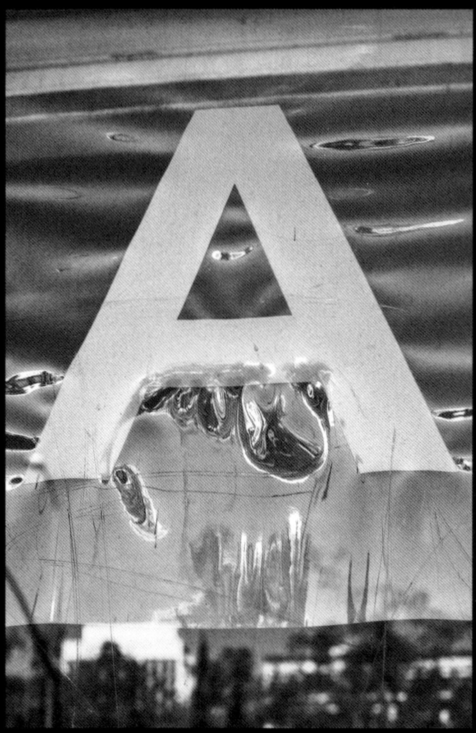
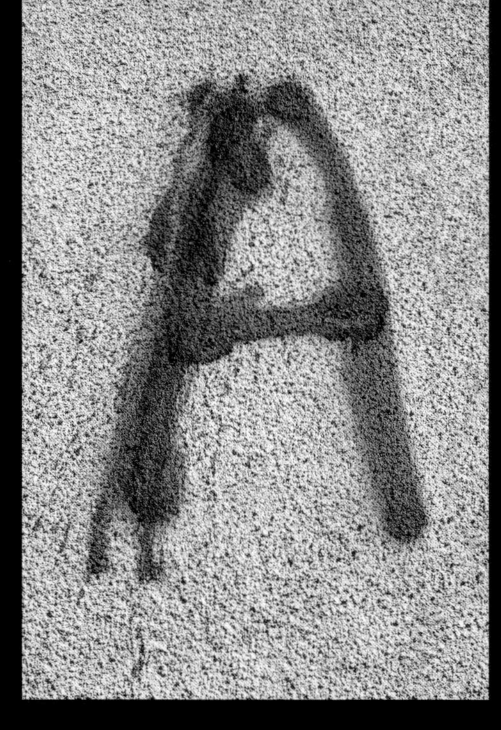

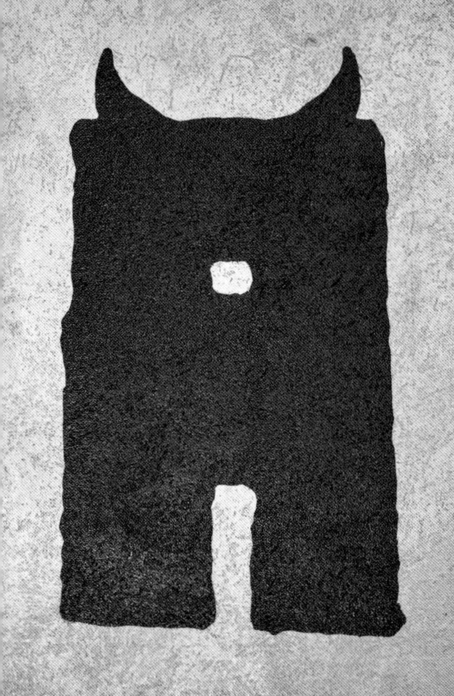

MOTO
TYA
& CO
ION

R   C   I

R

U T O

L L I S

FOUR

COLL

N &

RFNG

W A Y

I S I O

R S T P

MAXX LISI

COL
ON

ONYX LISI

COL
ON

I TAL

OLLI

I A C

S I O N

X C L U
      C O L
      C O L
O N

S I V E

L I S I

KING
LISI

COL ON

FEDE
COLL
N

RAL
ISIO

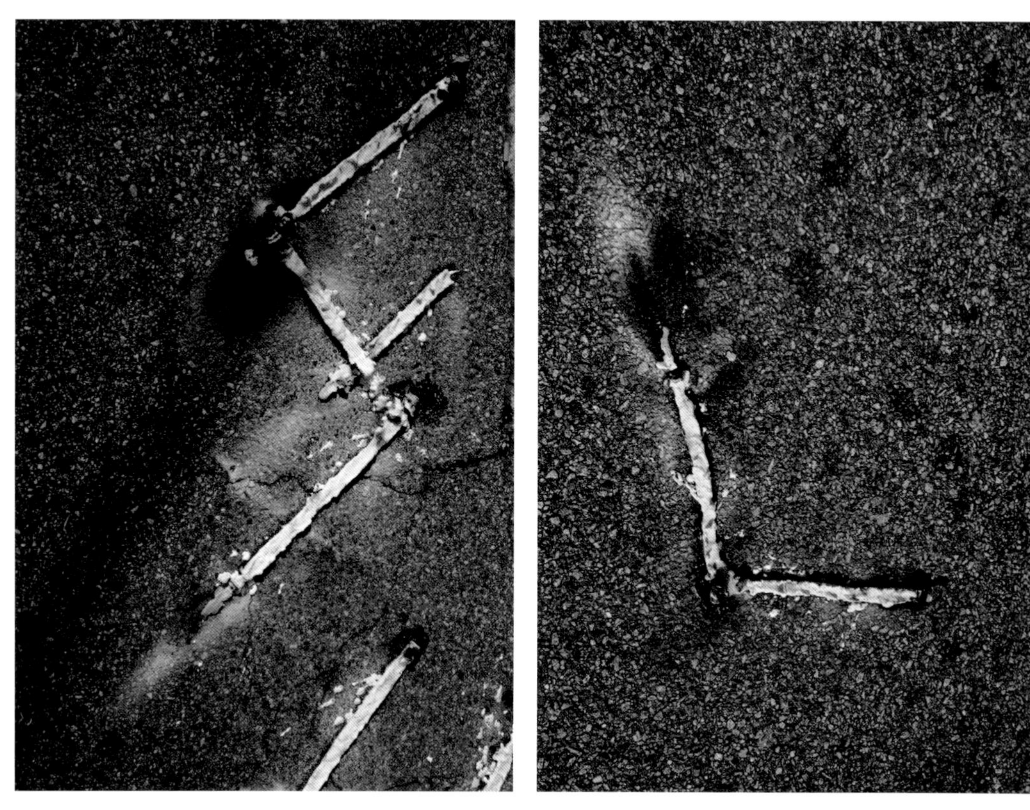

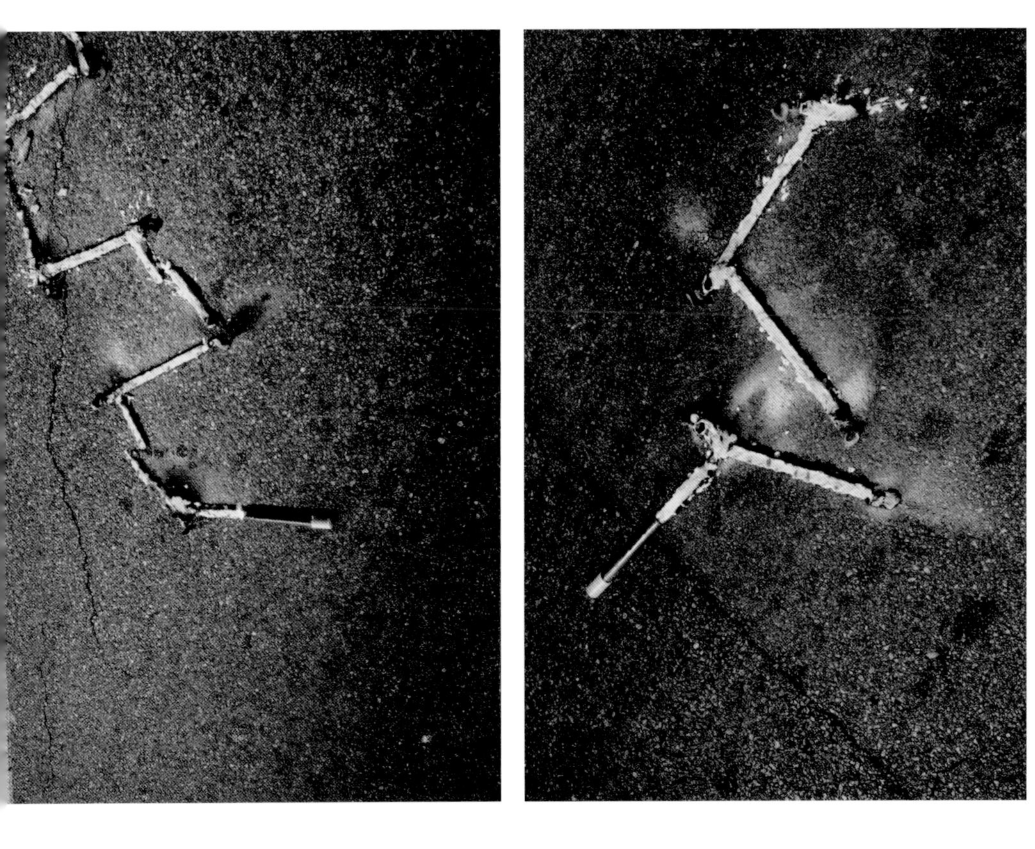

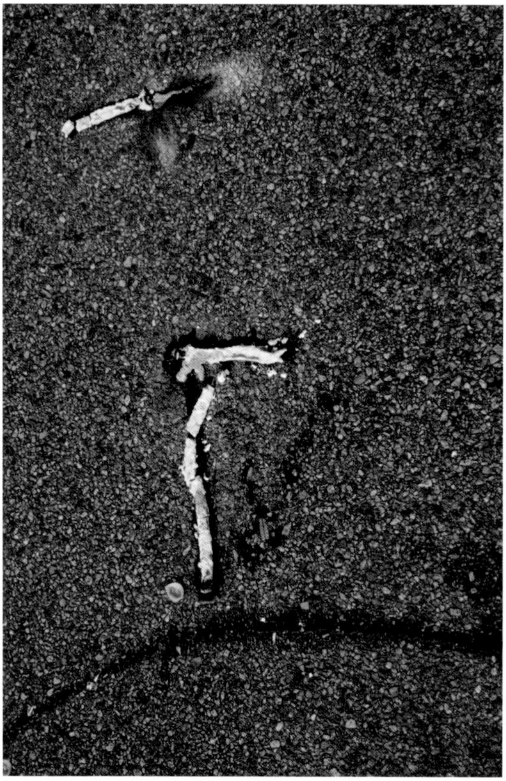

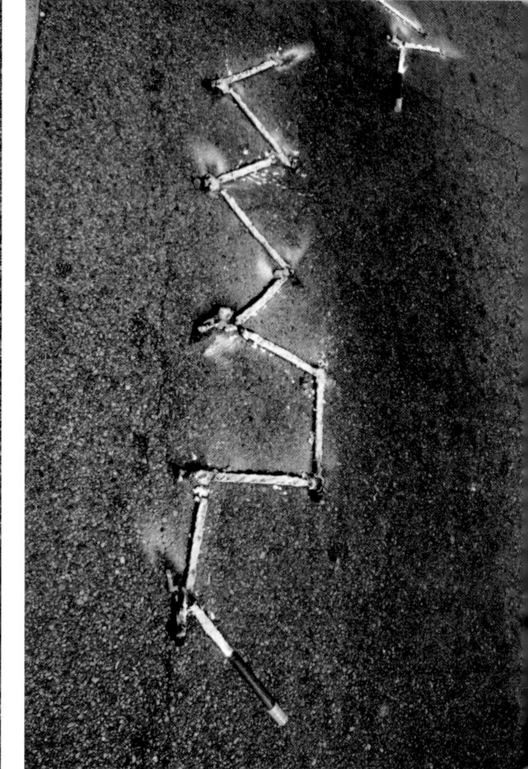

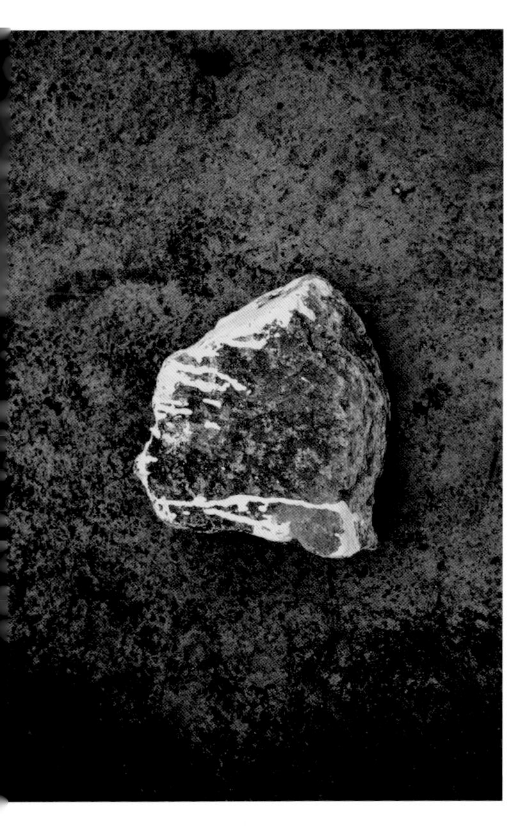

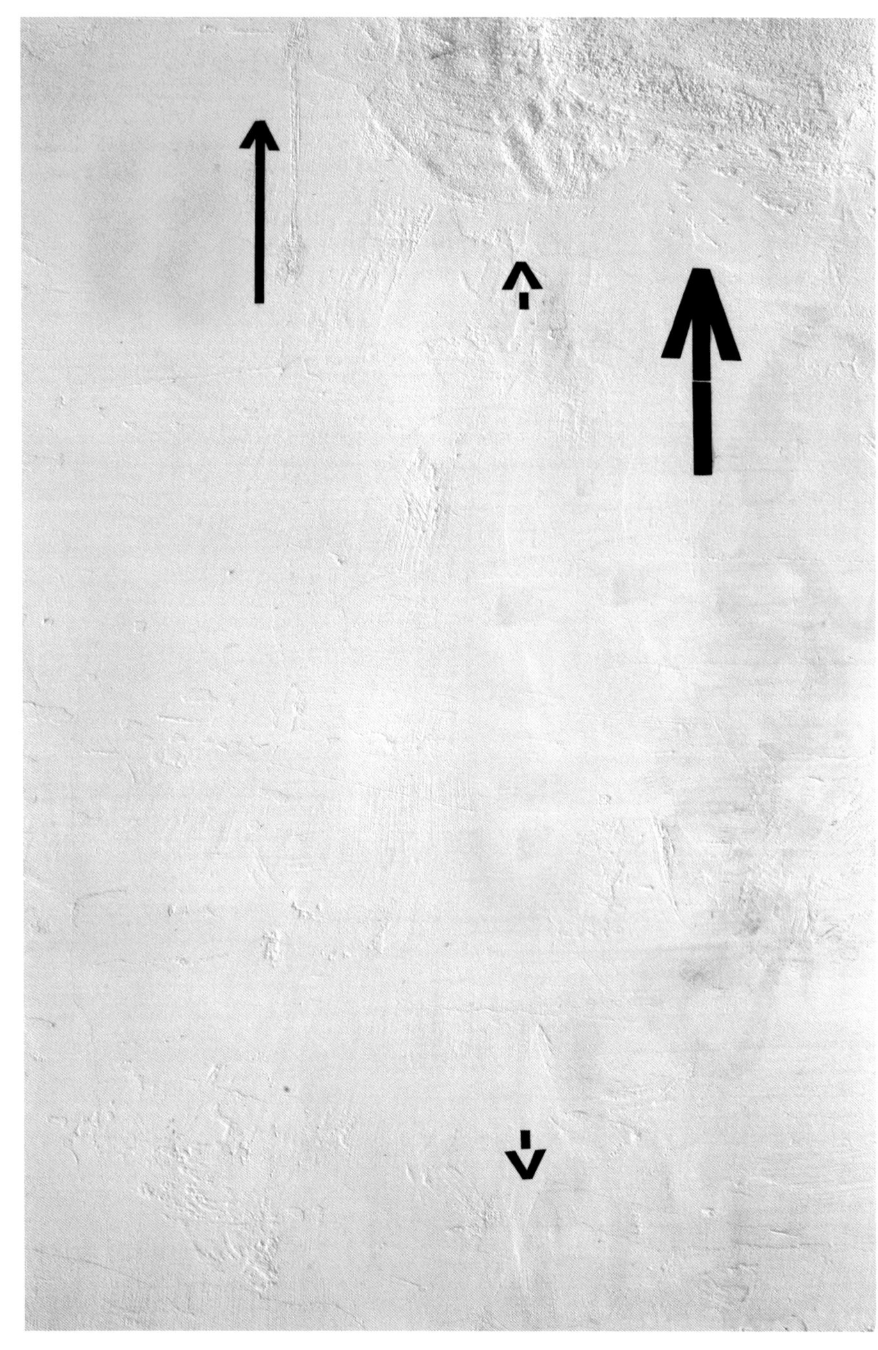

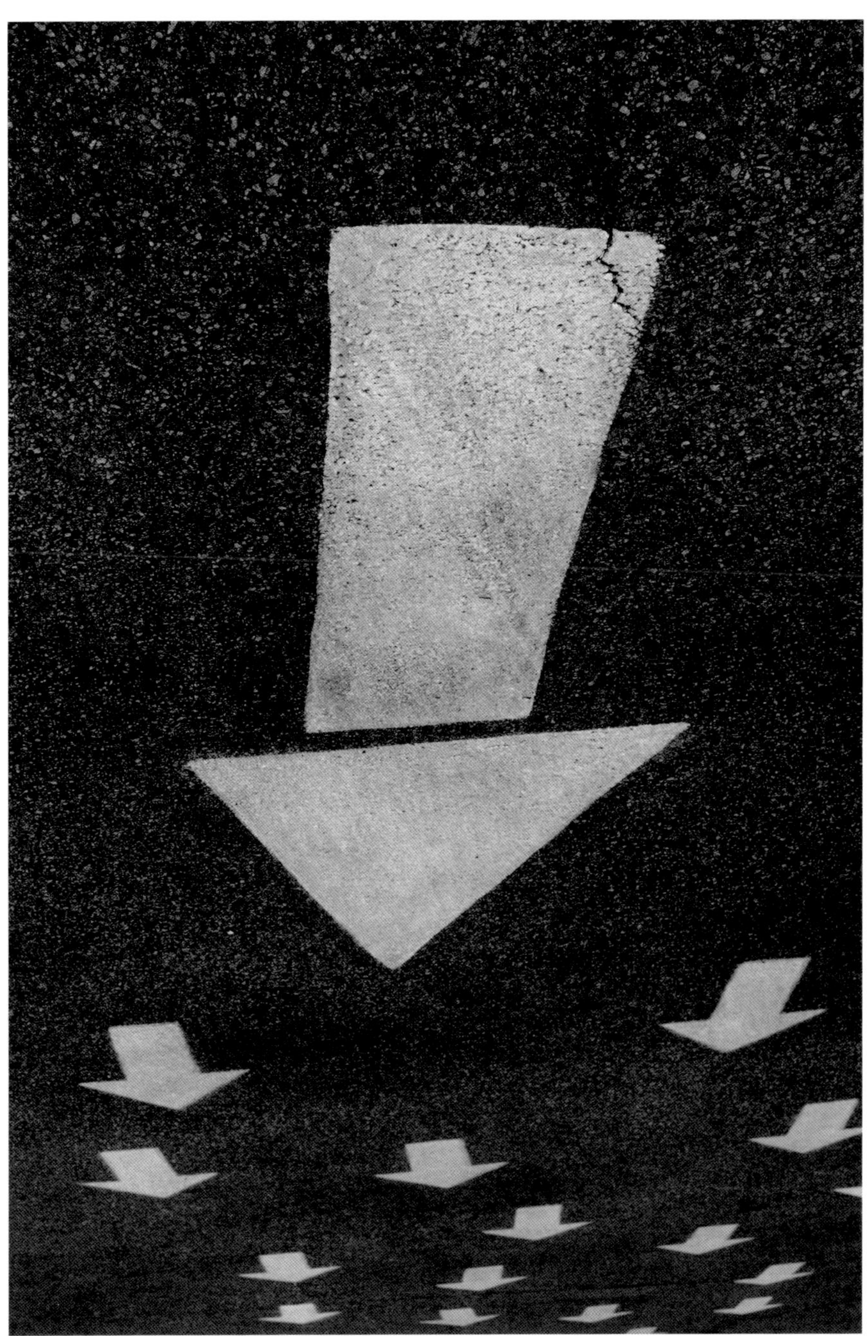

MARX

OLLI

’S C

SION

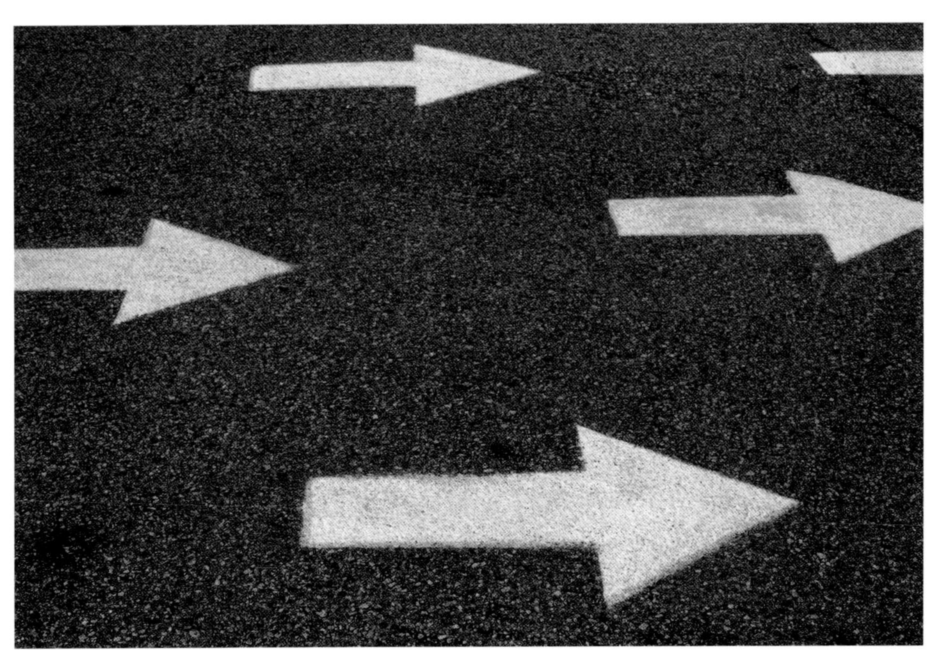

3 D   C

S I O N

OLLI

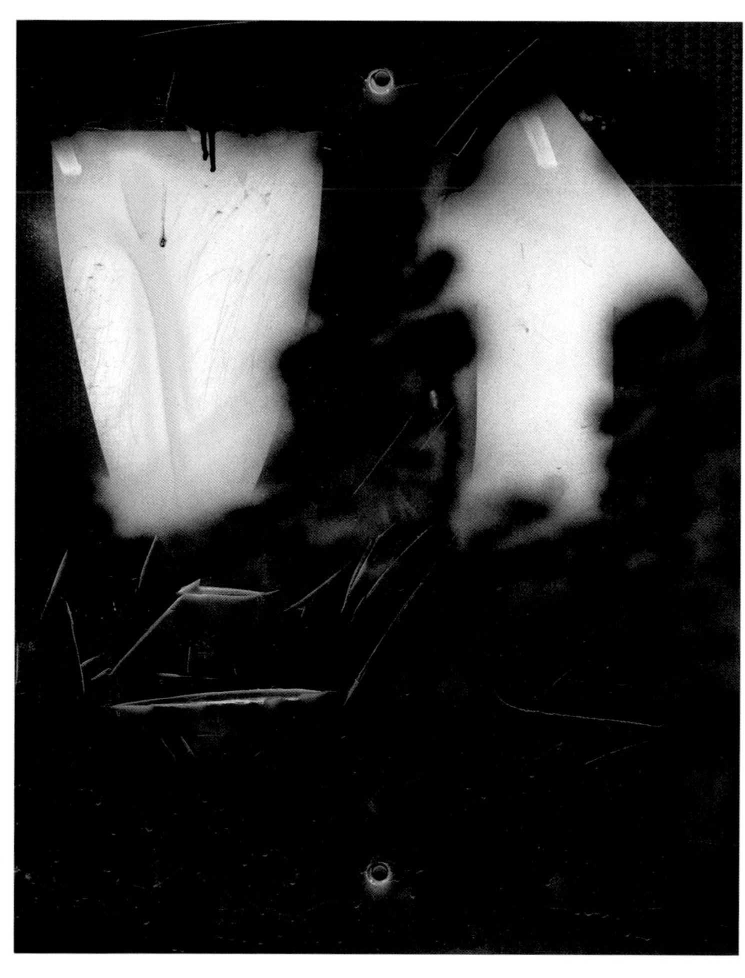

LUXU
OLLI

R Y   C

S I O N

CAMP OLLI

U S C

S I O N

C H E C

C O L L

N

KER ISIO

K R U I

O L L I

SE C
SION

SIX
COL
ON

MILE
LISI

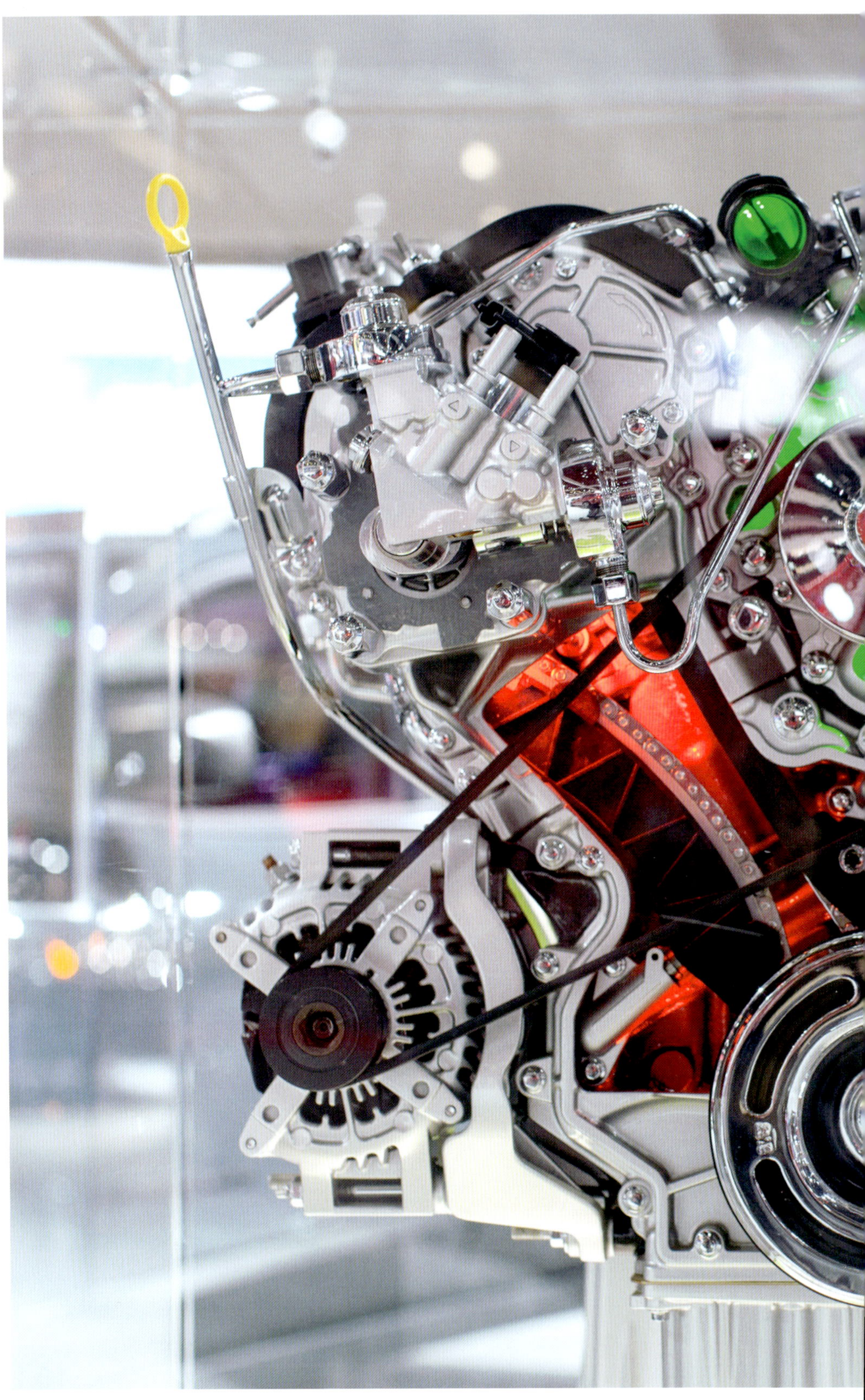

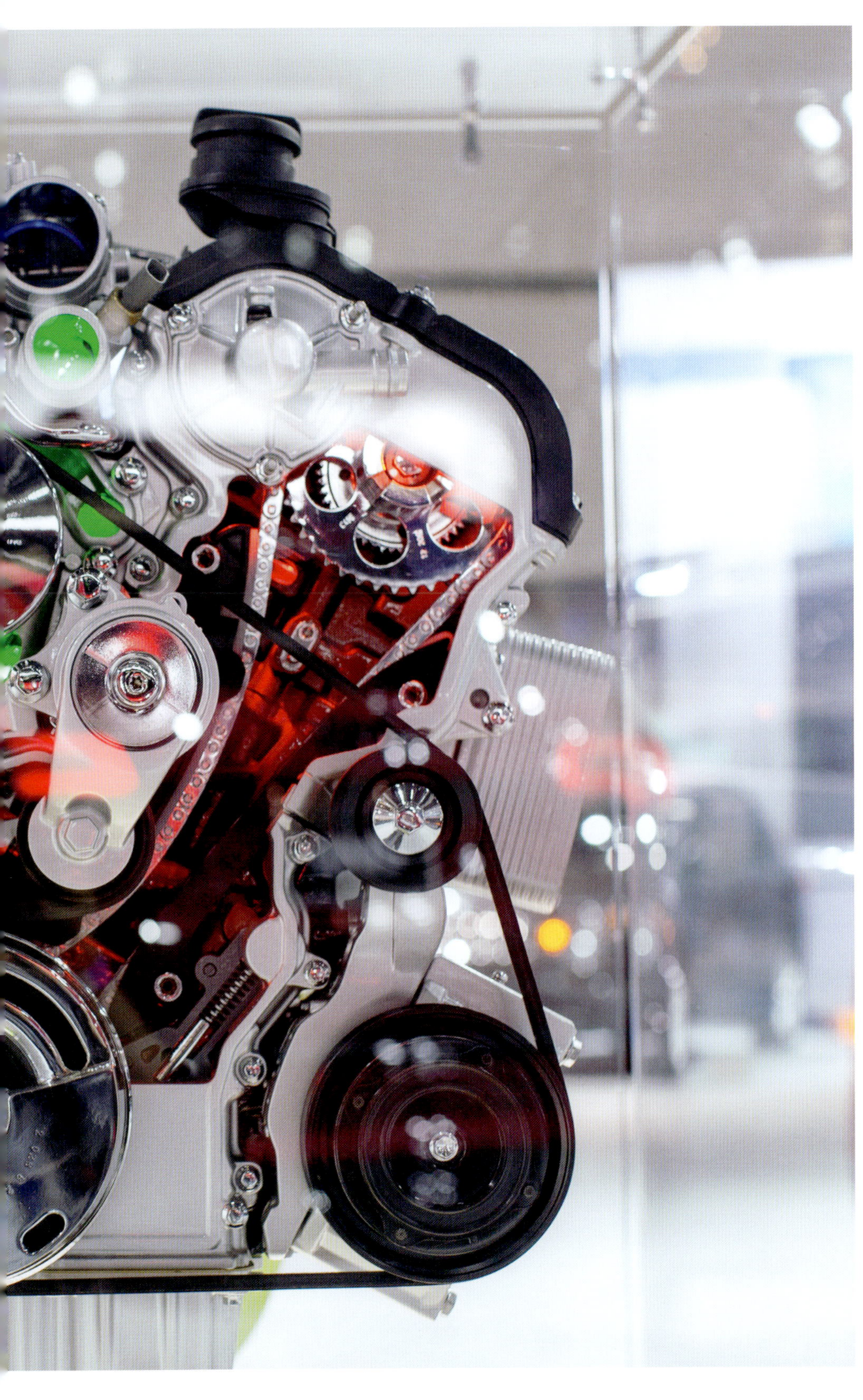

SPEC

M   CO

I   ON

K T R U L L I S

UNI-
COL
ON

BODY LISI

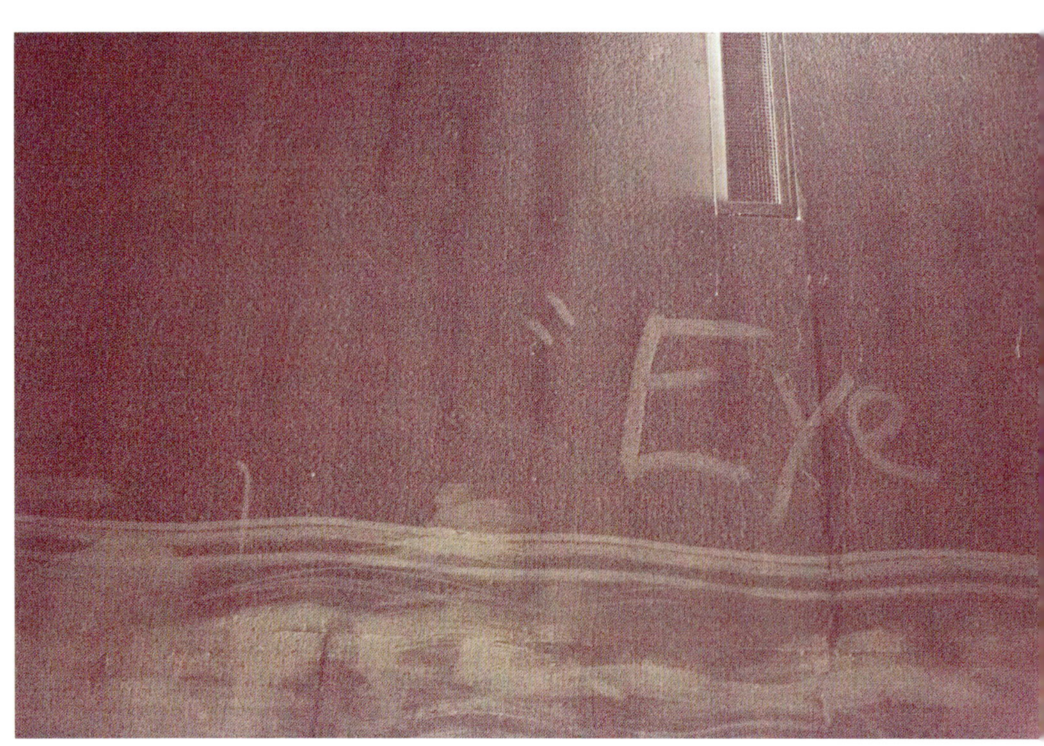

Eye

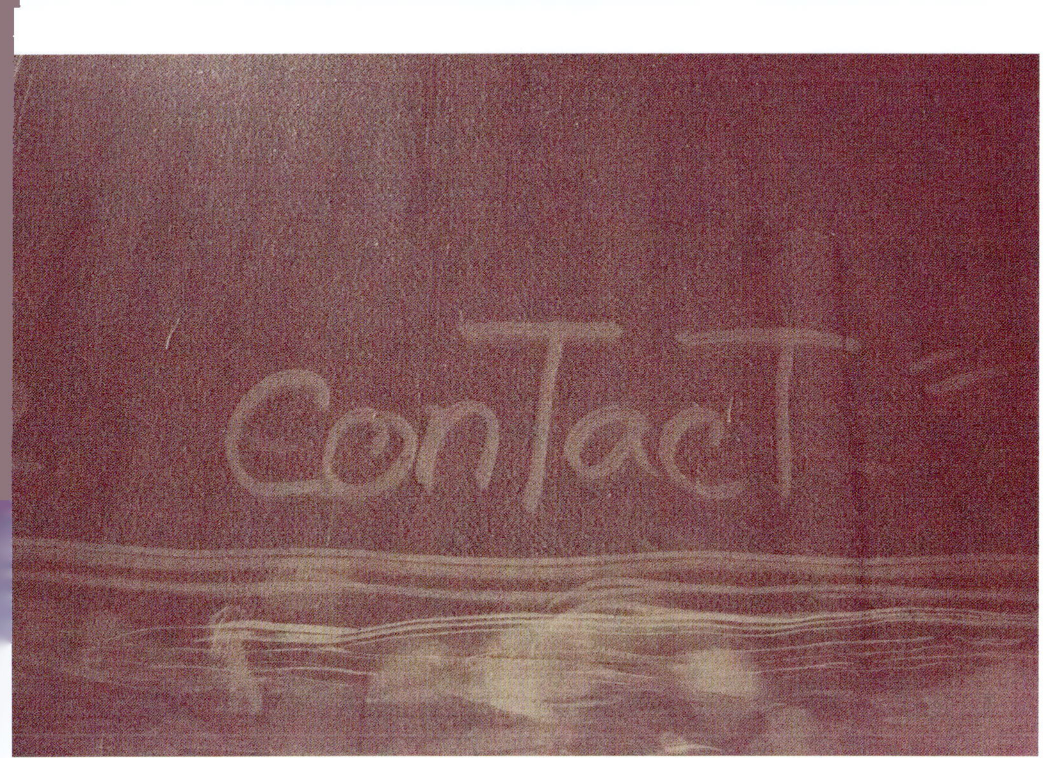

ConTacT

I - CA

R

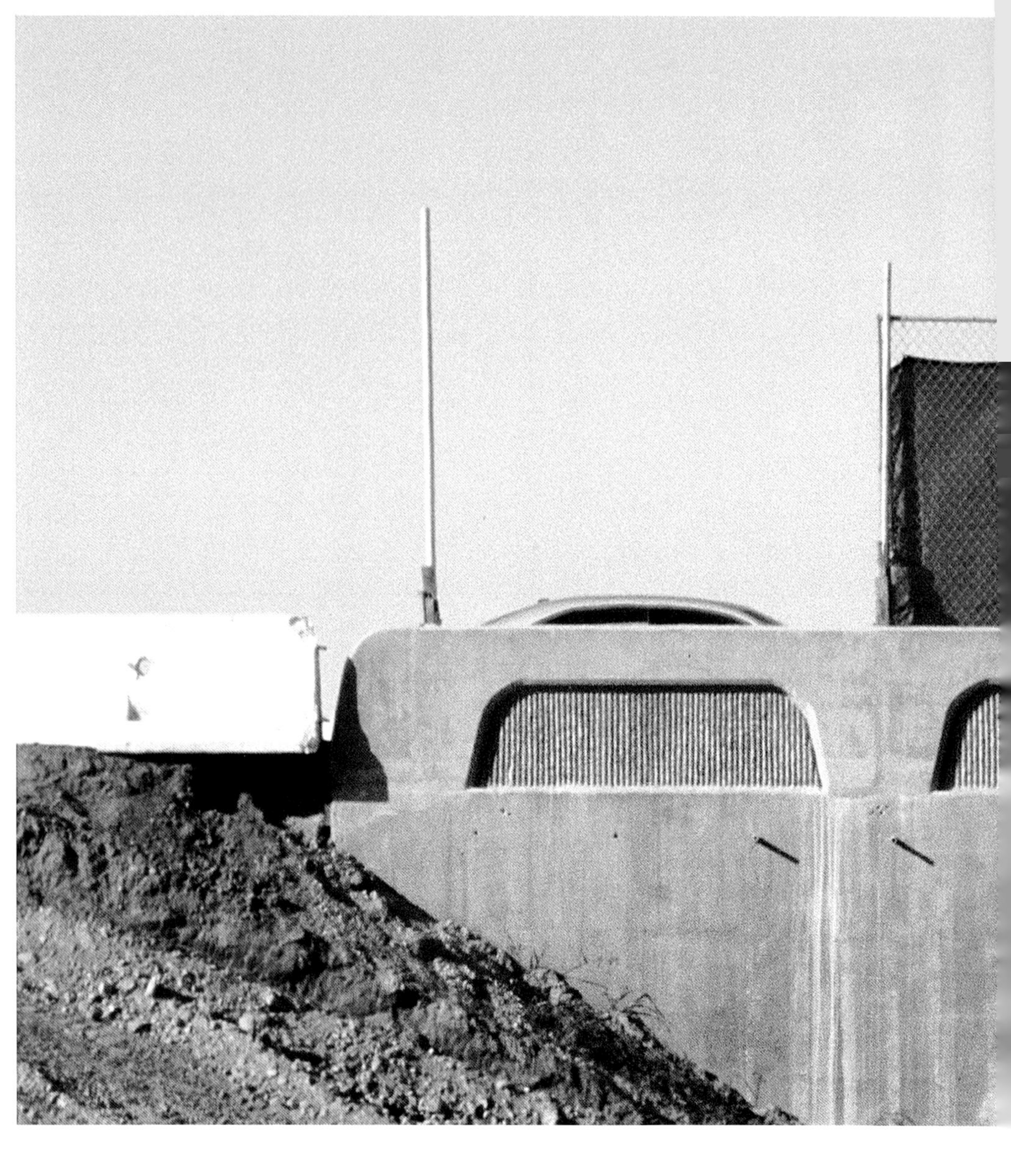

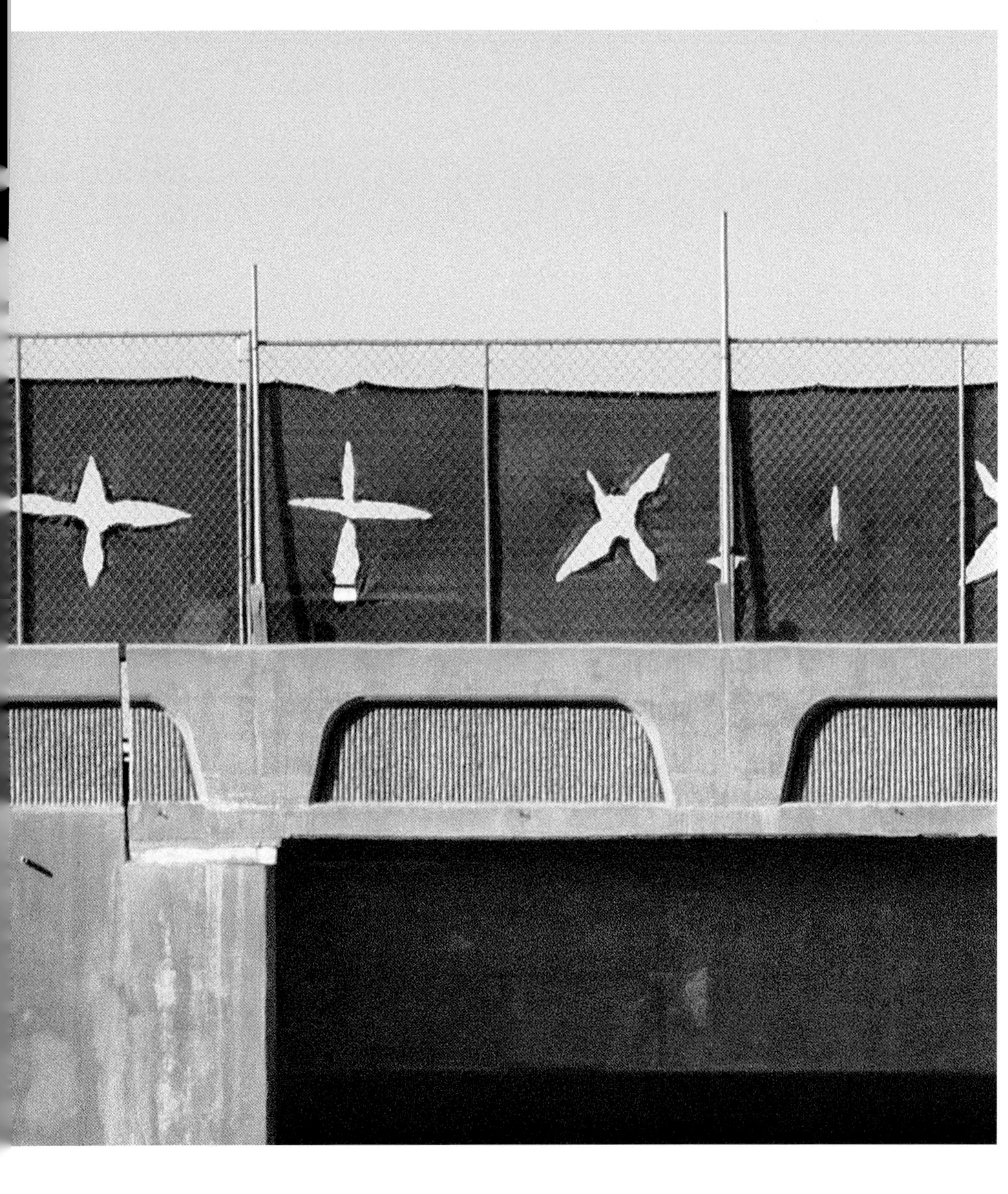

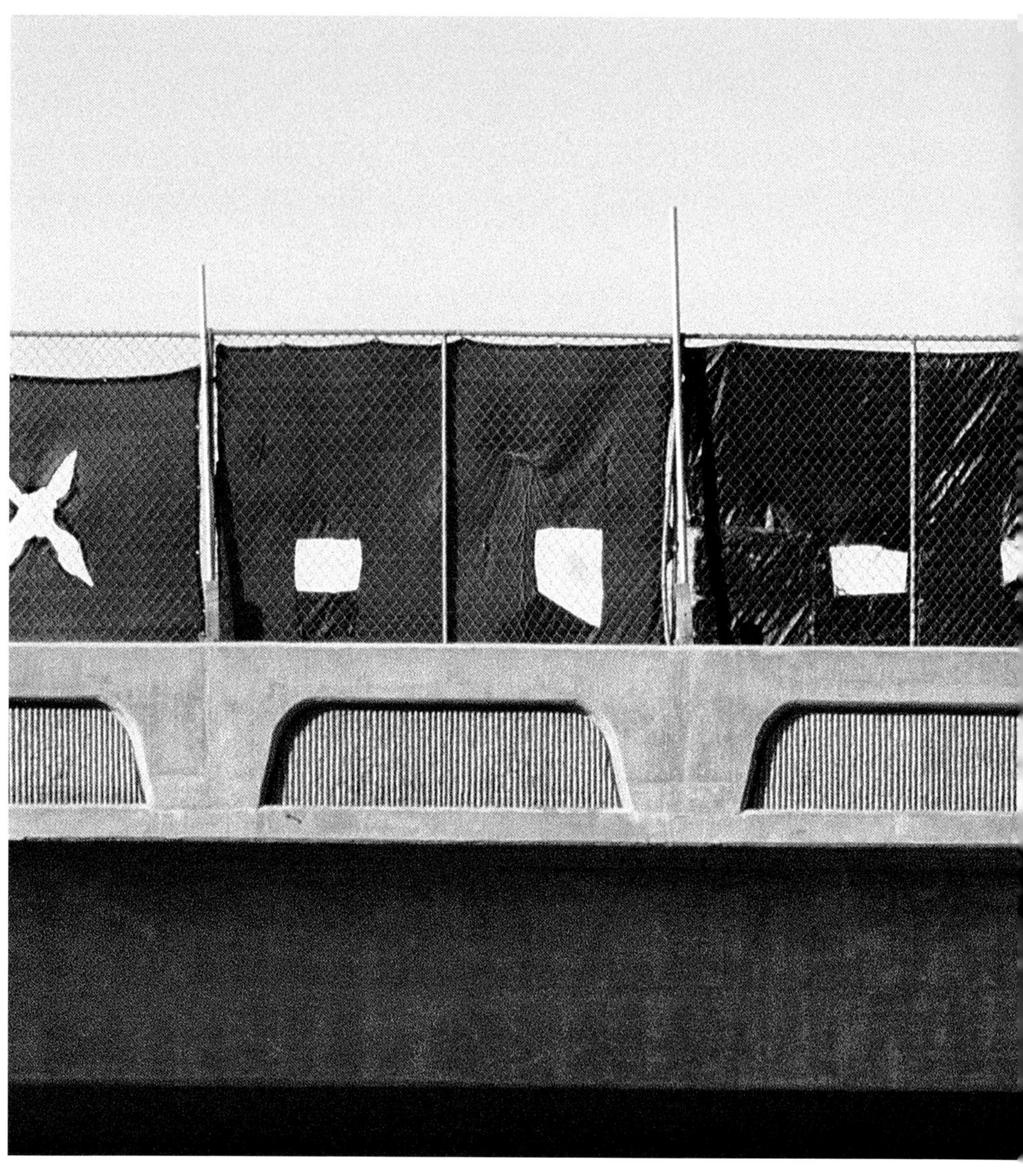

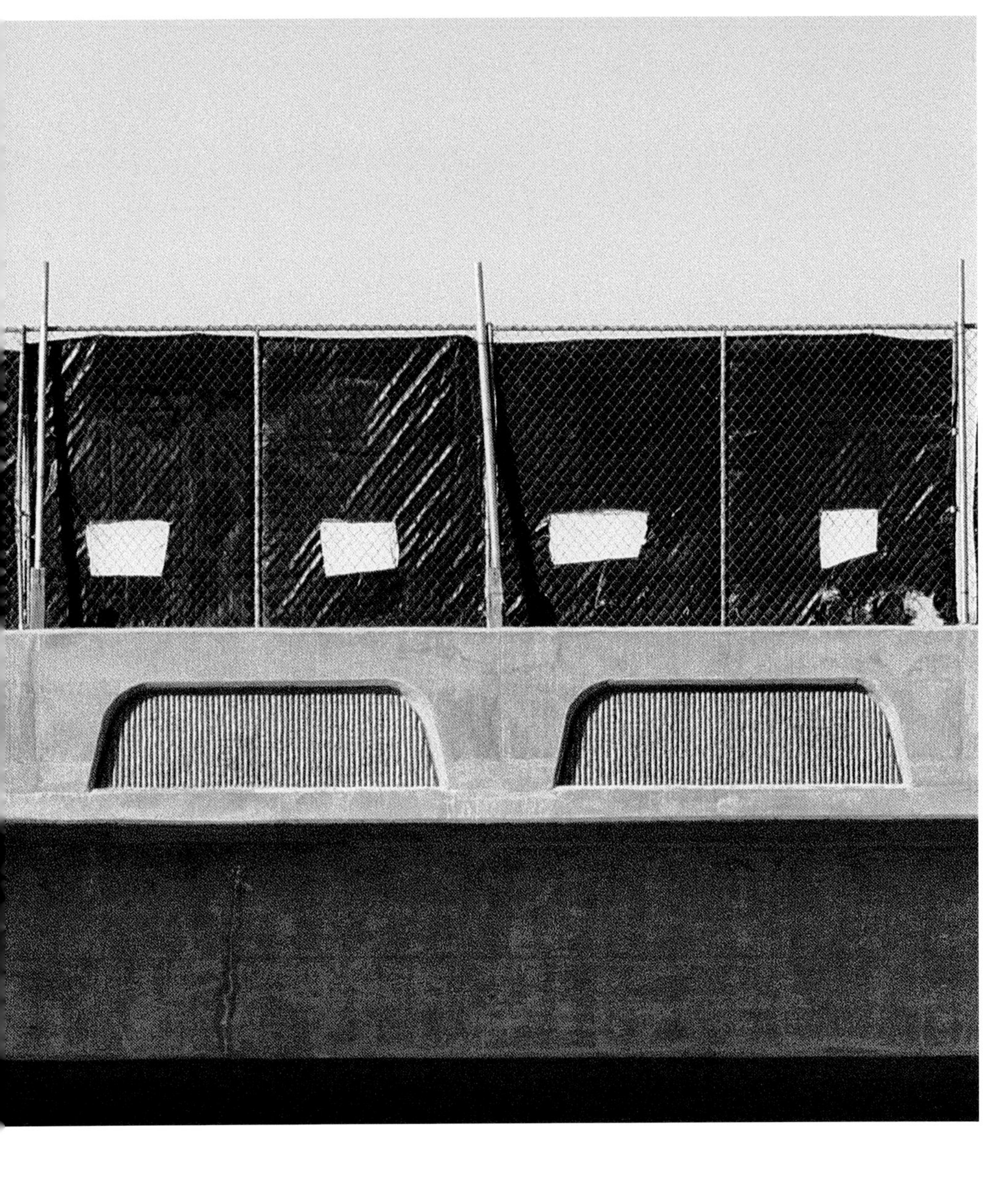

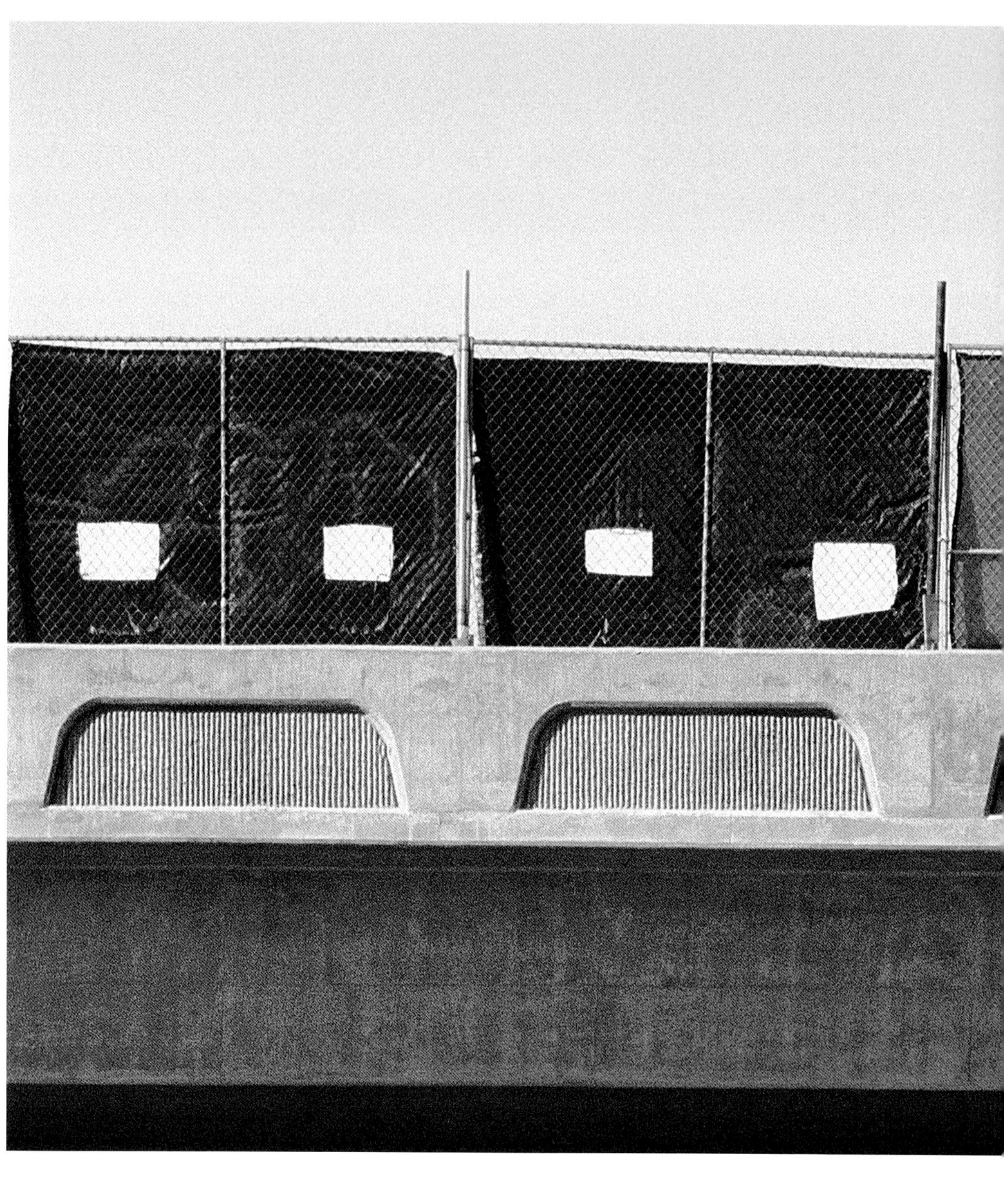

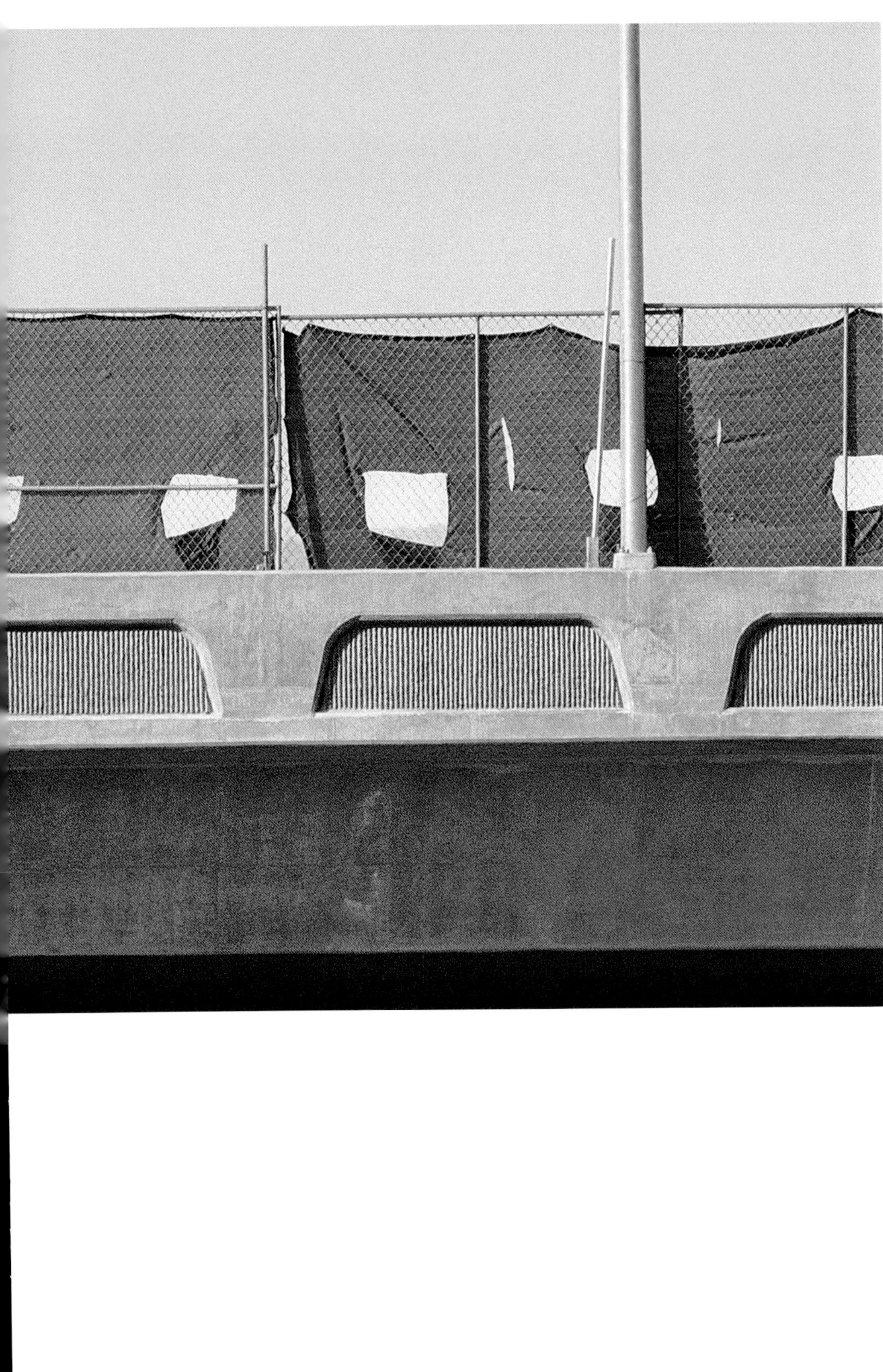

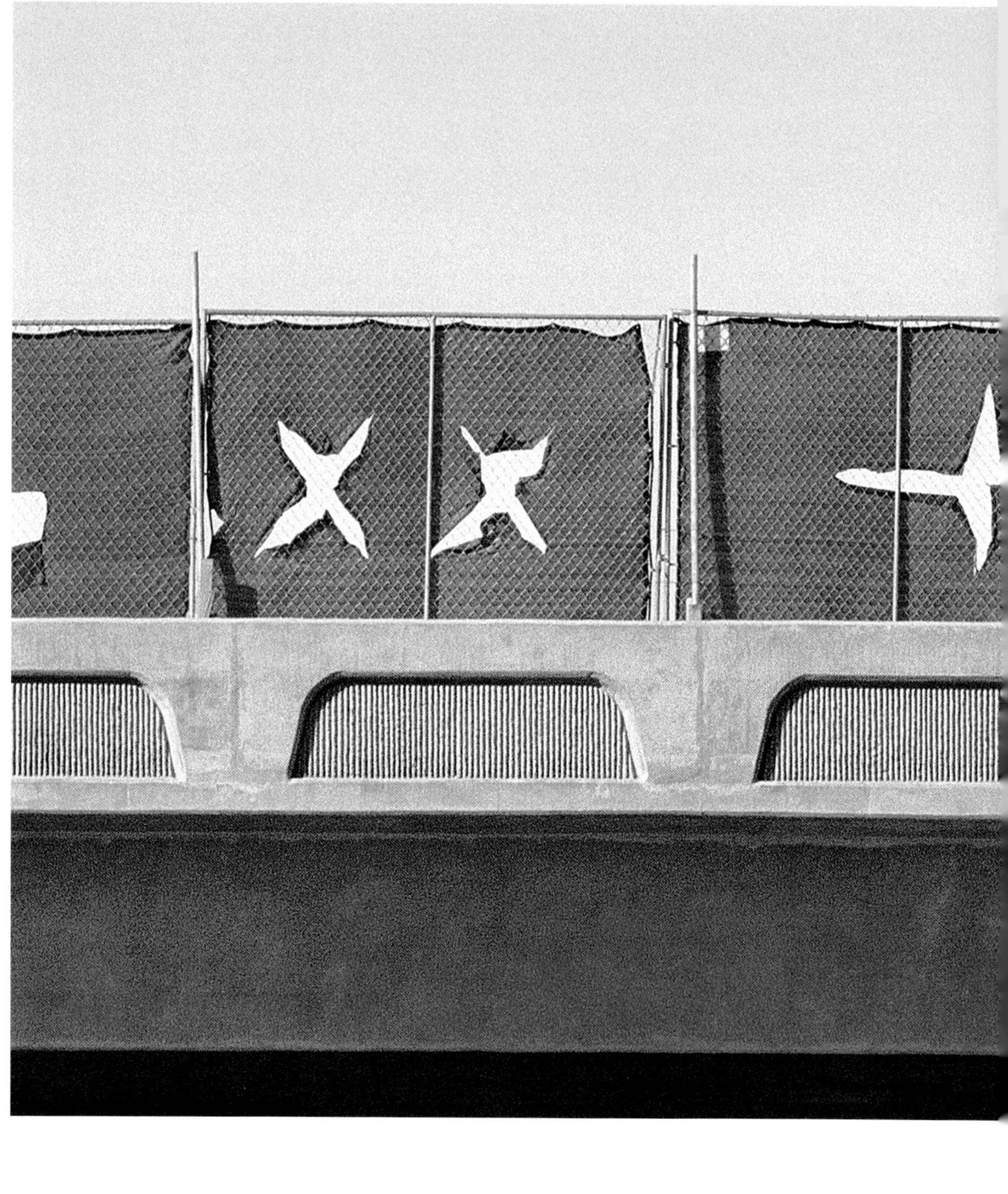

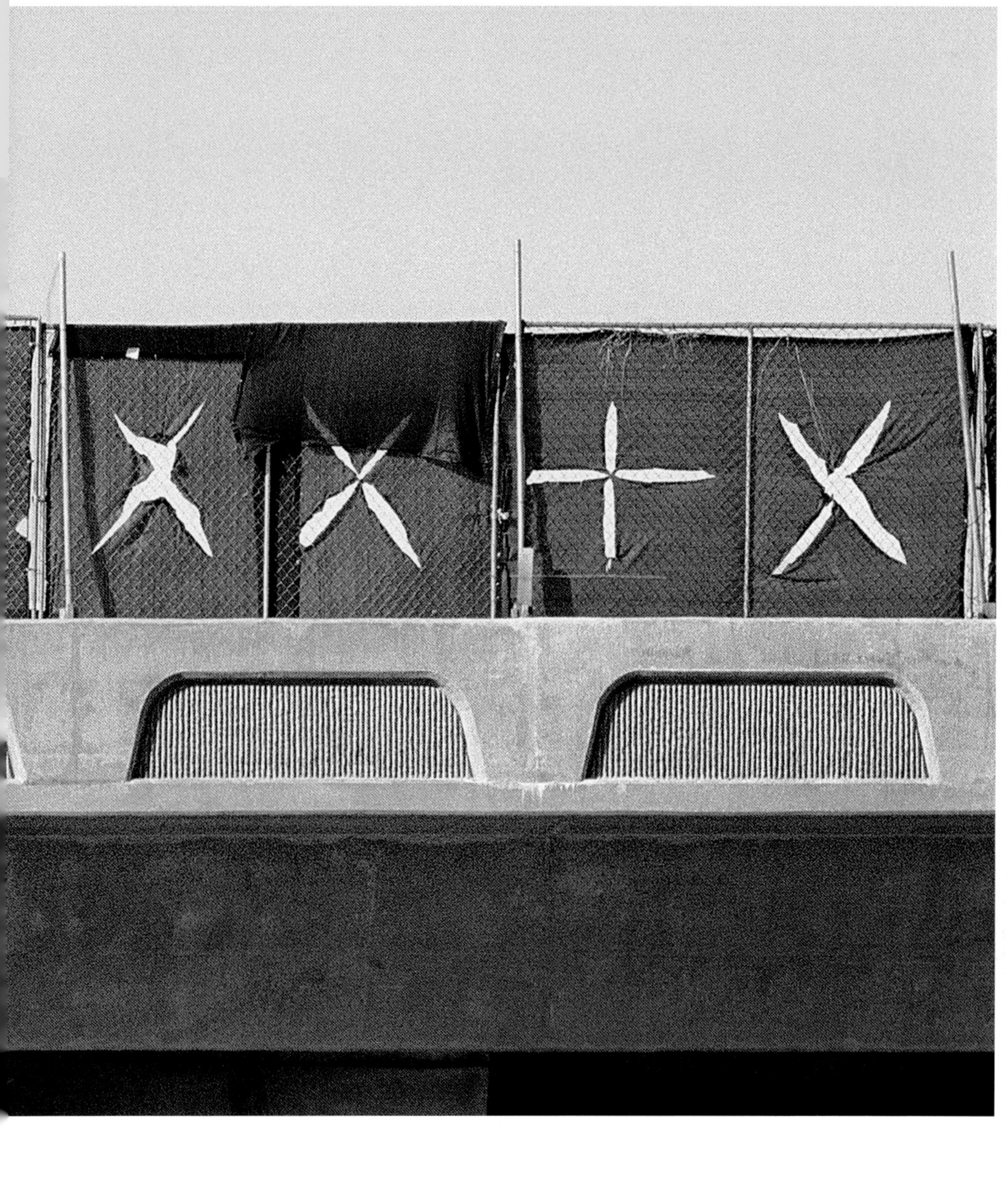

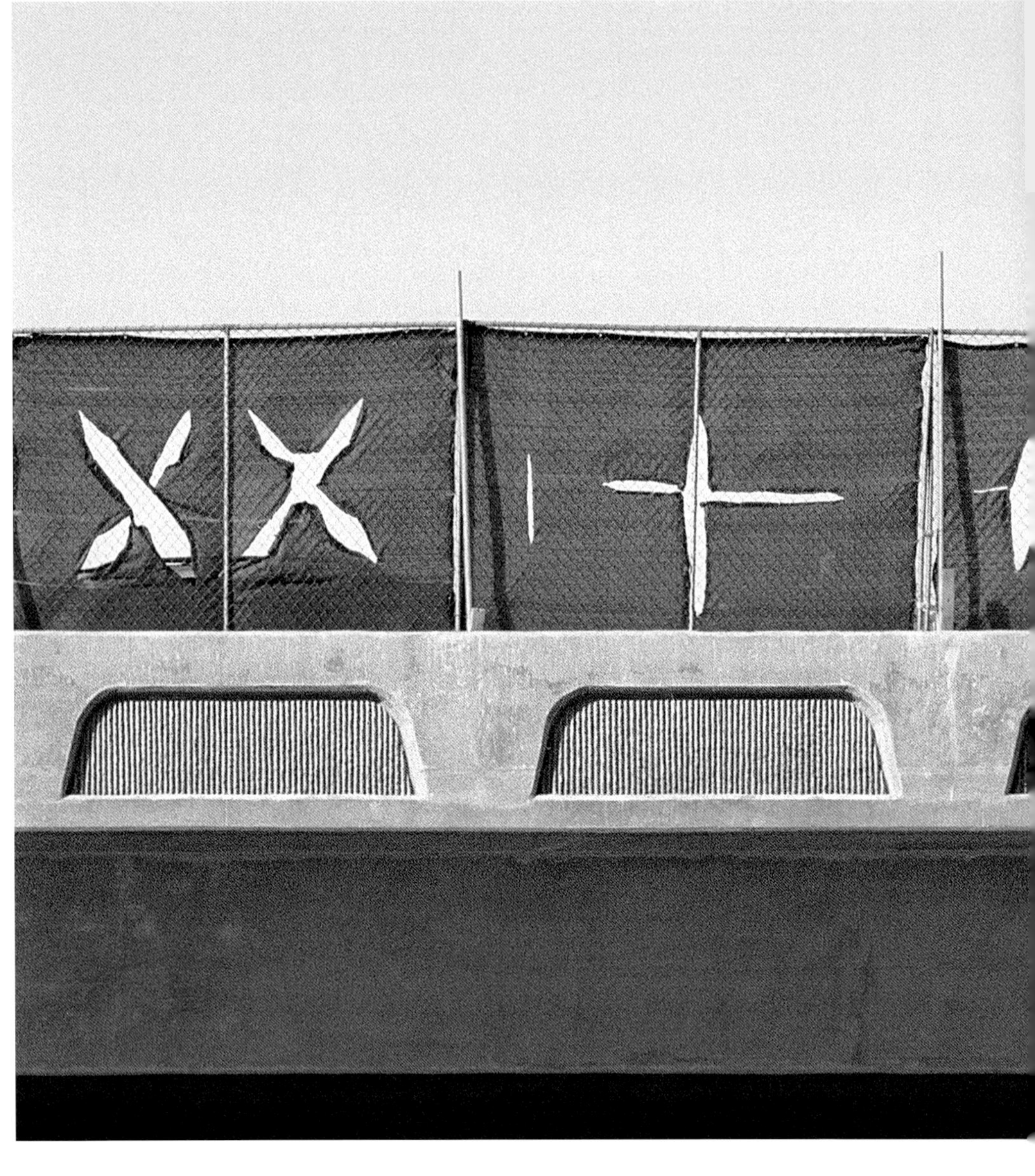

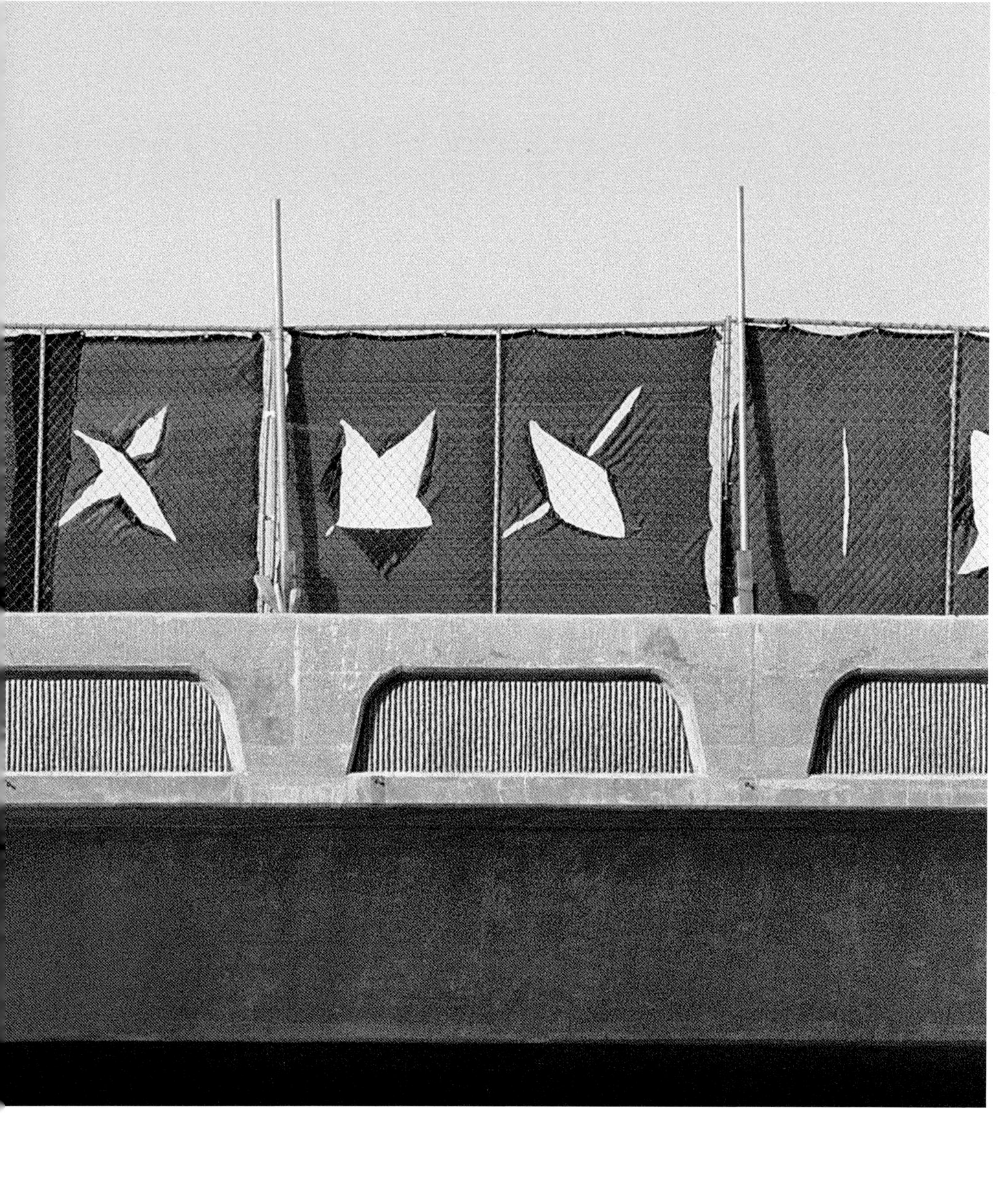

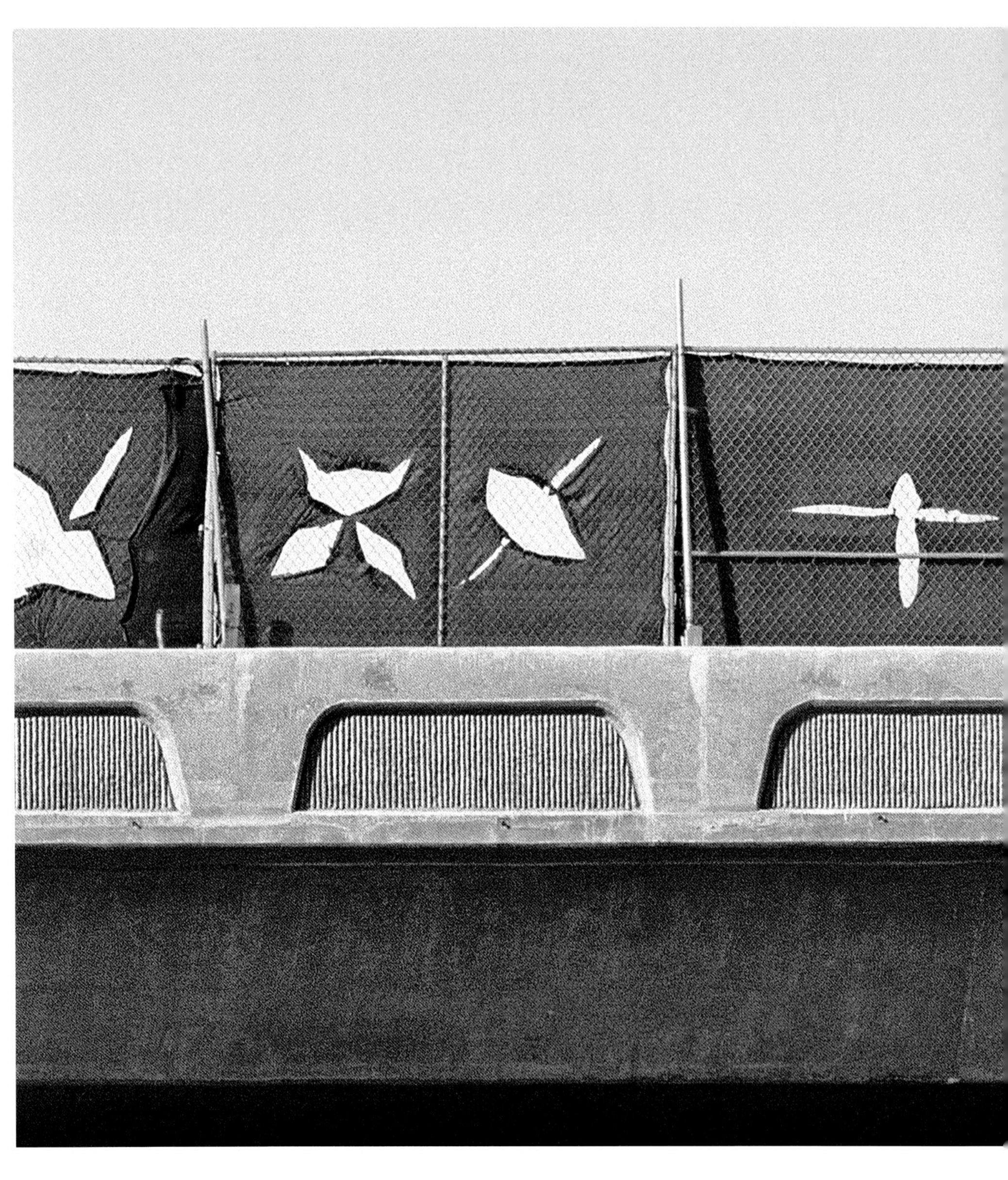

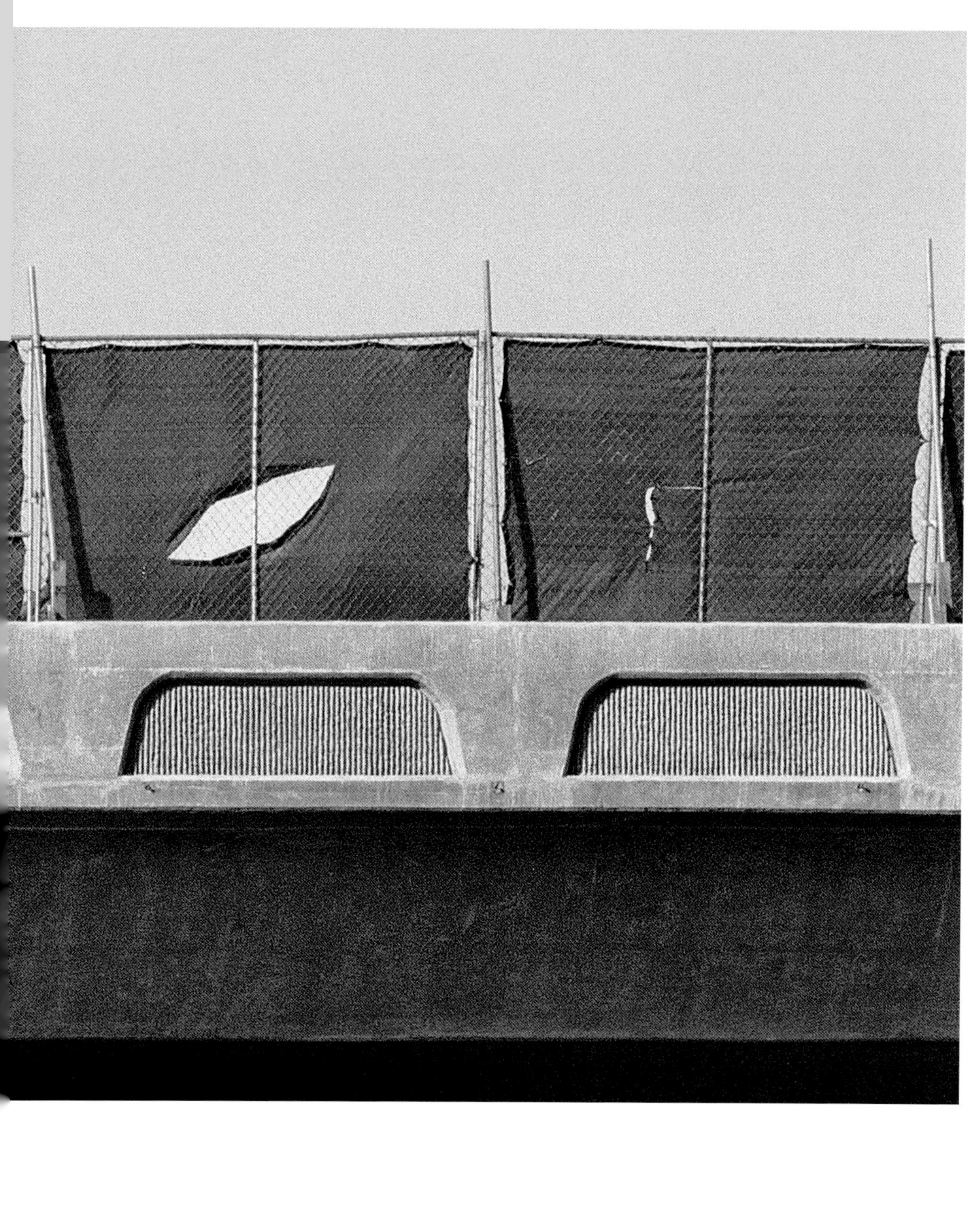

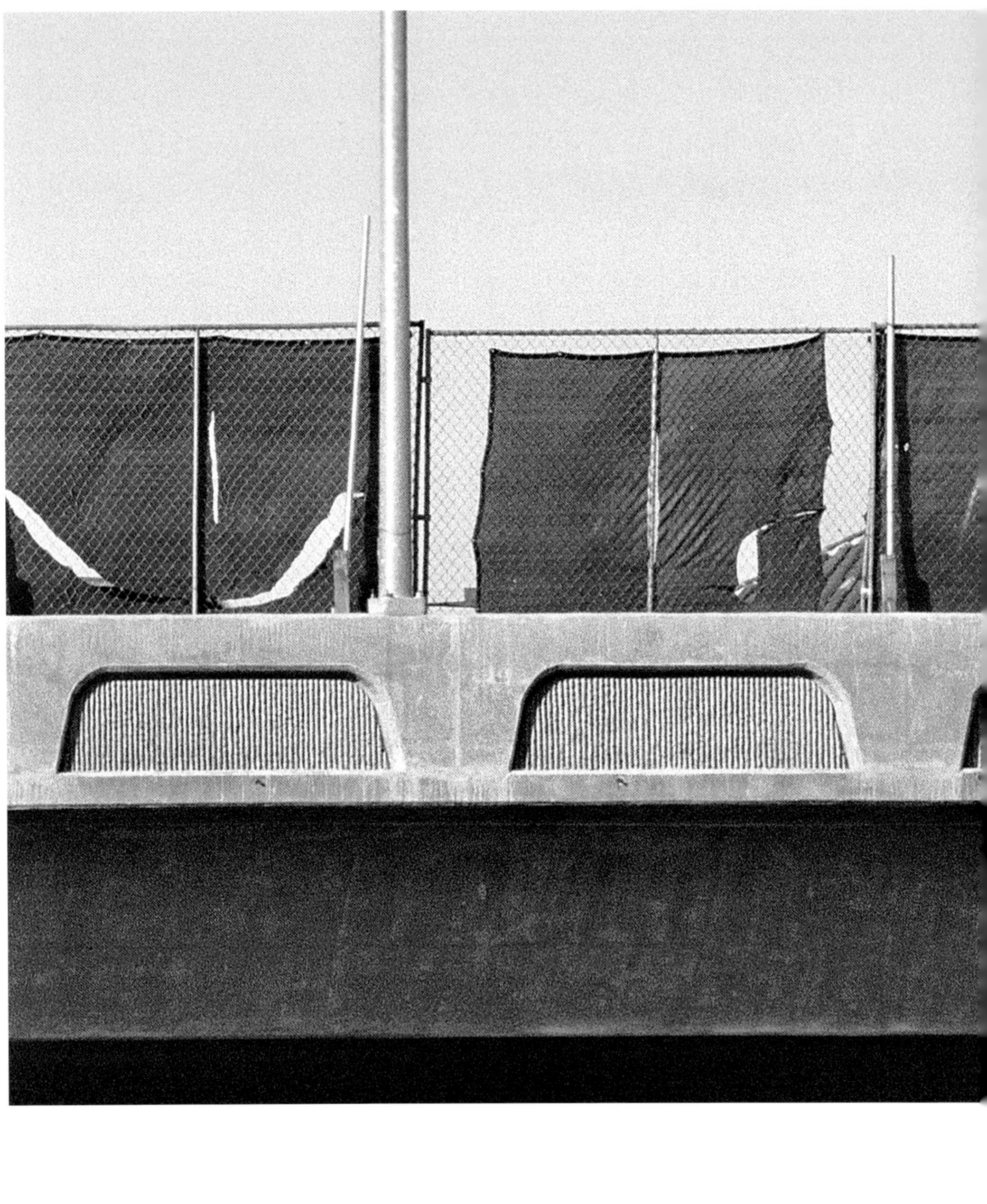

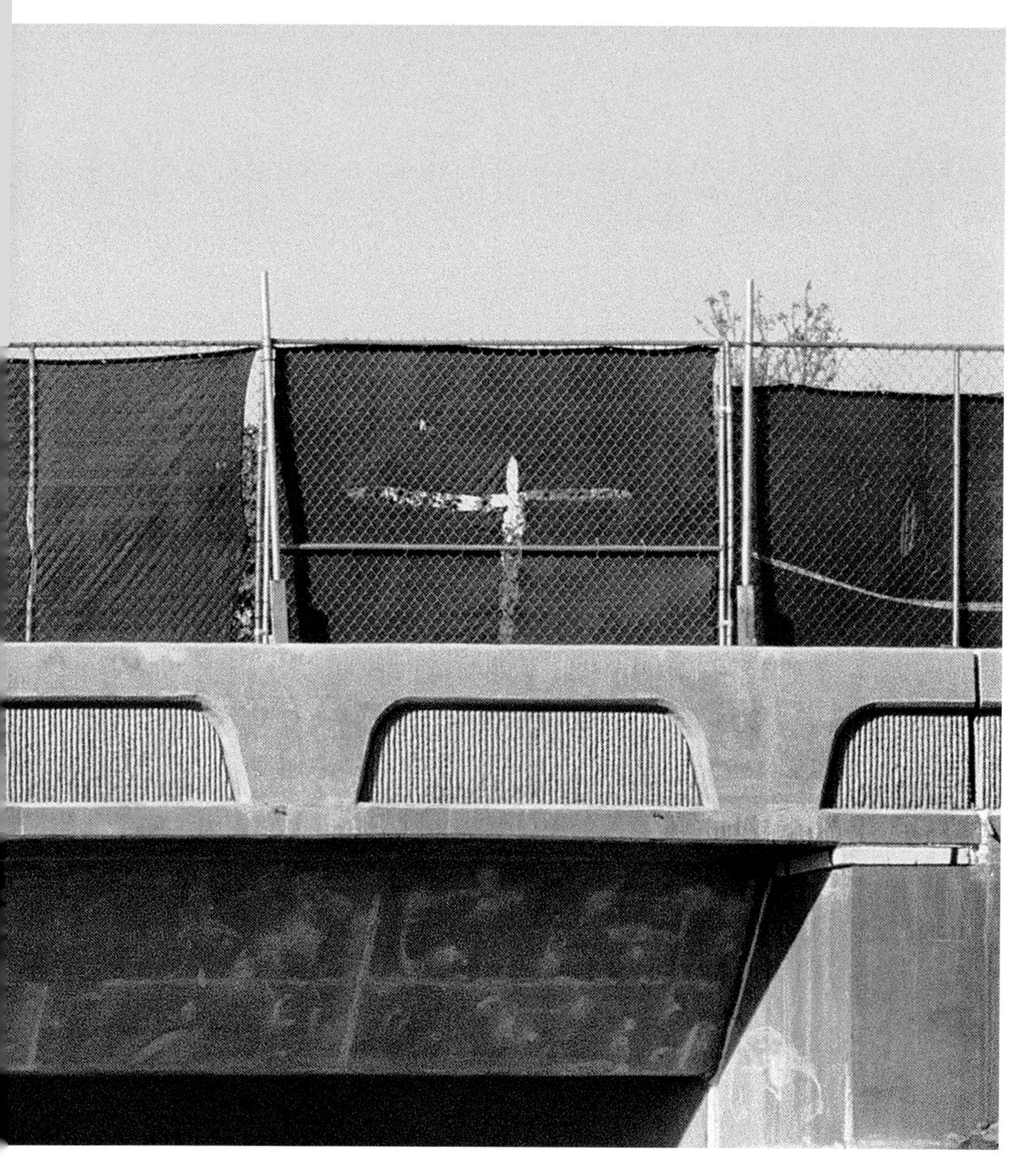

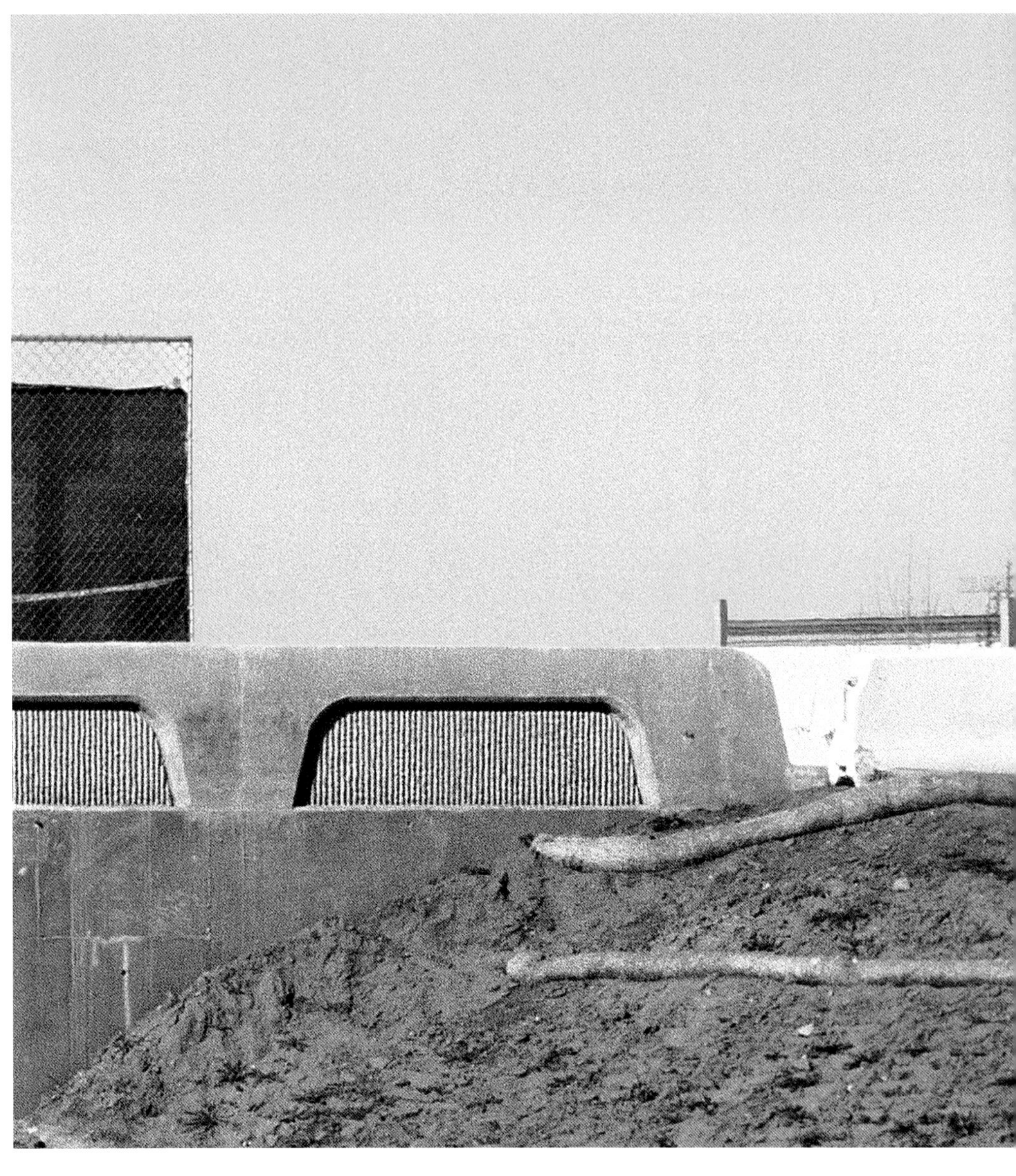

C E N T
O D Y

E R B

WORK

S I G N

E C O

I O N

A T U R

L L I S

W E   H

T H E M

182

AVE ALL

D E N T

I N G S

D A C

N T A L

S , D

, AN

,

C I D E

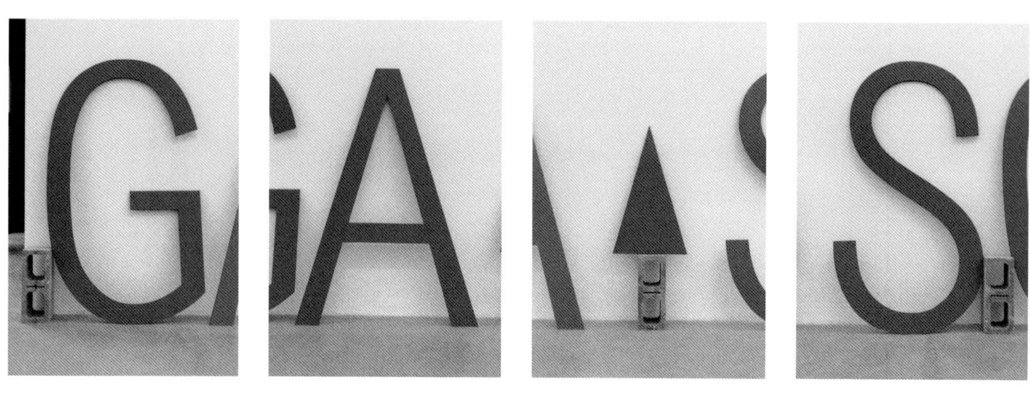

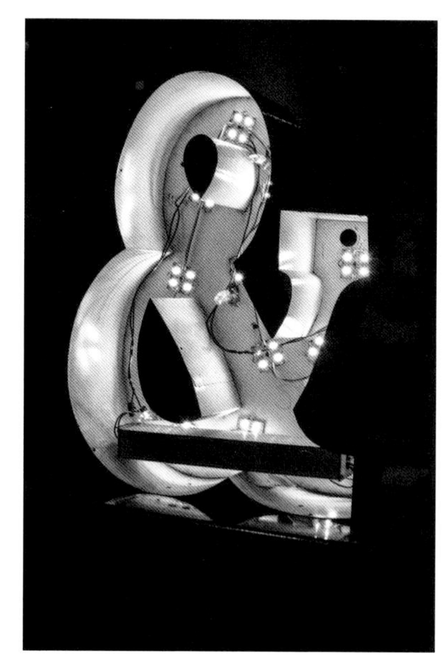

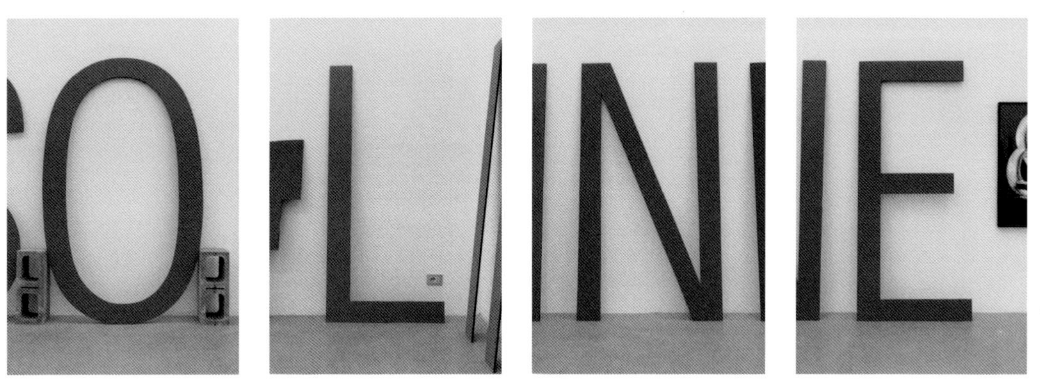

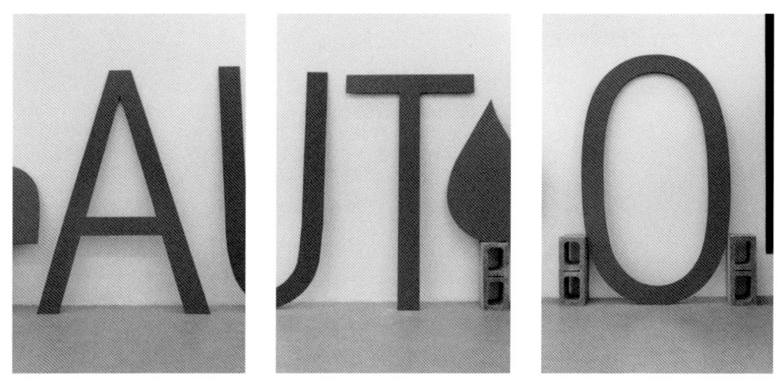

E L E C

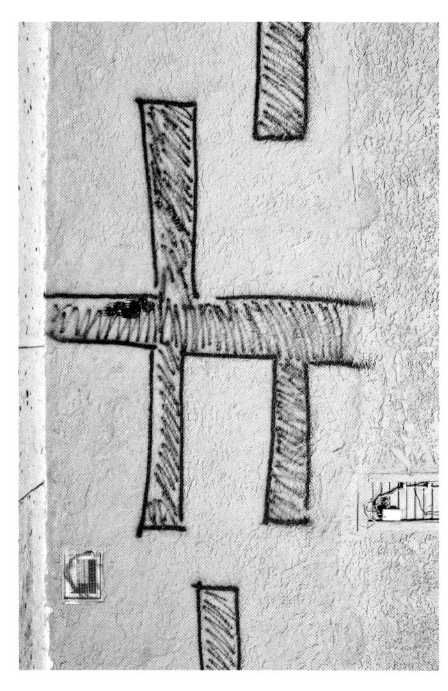

T R I C

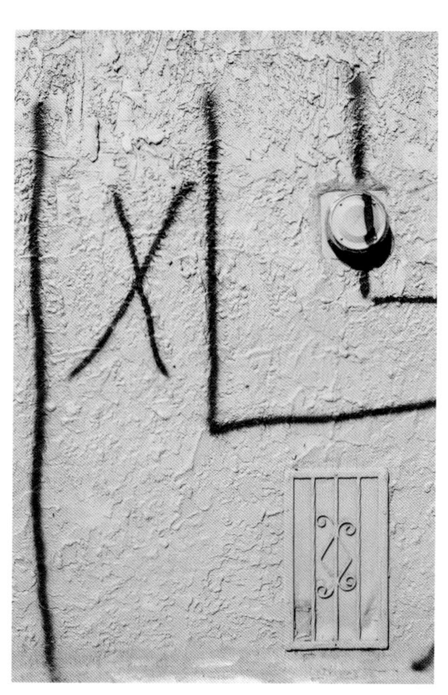

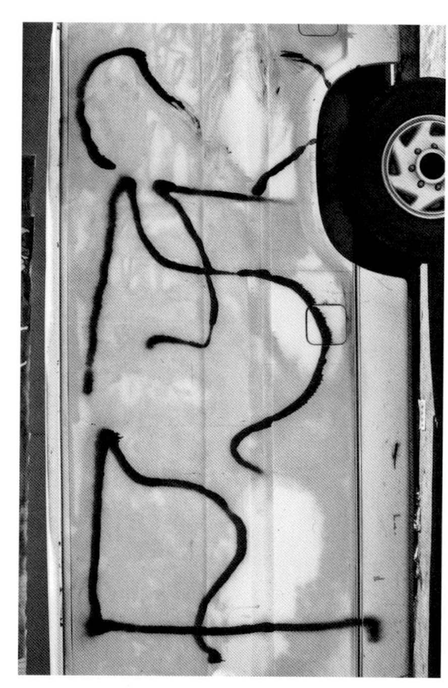

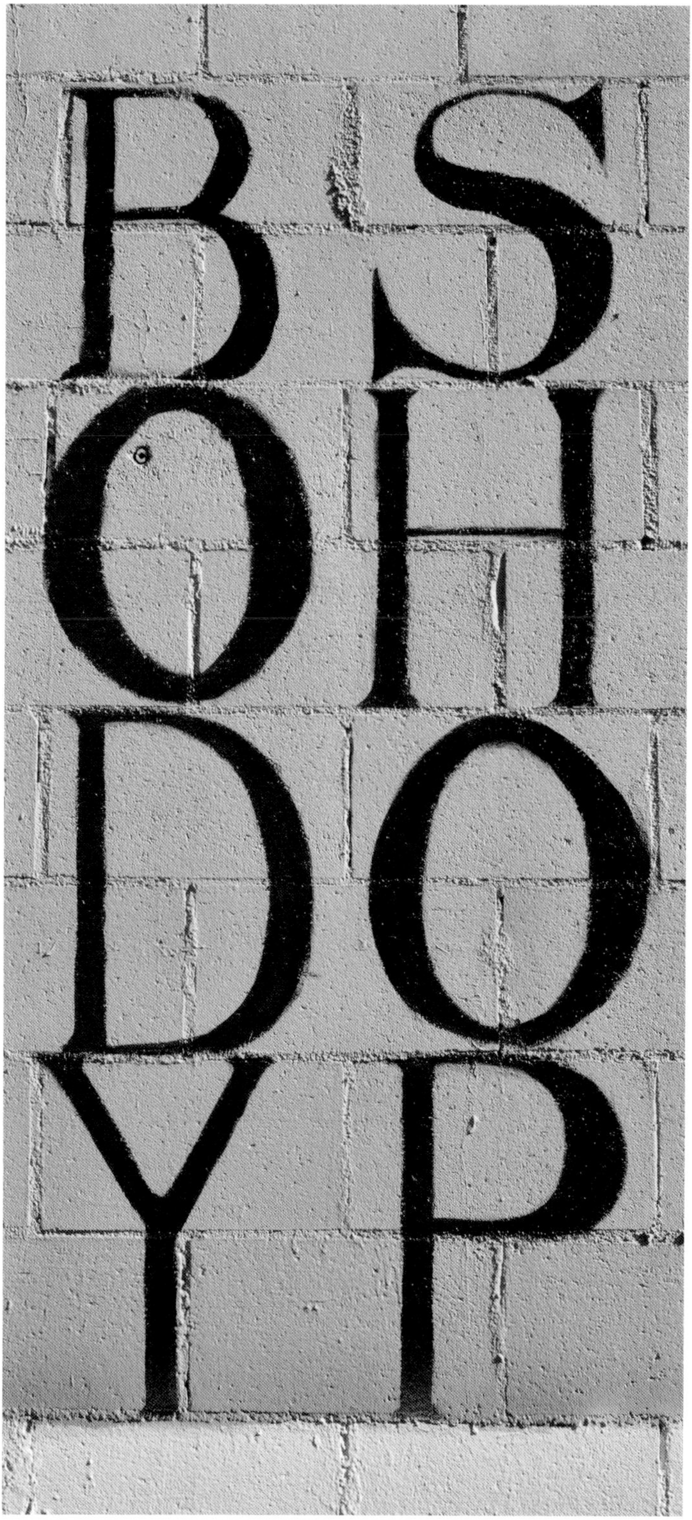

BODY
SHOP

SPEC
ATTE
N

IAL

NTIO

SPEC

SERV

I A L
I C E S

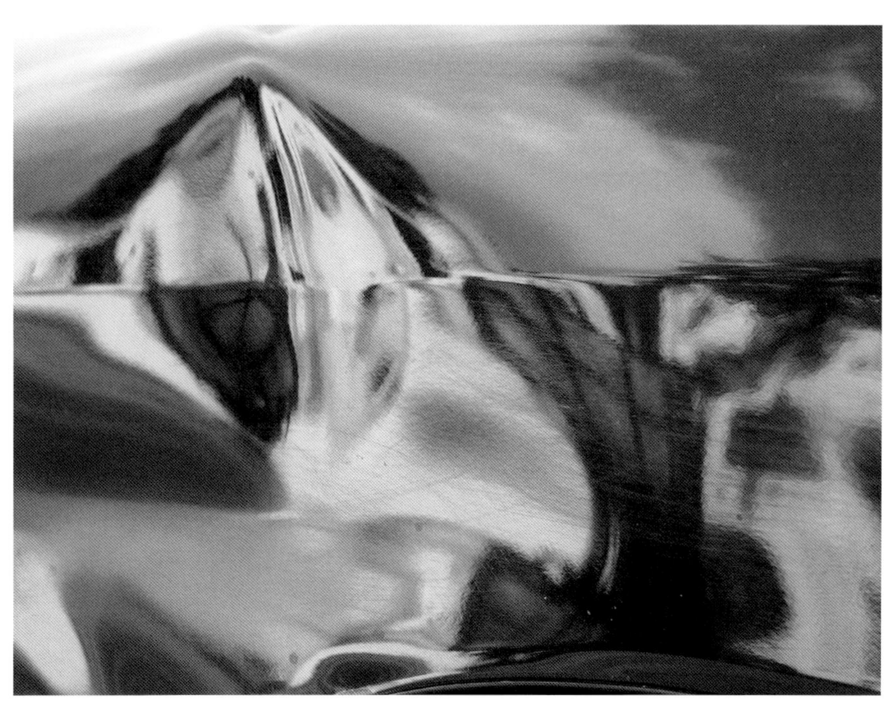

HYBR
DEMA

I D S

N D

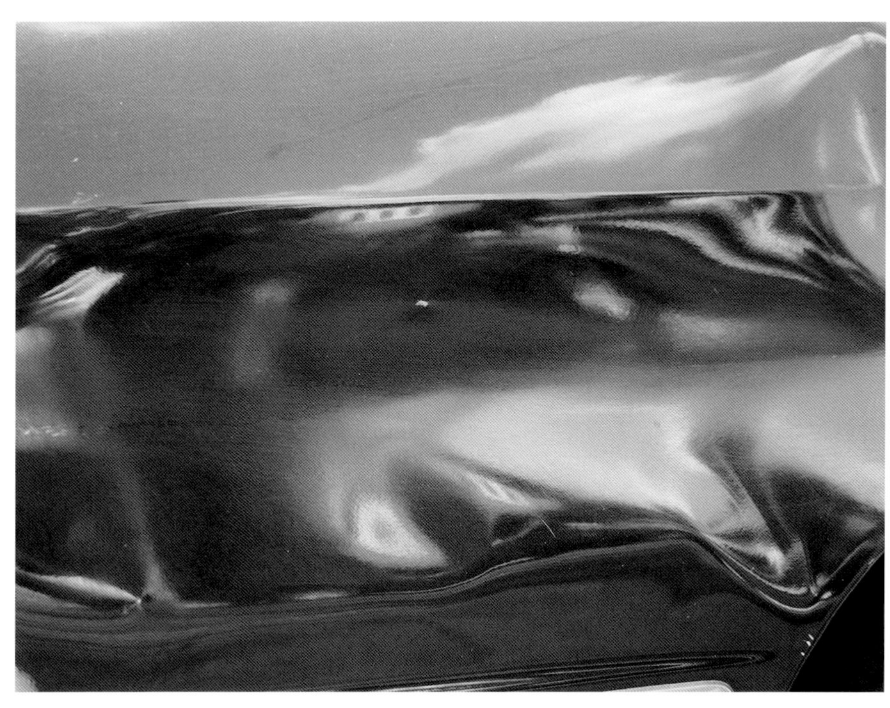

FACIES

L I T I

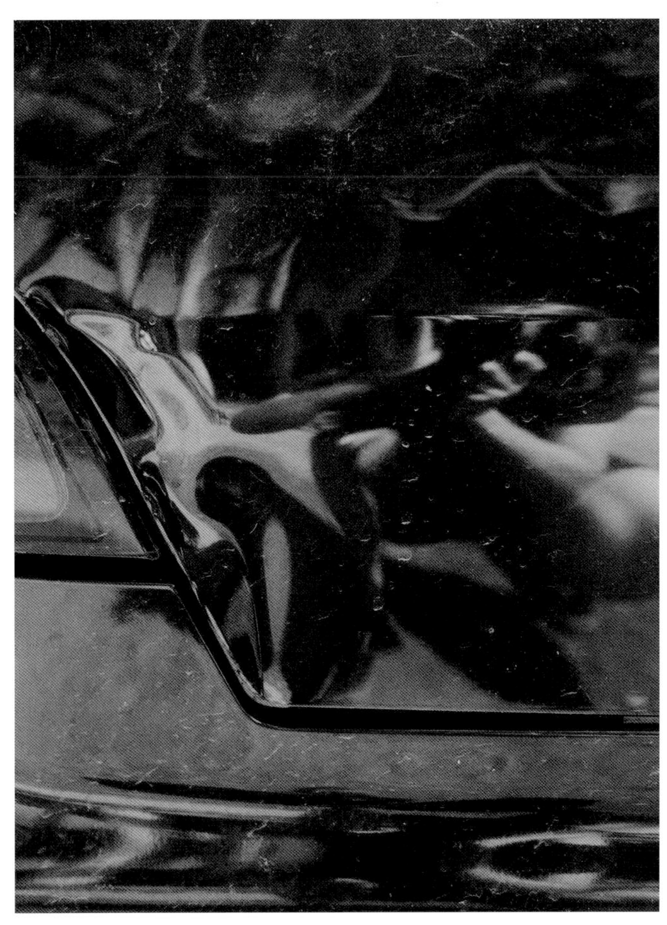

DAMA

GES

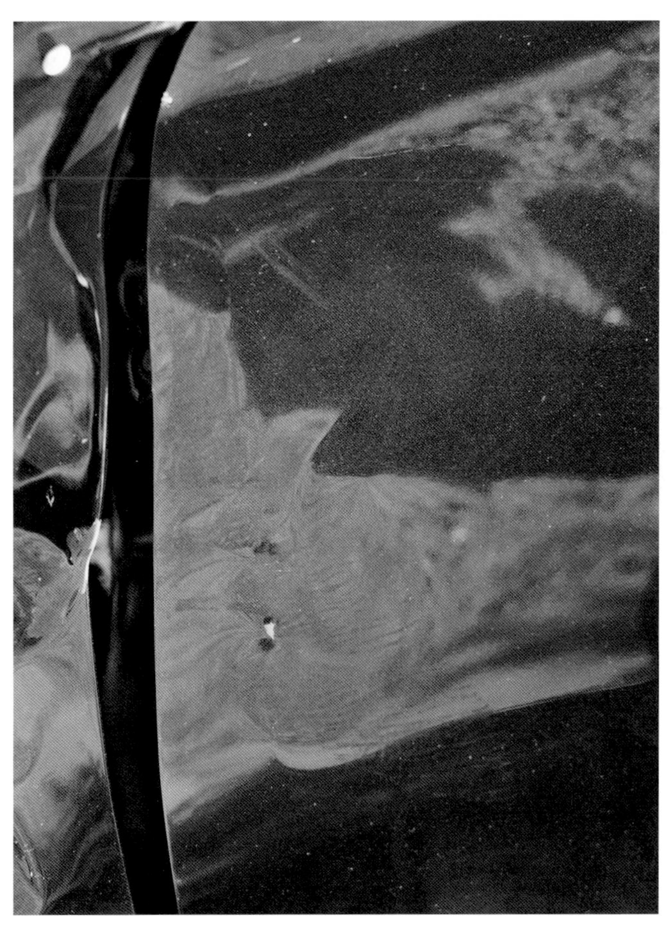

C O L L

N   R E

202

ISIO

PAIR

FULL

VICE

S E R

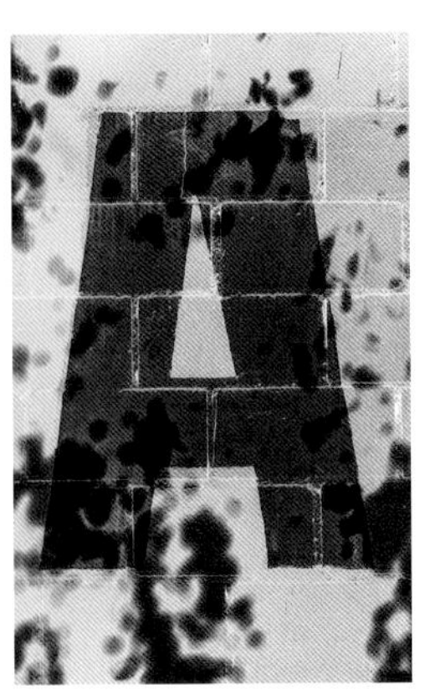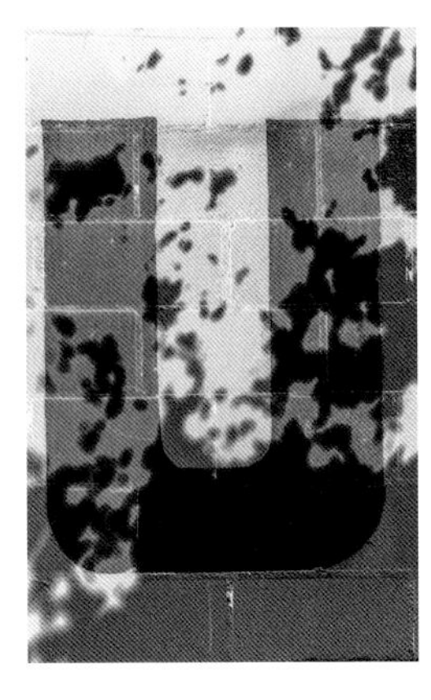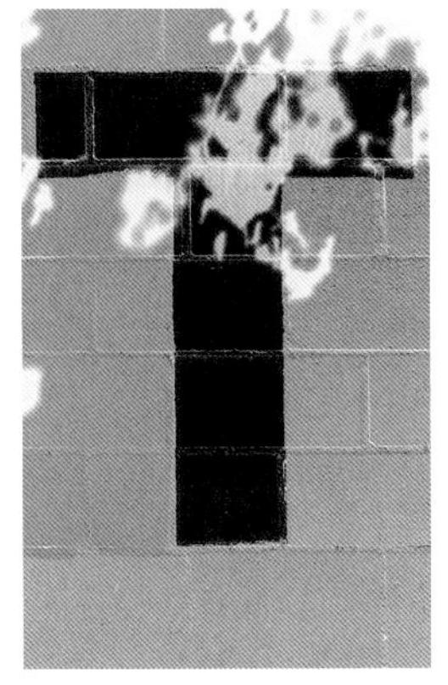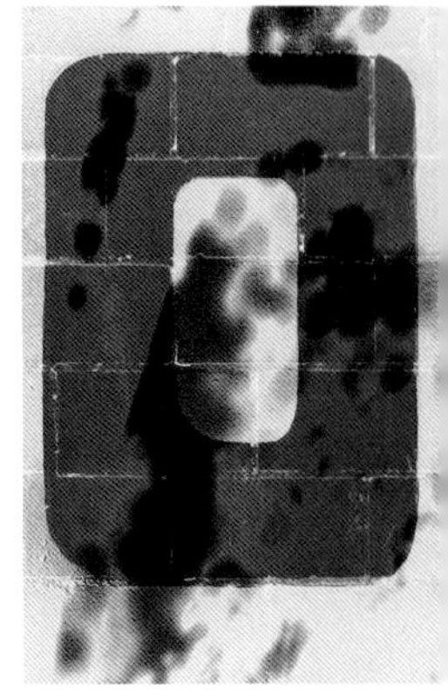

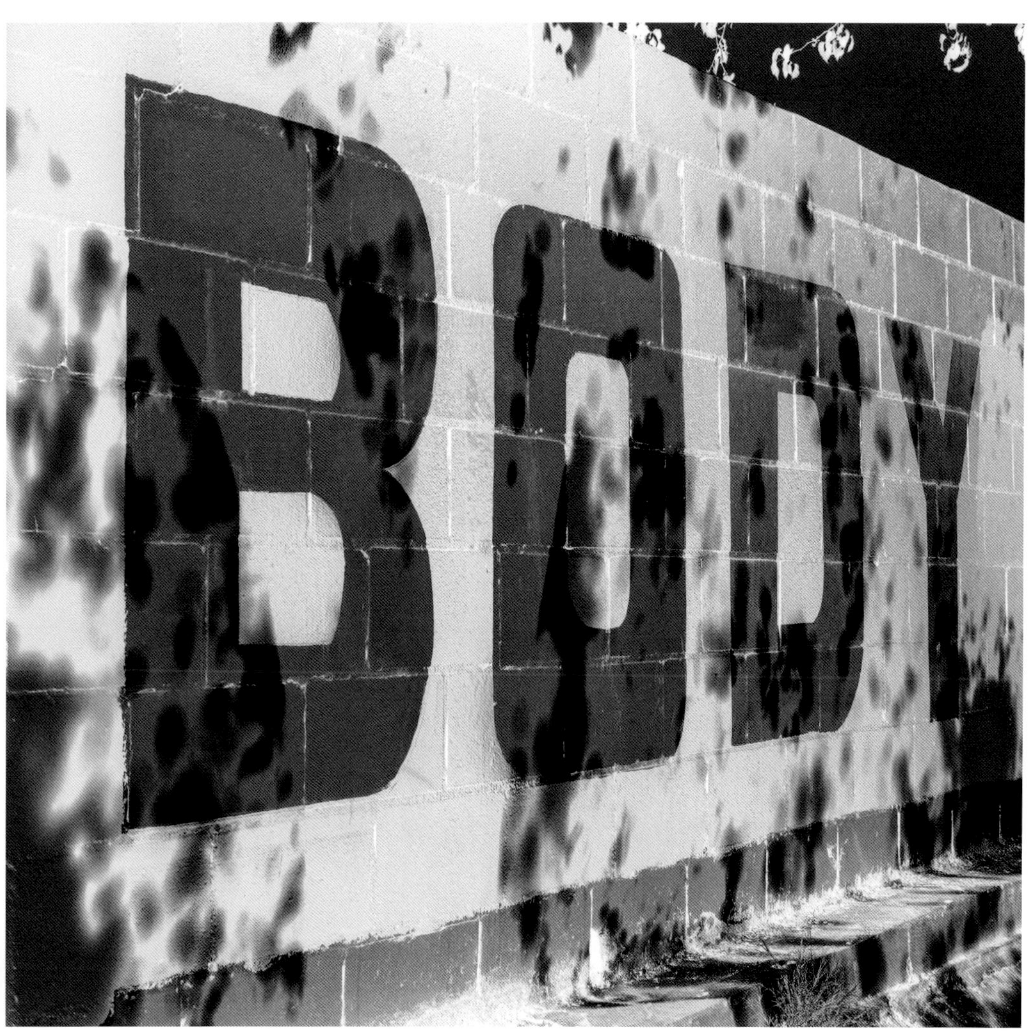

BODY

COLLISION

COLLISION AUTHORITY

COLLISION CENTERS OF AMERICA

TRUE QUALITY COLLISON CENTERS

CARSTAR COLLISION CARE OF AMERICA

AUTOMALL AUTOBODY/AMERICAN AUTO BODY

CHAMPIONS COLLISION CENTER

OXMOOR COLLISION CENTER

VISION COLLISION

3 MILLION COLLISION CENTER

A.C.E. AUTO WORLD COLLISION

A-1 COLLISION CORRECTION

ABC COLLISION CENTER

ABC COLLISION, INC

ACCENT COLLISION CENTER

ACCESS COLLISION CENTER

ACTION COLLISION CENTER

ADBU COLLISION

ADVANCED AUTO COLLISION REPAIR 2

ADVANCED FIRST AUTO AND COLLISION INC.

AFRICA AUTO REPAIR BODY SHOP

ALL AMERICAN COLLISION CENTER

ALL AMERICAN COLLISION OF ODESSA

ALL AUTO COLLISION

ALL CAR COLLISION

ALL CAR COLLISION & BODY, INC

ALL CITY AUTO BODY

ALL COUNTRY COLLISION

ALL MAKES COLLISION

ALL MAN AUTO BODY

ALL PRO BODY

ALL PRO COLLISION

ALL READY PAINT & BODY

ALL STAR BODY & PAINT

ALL STAR COLLISION CENTER

ALLEGHENY AUTO BODY

AUTO AXCESS COLLISION

AUTO BAKE COLLISION CENTER

AUTO BODY

AUTO BODY #1

AUTO BODY BY MACK

AUTO BODY CENTER

AUTO BODY CLINIC

AUTO BODY COLLISION & GLASS

AUTO BODY CONCEPTS - PHOENIX

AUTO BODY CRAFTERS

AUTO BODY CUSTOMS, LLC

AUTO BODY EXPERIENCE COLLISION

AUTO BODY INC

AUTO BODY PLUS, INC.

AUTO BODY SERVICE CENTERS, INC

AUTO BODY SERVICE CENTERS, INC.

AUTO BODY SERVICES

AUTO BODY SERVICES INC - IRVING

AUTO BODY SOLUTIONS COLLISION CENTER, LLC

AUTO BODY SPECIALIST - GARLAND

AUTO BODY SPECIALISTS - COLUMBUS

AUTO BODY SPECIALISTS - MESA

AUTO BODY SPECIALISTS - ROCKFORD

AUTO BODY USA

AUTO BODY WORLD - GILBERT

AUTO BODY WORLD - MESA

AUTO BODY WORLD - PEORIA

AUTO BODY WORLD - PHOENIX

AUTO CITY BODY SHOP

AUTO CITY REPAIR & BODY WORK

AUTO CLUB ASSOCIATION

AUTO COLLISION

AUTO COLLISION CENTER

AUTO COLLISION EXPERTS

AUTO COLLISION SERVICES

AUTO COLLISION SERVICES INC

AUTO COLLISION SPECIALISTS

AUTO COLLISION SPECIALISTS INC

AUTO COLLISION WORKS

AUTO CRAFT COLLISION REPAIR, INC.

AUTO CRAFTERS COLLISION CENTER

AUTO CRAFTERS PAINT & BODY INC.

AUTO ELITE COLLISION CENTER

AUTO EMERGENCY ROOM

AUTO ENHANCER'S, INC

AUTO FIXIT BODY SHOP

AUTO FRAME & BODY WORK'S INC

AUTO HAUS COLLISION CENTER

AUTO IMPACT # 2, LLC

AUTO PAINT & BODY AUTO GLASS

AUTO PAINT AND BODY SHOP

AUTO PAINT RENEW

AUTO PAINT SPECIALISTS

AUTO PLUS OF CHICAGO

AUTO PRO COLLISION CLINIC INC

AUTO PRO'S COLLISION CENTER

AUTO REPAIR CENTER 2000

AUTO R-US COLLISION CENTER

AUTO SERVICE AND COLLISION

AUTO SHAPE COLLISION CENTER - RTP

AUTO SPORT PRO BODY SHOP

AUTO TECH COLLISION

AUTO TECH COLLISION CENTER

AUTO WORKS

AUTO WORKS INC

AUTOBAHN PAINT & BODY

AUTOBODY AMERICA

AUTOBODY AMERICA - COVINGTON PIKE

AUTOBODY AMERICA - STAGE

AUTOBODY AMERICA - WINCHESTER

AUTOBODY AMERICA-CHATTANOOGA

AUTOBODY EXPRESS

AUTOBODY GARAGE

AUTOBODY OF DENTON

AUTOBODY SOLUTIONS BY SATURN

AUTOBODY SPA

AUTOCARE COLLISION CENTERS

AUTOCRAFT BODY SHOP

AUTOCRAFT BODY WERKS

AUTODENT CARE

AUTOEXACT COLLISION & PAINT

AUTO-GRAPHICS AUTO BODY & PAINT

AUTOIMPACT #1, LLC

AUTOMALL COLLISION

AUTOMASTERS COLLISION REPAIR

AUTOMOTIVE COLLISION TECHNICIANS

AUTONATION COLLISION CENTER

AUTOPRO COLLISION CENTER

AUTOPRO COLLISION CENTER INC

AUTOPRO COLLISION CLINIC INC.

AUTO'S R US

AUTOSPORT COLLISION CENTER

AUTO-TECH COLLISION CENTER

AUTOWAY COLLISION - AUSTIN

AUTOWEST COLLISION REPAIRS

AUTOWORLD COLLISION CENTER

CAPITAL COLLISION

CAPITAL COLLISION CENTER

CAPITAL FORD COLLISION CENTER

CAPITOL AUTO BODY

CAPITOL COLLISION REPAIR

CAPITOL COLLISION REPAIR SPECIALISTS

CAR SCANS COLLISION CENTER

CAR TECH COLLISION CENTER

DICK POE DODGE BODY SHOP

DICK SMITH BODY SHOP

DICK SMITH FORD BODY SHOP

DICK SMITH PAINT & BODY SHOP

DICK TAYLOR COLLISION SERVICES

DICKERSON'S COLLISION REPAIR

DICKEY'S BODY SHOP

DICKS AUTO BODY & FRAME

EPIC ONE COLLISION

ETHICAL PAINT AND BODY

FIRST CHOICE BODY SHOP

FIRST CHOICE COLLISION

FIRST CHOICE COLLISION CENTER

FIRST CLASS AUTO BODY, INC

FIRST CLASS COLLISIONS

FIRST COLLISION

FIRST COLLISION INC.

FIRST IMPRESSIONS COLLISION INC

FIRST STOP AUTO BODY REPAIR

FIRST STREET AUTO BODY & TOWING

FIRST TEAM COLLISION

INDIA'S AUTO COLLISION

INVISION AUTO BODY

JESUS COLLISION CENTER

KINO'S BODY SHOP

KUSTOM WERX AUTOBODY

LIFETIME AUTO COLLISION

LIKE NEW AUTO COLLISION REPAIR

LIKE-NU AUTO PAINT & BODY WORKS

LIL IKES AUTO COLLISION & FRAME REPAIR

LYK-NU COLLISION CENTER - NASHVILLE

MARS NATIONAL COLLISION

MAXIMUM COLLISION CENTER

NAT AUTOBODY

NATIONAL AUTO COLLISION

NATIONAL AUTO COLLISION CENTERS

NATIONAL AUTOBODY CO

NATIONAL COLLISION CENTER

NATIONAL COLLISION CO., INC.

NATIONAL COLLISION REPAIR

NATIONAL DENT PAINTLESS DENT REPAIR

NATIONWIDE AUTOBODY INC.

NATIONWIDE COLLISION CENTER

NATIONWIDE COLLISION CENTERS

NATIONWIDE COLLISION EXPERTS

NEAT STREET AUTO BODY

NETWORK AUTO BODY & PAINT SHOP

NEW GENERATION AUTO BODY INC

NEW IMAGE AUTO BODY

NEW IMAGE PAINT AND BODY SHOP, INC.

NEW LIFE AUTO BODY

NEW TECH AUTO BODY

NEW UNITED AUTO BODY

ONE BY ONE AUTO & BODY REPAIR

ONE STOP AUTO

ONE STOP AUTO BODY & TOWING

ONE STOP COLLISION CENTER

ONE WAY AUTO BODY INC.

ORION BODY SHOP

ORLANDO AUTO BODY

ORLANDO AUTO TOP, INC.

PATRIOT COLLISION CENTER

PAYNE COLLISION CENTER

PERFECT AUTO BODY

PERFECT COLLISION

PERFECT COLLISION CENTER, INC.

PERFECT TOUCH PAINT & BODY

PERFECTION AUTO BODY

PERFECTION BODY CO

PERFECTION ONE COLLISION CENTER

PERFECTION PAINT & BODY

PERFORMANCE AUTO BODY - RALEIGH

PERFORMANCE AUTO COLLISION CENTER

PERFORMANCE BODY AND PAINT

PERFORMANCE BODY SHOP - HOUSTON

PERFORMANCE COLLISION

PERFORMANCE COLLISION REPAIR
SPECIALIST, INC.

PERFORMANCE PAINT & BODY

PERFORMANCE TRUCK BODYSHOP

POWER COLLISION CENTER

PRECISE COLLISION

PRECISE COLLISION CENTER

PRECISION AUTO BODY

PRECISION AUTO BODY - CINCINNATI

PRECISION AUTO BODY - LUFKIN

PRECISION AUTO BODY - SAN JOSE

PRECISION AUTO BODY - TEMPE

PRECISION AUTO BODY, INC.

PRECISION AUTOBODY

PRECISION BODY WORKS

PRECISION BODY WORKS - LUBBOCK

PRECISION BODY WORKS - RICHMOND

PRECISION BODY WORKS #2

PRECISION BODY WORKS #3

PRECISION BODY WORKS, INC.

PRECISION COLLISION - HOUSTON

PRECISION KUSTOMS PAINT & AUTO BODY LLC

PRECISION PAINT & BODY

PRECISION TUNE AUTO CARE

PRO AM COLLISION

PRO AUTO BODY

PRO AUTO BODY INC

PRO AUTO SERVICE

PRO AUTOMOTIVE & BODY

PRO BODY WORKS

PRO CARE COLLISION

PRO CLASS AUTO BODY

PRO COLLISION

PRO SPEED AUTO BODY

PRO STAR COLLISION

PRO TECH BODY SHOP

PRO TECH COLLISION CENTER

PRO TECH COLLISION REPAIR CENTER

PRO TRUCK BODY REPAIR & SERV., INC.

PROCARE AUTOMOTIVE & COLLISION

PROCARE AUTOMOTIVE & COLLISION N.E.

PROFESSIONAL AUTO COLLISION

PROFESSIONAL AUTO COLLISION CENTER

PROGRESSIVE BODY WORKS

PROGRESSIVE COLLISION REPAIR

PRONTO PAINT AND BODY

PRONTO REBUILDERS

PROS COLLISION CENTER

PRO'S COLLISION CENTER

PRO'S TRUCK & AUTOBODY

PROTECH COLLISION REPAIR CENTER

PUSH & PULL AUTO BODY & FRAME WORKS, INC.

QUICK COLLISION CENTER

SIGGY'S AUTO BODY

SIGNATURE AUTOBODY

SIGNATURE COLLISION SERVICES

SIGNATURE COLLISION SPECIALISTS, INC

SUMMIT COLLISION CENTER, INC.

SUN AUTO WERKS, INC.

SUNDERHAUS AUTO BODY REPAIR

SUNNY AUTO BODY

SUNRISE COLLISION CENTER

SUNRISE PAINT & BODY INC

SUNROAD AUTOMOTIVE COLLISION CENTER

SUNROAD COLLISION CENTER

SUNSET PAINT & BODY INC.

SUNSET PAINT & BODY WORKS

THE CARNAGIE BODY COMPANY

THE COLLISION CENTER INC.

THE COLLISION CENTER SLOANE/CHAMPION

THE COLLISION SHOP

THE COLLISION SHOP OF WARREN

THE COLLISION SOLUTION

THE COLOR WORKS COLLISION

THE PAINT & BODY

THE PAINT & BODY FACTORY

THE PAINT AND BODY SHOP

THE SHOP AUTO BODY

UNIVERSITY COLLISION CENTER

URBAN COLLISION

USA AUTO COLLISION CENTER

VELOCITY COLLISION CENTER

VISION COLLISION CENTER LLC

VIVA COLLISION CENTER EAST

VIVA COLLISION CENTER WEST

WORLD COLLISION CENTER

XTREME COLLISION CENTER

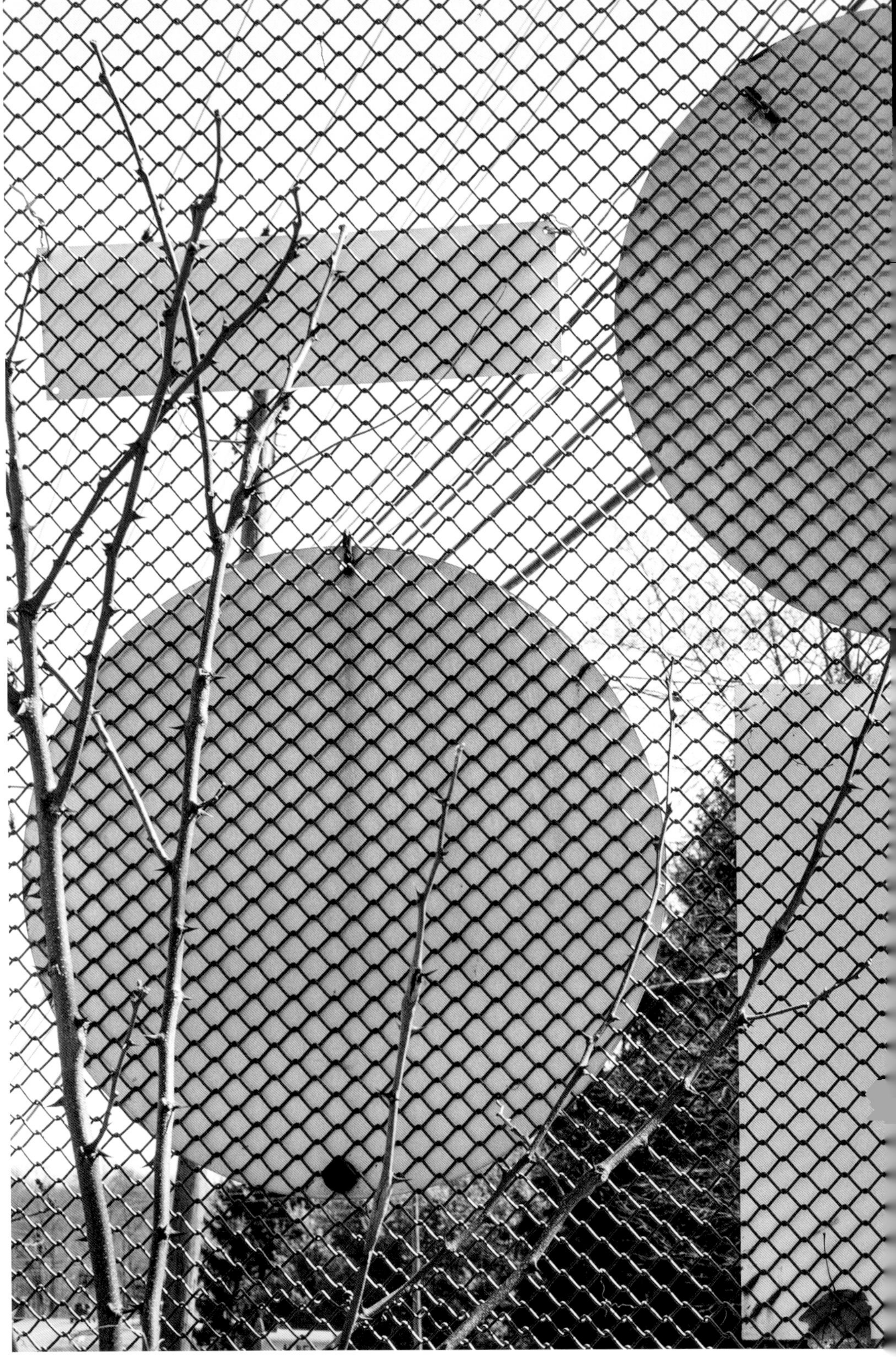

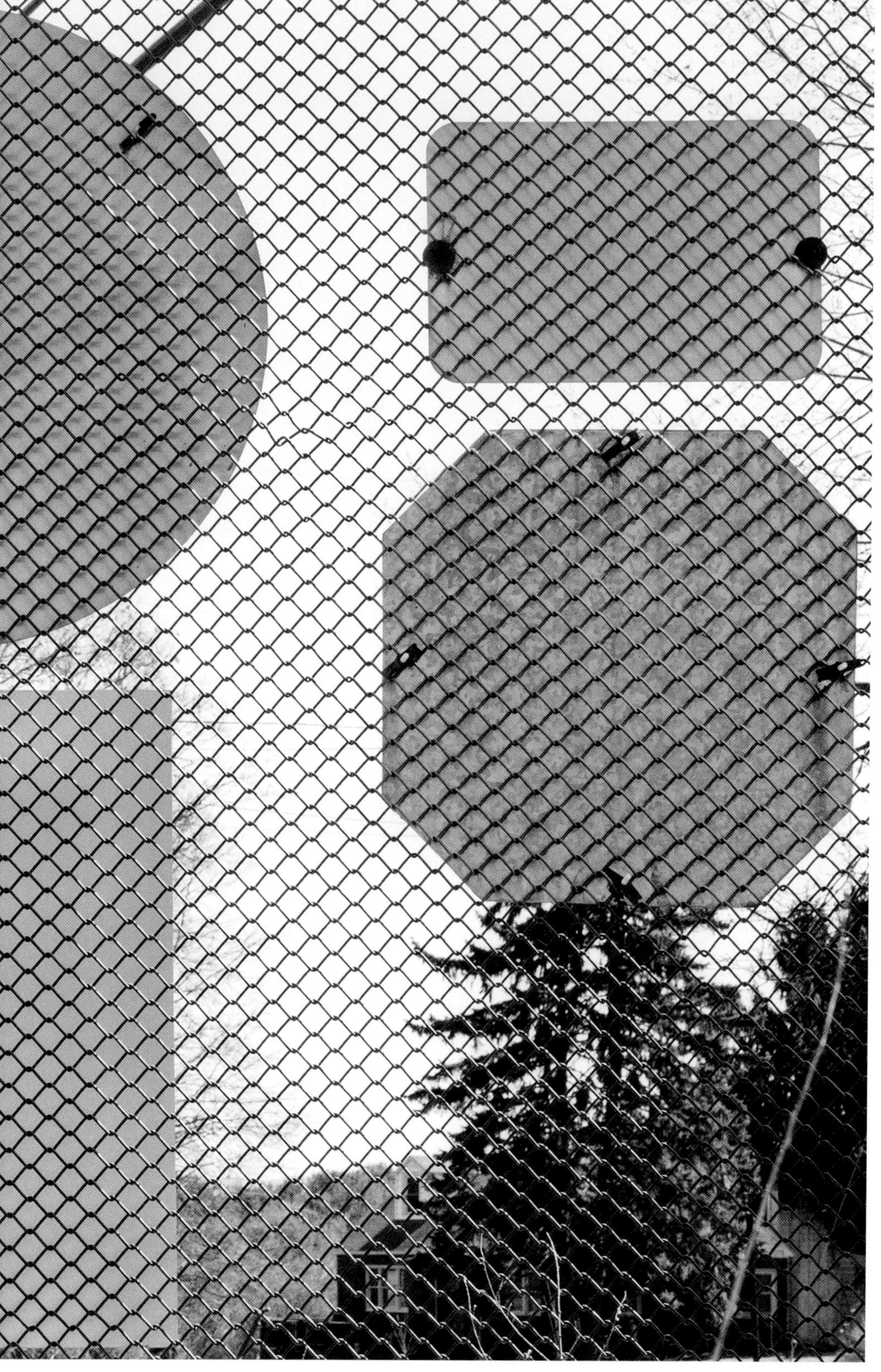

Tina Kukielski

The Transmission System

Talk to any mechanic long enough about the inner workings of a car and the analogy between "vehicle" and "body" soon manifests itself. If looking for a diagnosis on a suspicious whining or thumping sound coming from the rear, or a noxious smell emerging from the exhaust, that mechanic will inevitably use a combined method similar to that of a medical doctor: inquiring after symptoms and then peeking under the hood. The transmission system, a complex set of mechanical parts that connects the engine to the gears—the seat of the car's speed and mobility—is perhaps the closest thing to the inner "body" of a vehicle; like our own bodies, it suffers wear and tear due to its many moving, interacting parts. The metaphor is not lost on artist Shannon Ebner. And while *Auto Body Collision*—its collected language and its photographic sequencing—is by no means a study of automobiles, it offers allusions to the interchangeability between body and vehicle, auto and the self. Collisions and breaks in the system are central to Ebner's photo-linguistic program.

Ebner's poem of the same name, spread throughout the pages of this book, builds on select sets of pre-existing data, most notably words found on warehouses and auto body shops around Los Angeles, where the artist lives and works, or noticed during her travels on invitation to other cities, like Rome or Milan. In this and other projects, appropriated bits of language give the work its essential form: material forces chosen and calculated for their ability to transmit. The meaning of the term "transmission" extends here beyond the automobile to its usage across present-day telecommunications networks. In so doing, the overlooked figure of engineer-mathematician Claude Shannon emerges in the interest of comparison. Highly regarded in engineering circles, yet little known popularly, Shannon laid

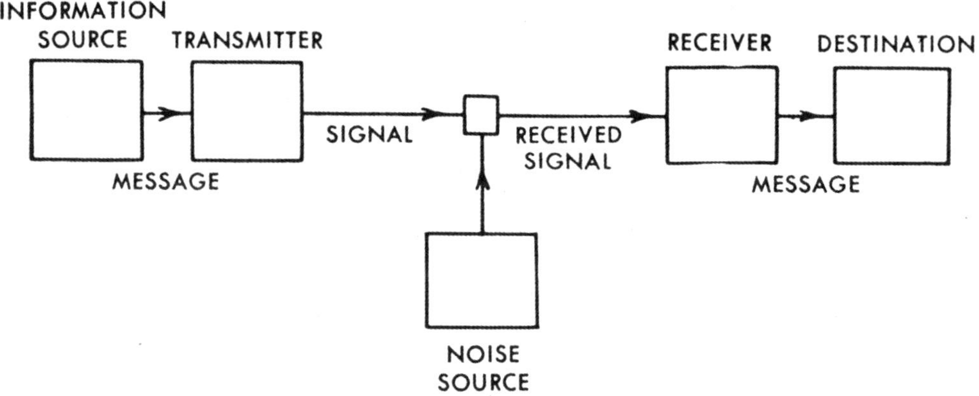

Fig. 1. Claude Shannon, *Schematic Diagram of a General Communication System*, 1948

1.
Claude E. Shannon, "A Mathematical Theory of Communication," originally printed in *The Bell System Technical Journal* 27 (July 1948): 379–423 and (October 1948): 623–56.

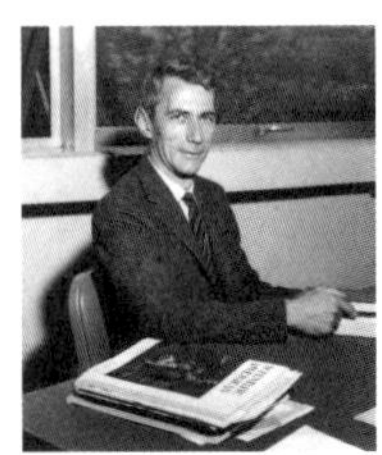

the groundwork for modern-day telecommunication as early as 1948 in his paper "A Mathematical Theory of Communication."[1] In that text, Shannon predicted transmission systems that today define the way digital technology operates through telecommunication channels like the Internet. He speculated that information could be stored in binary code or bits, thereby providing greater ease of movement across various media and barring significant loss (fig. 1). It was a theoretical proposition that gave birth to present-day information theory. Ebner's words-as-data mimic the shape and function of Shannon's coding system; in sequence, they operate as vehicles to carry information. In Shannon's mathematical program, the meaning of the information stored divorces from its transmission through established channels. In Ebner's work the effect is similar; we learn quickly that what words say are less important than what they do.

As such, the language of *Auto Body Collision* speaks to potential over program, forward movement over past reflection, transmission over interpretation. As a materialized force, the linguistic program is omnidirectional. A similar analysis might be made of her pictures. While Ebner's aesthetic preferences, such as her choice to print predominantly in black-and-white, fit squarely within a photo-conceptualist lineage promoted by the likes of Bernd and Hilla Becher, I would instead align Ebner's work with that of a more recent genealogy, invoked in the work of writer-photographer Moyra Davey. In Davey's own photo-linguistic

226

approach to the medium, the photograph, as noted by critic-historian George Baker, assumes a concealed role as "absent" agent, in lieu of a more traditional assignment such as that of evidence or index.[2] Documentation cast aside, the photograph's primary role is to germinate, making its position in the world one suggestive of potential, of a becoming. Davey's photographs build their character in relationship to other images and through the connections conjured in their "receivers."[3] *Copperheads* (1990, fig. 2) is a series of photographs Davey shot in extreme close-up that focus on Abraham Lincoln's portrait as engraved on the US cent; as she has done in a number of her photographic series, Davey found her 100 subjects while trolling the city streets. Shown customarily in a grid, *Copperheads* is a typology of scuffs, marks, dings, and imperfections on the coins' surfaces. And yet Baker notes that Davey's photographs are "latent" in that they suggest destruction as much as the marks on their receptor surfaces suggest a means for new life, a kind of rebirth.[4] The title *Copperhead* was the name given to a group of nineteenth-century Democrats who opposed the North's use of war to protect national unity under threat of secession. They wore copper coins as symbols of their pacifist position. But the label soon became an epithet of treason and betrayal,

2.
George Baker, "The Absent Photograph," in *Moyra Davey: Speaker Receiver*, ed. Adam Szymczyk (Berlin: Sternberg Press, 2010), 53–99. Baker attributes the idea of the "absent photograph" to Davey, as described in her work *Fifty Minutes* (2006). See also Roland Barthes, *Camera Lucida: Reflections on Photography*, trans. Richard Howard (New York: Hill and Wang, 1981).

3.
Baker, "The Absent Photograph," 89–90, 96.

4.
Here, Baker is comparing the skin of the penny to the photograph as a site of contact. Ibid., 68.

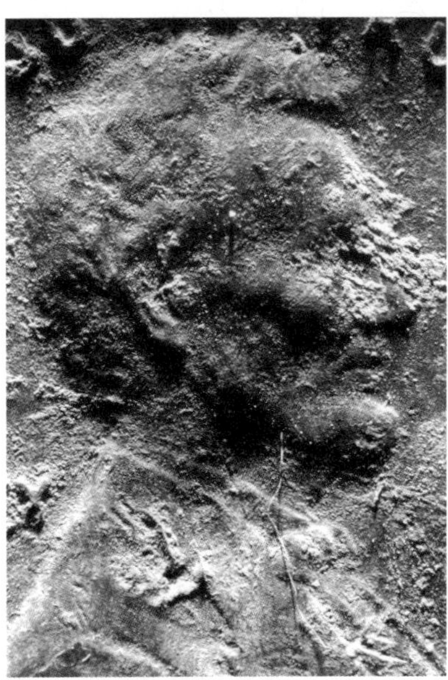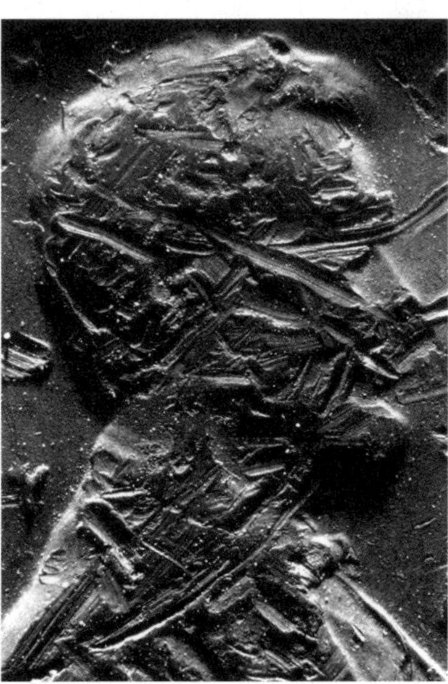

Fig. 2. Moyra Davey, *Copperhead No. 76* and *Copperhead No. 77*, 1990
Chromogenic prints, 24 × 18 in. (61 × 45.7 cm) each
Courtesy of the artist and Murray Guy, New York

227

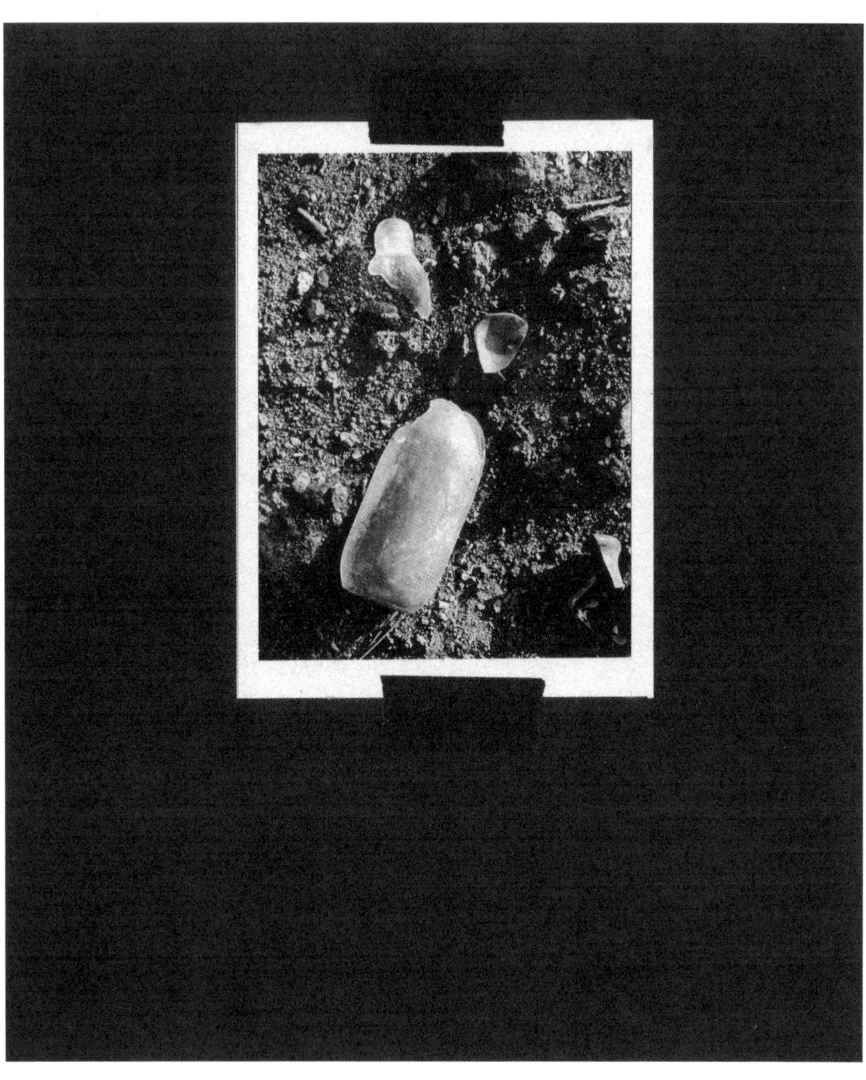

Fig. 3. Shannon Ebner, *Fire Bottles*, 2002–4
Color Xerox on newsprint, 8 ½ × 11 in. (21.6 × 27.9 cm)
Courtesy of the artist and Wallspace Gallery, New York

228

and a number of followers were forced to migrate
to Canada. Ebner's series *Fire Bottles* (2002–4, fig. 3),
which emerged more than a decade after Davey's
Copperheads, has a similarly doubling title. New to
Los Angeles in the early 2000s, Ebner and her partner,
the artist Erika Vogt, were exploring their newfound
landscape. Fires had recently ripped through the Sierra
Nevada forests, three hours east of the city. Out for
one of many exploratory drives, Ebner found a pattern
in the ruined landscape: broken shards of bottles in
various states of repose on the mostly barren forest
floor. As the last survivors in a decimated land, their
presence was haunting. Ebner photographed the
bottles in situ at the point where the sun reflected
back on the lens of the camera, trying to capture the
momentary obstruction between subject and photographer caused by a break in vision—that split-second
blinding as light infiltrated the aperture and pierced
the photographer's eye.[5] One notable presentation
of these works evoked that of specimen in a lab,
simple gelatin silver prints taped to black mat boards,
signaling a typology of *Informe* forms. As a multi-
valent work, the series bears striking resemblances to
Ebner's recent photographs of automotive junkyards
(pp. 50–51, 62–65). As pictures of everyday detritus,
the junkyards and the bottles push in two directions
at once. *Fire Bottles*—whose secondary meaning
suggests a homemade incendiary weapon—records
a natural world on the brink of change; as landscape
and image-surface in the process of breaking down,
both also anticipate their own rejuvenation.

Off the Grid

An attempt at recording a collision or disjuncture
between vision and experience, the artist's action in
Fire Bottles is an almost futile task. It necessitates an
instantaneous and immediate sync of movement and
vision that is not humanly possible—the impossibility
of capturing on film what the mind really sees. The
implied system breach has been a long time coming
in an artistic practice that initially relied on the grid
for its formal logic. The grid (or grids) appearing in
Ebner's work arrived in support of "language, without a ground."[6] In sets and series of photographs that
she calls "photographic sentences," Ebner sometimes
shot from a gridded platform—a white pegboard that

5.
Ebner, in e-mail
exchange with
the author,
March 11, 2015.

6.
Ebner, in interview
with Amanda Law,
"Q&A with Shannon
Ebner," September
6, 2011, Hammer
Museum, UCLA,
http://hammer.ucla.
edu/blog/2011/09/
qa-with-shannon-
ebner/.

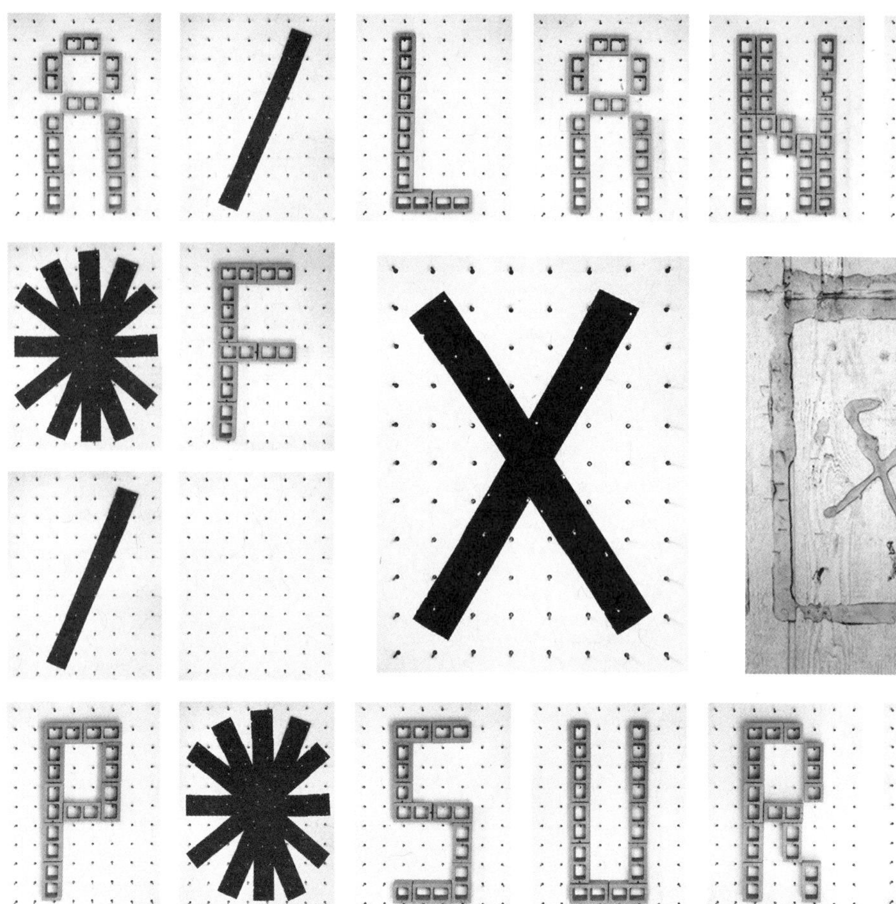

could hold up to twenty cinderblocks she arranged to make individual block letters. This "photographic modular alphabet" is employed in her work *STRIKE* (2008–15). Alternately, other photographic sentences could be hung as separate prints yet arranged in a grid such as *A Langauge of Exposures*, Ebner's contribution to the 2011 Venice Bienniale (fig. 4), or her growing collection of *Black Box Collision A*'s: cropped capital letter A's found in print or scrawled on storefront or warehouse façades (pp. 107–115). In her *Electric Comma* series (pp. 92–93), Ebner replaced the do-it-yourself pegboard grid of *STRIKE* with digitized language. She rented, programmed, and photographed a Portable Changeable Message Sign—the kind of boxed LED lights that you see flashing an alert message alongside the highway—resulting in an evocative thirteen-line poem that breaks into smaller strings of word-images.

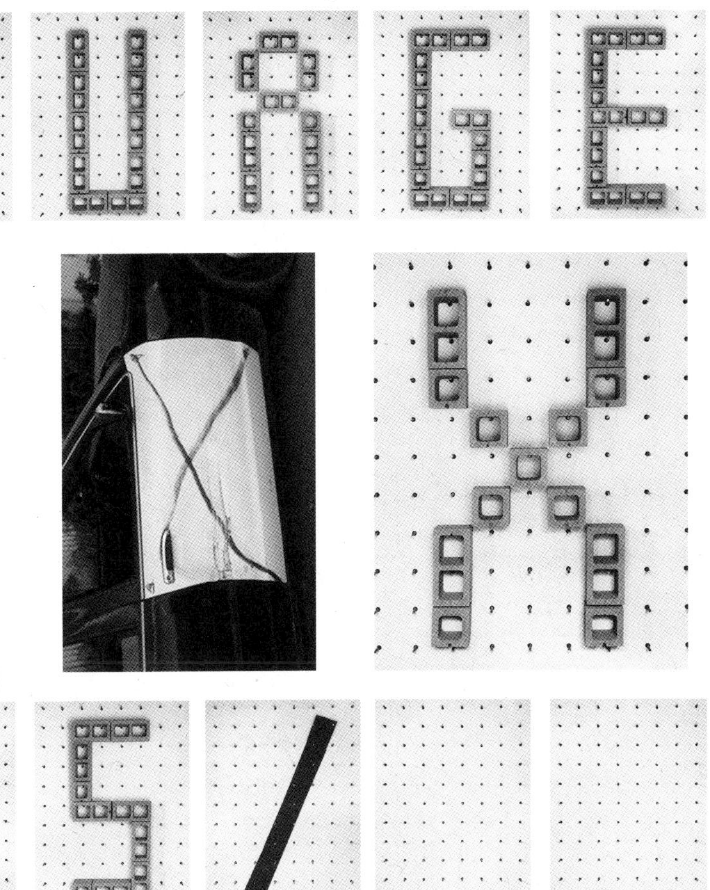

Fig. 4. Shannon Ebner, *A Language of Exposures*, 2011, from *The Electric Comma* series (2011–13) Twenty-eight chromogenic prints, 136 × 283 in. (345.4 × 718.8 cm) overall Courtesy of the artist and Wallspace Gallery, New York

In *STRIKE* (fig. 5), we see the grid hold shape but slowly begin to erode, like bottles in the landscape. *STRIKE* is composed of singular photographs of singular letters that when combined make up eighteen separate, English-language palindromes that explore reciprocal relationships and the multiple meanings ascribed to language, especially that surrounding the rhetoric of war. Ebner's borrowed words stand at attention in these pictures despite their quality of being scrambled or garbled from a political speech or military training exercise:

NO / IT CAN / AS IT IS / IT IS A WAR /
RAW AS IT IS / IT IS AN ACTION/
NO/ IT IS OPPOSITION / NO / SIR /
PREFER PRISON / RISE TO VOTE SIR /
RISE / SIR LAPDOG / REVOLT

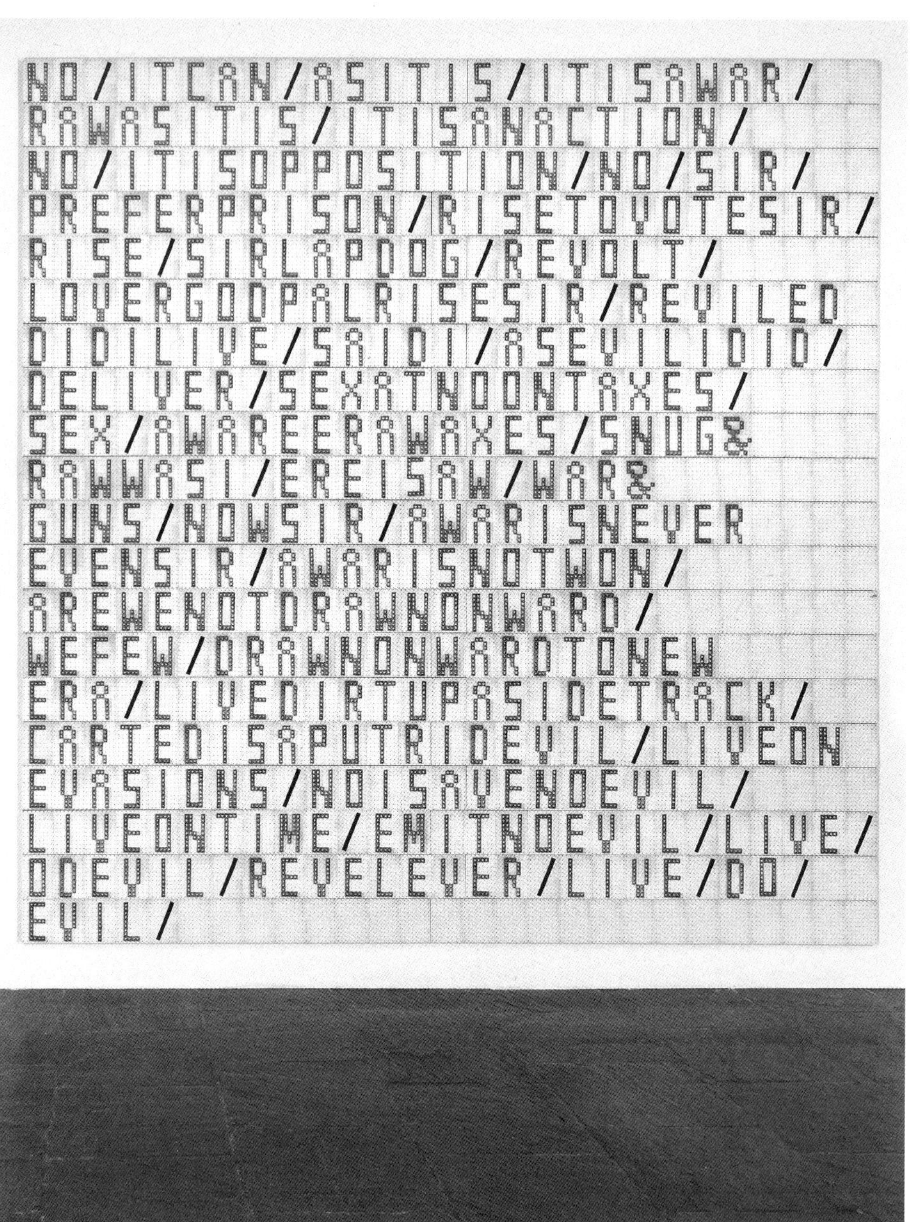

Fig. 5. Shannon Ebner, *STRIKE*, 2008
540 chromogenic prints, aluminum, wood, approx. 150 × 155 in. (381 × 394 cm)
Courtesy of the artist and Wallspace Gallery, New York

And yet the nature of Ebner's palindromes are such that their physical traits, the object-ness of their reading left to right, or right to left, supersedes what the words are meant to convey; meaning is overruled by form, and the illogical supplants the logical. The work exists as both a book and a large panel photograph. It insists on sequence and continuity, one piece contingent on the next, bound by the grid as both a formal device and an overarching ordering system. And yet *STRIKE*, like *Auto Body Collision*, is really a testament to the interchangeability of language.

Ebner exploits the inherent objectness of the palindromes to build tension between the photograph as a physical object and the image-language that it describes: "For me a palindrome is one manifestation of the objecthood of language because it gives language a form much in the same way that Minimalist sculpture functions to make a space for something that barely exists."[7] Ebner cites Mel Bochner's serial photography of his minimalist sculpture as an influence on *STRIKE*. As in Bochner's photographs of the late 1960s (the artist abandoned the medium around 1970), the linguistic schema becomes the subject of systemic, controlled, and sequential changes to the arrangements of his sculptural forms. And yet *STRIKE* carries with it yet another referent, that of concrete poetry. The cinderblocks themselves evoke the fragility or concreteness of language and the stability and instability of architecture, not to mention the fleeting rhetoric of war. Remember Weapons of Mass Destruction? The assumed logic of the grid here is supplanted by the detourned language that *STRIKE* activates and describes.

7.
Ibid.

At Intervals

Ebner's work in photographs and in text builds on strings of flexible data that recall their cut-and-paste origins. Digitized language can be reused anywhere, such that words, like their sibling images, spread when shared or manipulated through today's open communication channels and via social media. We live in the era of cut-and-paste aesthetics that dictate and inform our formal strategies toward language on the one hand and image collection on the other. In that sense, Ebner's word-image combinations function like data packages in a network; they beg to be clicked on, digested, regurgitated, repeated, and redeployed. "Computer vision is the next frontier" appears in a line of text in a single image that belongs to a group of stunning photographs in *Auto Body Collision* that the artist took at a Los Angeles car expo, suggesting that Ebner herself has begun to employ the computer language that will one day soon automate our cars, and eventually much more (pp. 24–25).

Apart from the grid, a consistent characteristic in Ebner's artistic lexicon is the blank. In her photographic sentences, some letter cells are left empty, or replaced with a slash, pound sign, or asterisk, creating a break in the continuity of the line. In *STRIKE*, words run together such that the visual rhythm breaks down, a condition amplified by the insertion of black forward slashes that appear so frequently that reading takes place in jerky on-and-off segments. In an interview Ebner explains: "I guess what I like about photographs of symbols is that they can redirect an image or create uncertainty and indeterminacy and suggest that one thing is two things or one thing is an incomplete thing, an incomplete picture."[8] As silence, as a muting of the system, the uncertain pauses introduce a mode of resistance, like a détournement. Concrete poetry displaced language away from the concept of verse toward what is referred to as "verbivocovisual expression," thereby introducing space, geometry, and material and graphic patterns into their poems.[9] Experiments have included the use of ideograms as a substitute for verbal forms. The idea that words themselves could be ideograms is made apparent in a poem like "sem un numero" by Augusto de Campos (fig. 6). Again, the comparison here to concrete poetry is relevant and especially notable in Ebner's use of discarded scraps of language, what can be referred to as "counterforms." "Counterforms" refer to the spatial areas in-between closed letterforms, or in other cases the negative space between characters. Attention to the white space surrounding a graphic mark is a hallmark of a concrete poem. The artist has noted the "limb-like or prosthetic" qualities of text and its negative form, suggesting another kind of body or a monument to meaning lost.[10] As material, Ebner's "counterforms" (fig. 7) plumb the detritus of both linguistic and visual correspondences.

8.
Lauren O'Neill-Butler, "Shannon Ebner: The Continuous Present," *The Paris Review*, October 4, 2011, http://www.theparisreview.org/blog/2011/10/04/shannon-ebner-the-continuous-present/.

9.
Brothers Augusto de Campos and Haroldo de Campos with fellow poet Décio Pígnatarí coined this term in "Plano-piloto para poesia concreta," in Augusto de Campos, Haroldo de Campos and Décio Pígnatarí, *Teoria da Poesia Concreta: Textos Criticos e Manifestos (1950–1966)* (São Paulo: Edições Invenção, 1965).

10.
Ebner, in e-mail exchange with the author, April 9, 2015.

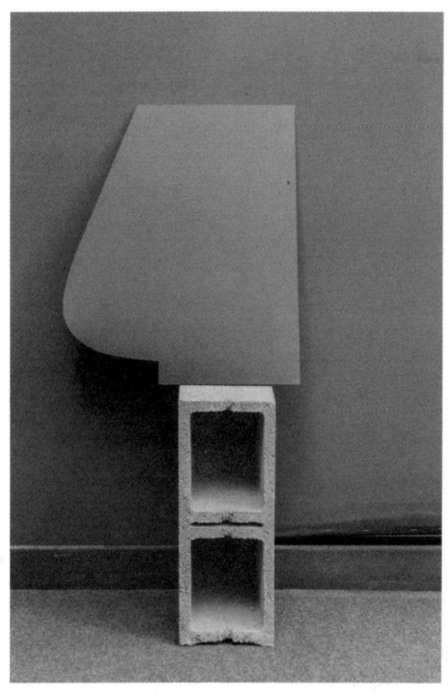

Fig. 6. Augusto de Campos, "sem um numero," 1958

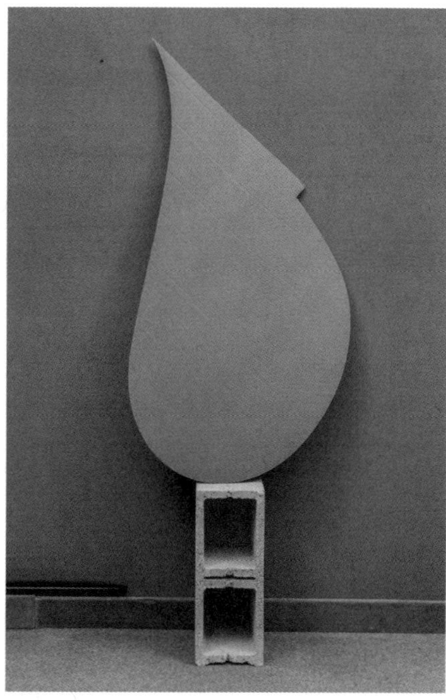

Fig. 7. Shannon Ebner, *Counterform Times New Roman A*, 2015
and *Counterform Times New Roman S*, 2015
Archival pigment prints, 50 × 33 ¼ in. (127 × 84.5 cm)
Courtesy of the artist and Wallspace Gallery, New York

Fig. 8. Susan Howe, from *Tom Tit Tot*, 2014

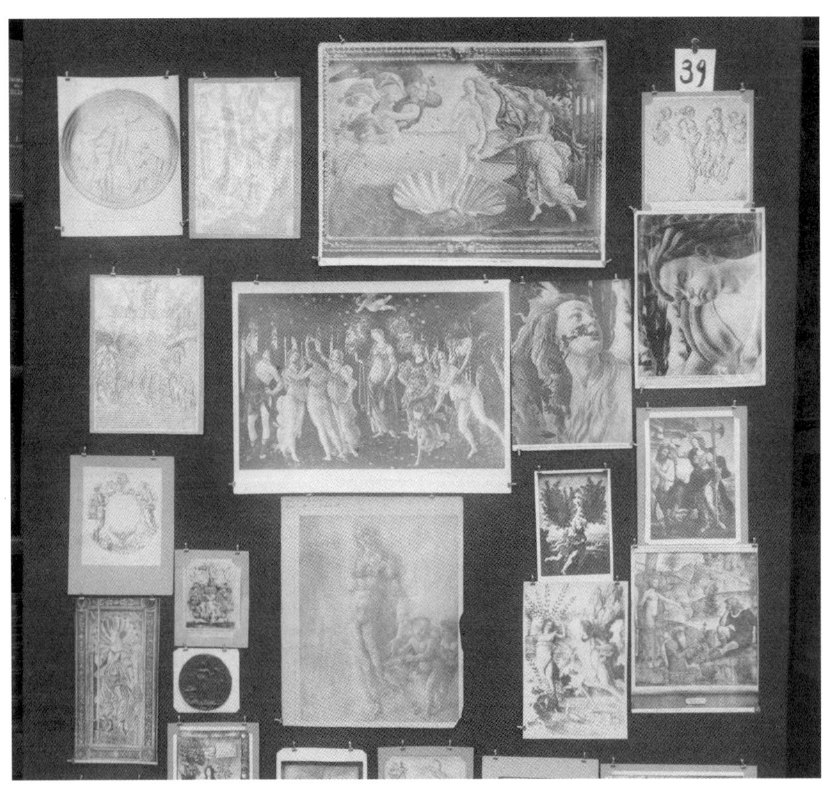

Fig. 9. Aby Warburg, *Mnemosyne Atlas*, Panel 39, 1929

A further move toward the "verbivocovisual expression" promoted by concrete poets occurs in Ebner approach to image isolation; cropping and fragmentation are defining characteristics of this work. The space between Ebner's letters, the awkward pauses, the glitches, and even the "counterforms" (cover and pp. 40–41) comprised of crude symbol fragments disrupt continuity. These are not clear and polished market-savvy messages; there are too many rifts and wounds. On pages 34–35, Ebner's words yell out to us with visible and audible clues: "Network have some damage." It continues: "Perform Accidents. Expect Delays." At times, her language wrestles free from functionality as words drop off or transform their meaning through dislocation. Pushed to the point of gibberish, Ebner's words are both there and not there. When absence and presence hold equal weight, there emerges a third category: the interstitial or the in-between. Here the words of Susan Howe, a poet admired by Ebner, apply (fig. 8). She describes her own work as being "about the impossibility of putting into print what the mind really sees and the impossibility of finding an original in a bibliography."[11] Here is where Ebner goes off grid, to that interstitial space marked by breaks, pauses, and silences: in the chasm between what language is and what it represents.

One of the greatest art historians of the twentieth century, Aby Warburg built a collection of image relationships in a bold unfinished work called the *Mnemosyne Atlas* (1927–29, fig. 9). The collection has been called "an iconology of intervals" because it involves not singular objects but the tensions, analogies, contrasts, and contradictions among them.[12] Curator and art historian Philippe-Alain Michaud notes in his seminal book on Warburg that each of *Mnemosyne*'s image panels re-create a theme in art history that symbolize a movement and a jump through time, history, and thought patterns, creating "a network of the intervals" that describe in broad terms ideas of representation.[13] This is a crucial comparison; for Ebner is, like Warburg, a collector of intervals. Her work captures the language-based and mark-making intervals that comprise contemporary experience. Putting emphasis on the lacuna, Ebner's discontinuous sequences find expression only when analyzed in an arrangement of complex

11.
Susan Howe, "Talisman Interview with Edward Foster," in *The Birth-Mark: Unsettling the Wilderness in American Literary History* (Middletown, CT: Wesleyan University Press, 1993), 175.

12.
Philippe-Alain Michaud, *Aby Warburg and the Image in Motion*, trans. Sophie Hawkes (New York: Zone Books, 2004), 244.

13.
Ibid., 253.

interconnections. Toward the end of the book, Ebner's lists proliferate so that repeating words like "auto," "body," and "collision" detach and begin to spread like a virus. It is here that language transforms again, like a child repeating the same words ad infinitum, described by theorist Frederic Jameson as the point where "a signifier that has lost its signified has thereby transformed into an image."[14]

The process of assembling her poem only reinforces our ever-changing relationship to words in the digital and networked reality of present-day computing. Again it is important to note that this is not a book about cars. Less attached to the content, Ebner is more interested in the structural role played by the system. As critic and artist Hito Steyerl writes: "Capital's semiotic turn, as described by Felix Guattari, plays in favor of the creation and dissemination of compressed and flexible data packages that can be integrated into ever-newer combinations and sequences."[15] It is here that language takes on its non-linguistic or extra-linguistic properties. Beyond the limits of meaning is where language abandons its referent, and a photograph divorces from its content. Interestingly Shannon—the other Shannon, Claude Shannon—responsible for the structure of those now-widespread data packages, was at the same time also masterminding early landmark inventions in crytopgraphy as a contractor for the US military during World War II. Two sides of the same coin, encryption and encoding information differ in one essential way: one requires a key for translation. In Ebner's work there is no key for decoding. *Auto Body Collision* reveals nothing that is otherwise hidden; instead, it reminds us of exactly that which we see out in the world. As information digested, its program infiltrates our minds, to be slowly decrypted.

14.
Frederic Jameson, "Postmodernism and Consumer Society," in *The Anti-Aesthetic: Essays on Postmodern Culture*, ed. Hal Foster (New York: The New Press, 1983), 138.

15.
Hito Steyerl, "In Defense of the Poor Image," *e-flux* 10 (November 2009). Available online at http://www.e-flux.com/journal/in-defense-of-the-poor-image/.

Alex Klein

Crash Course

In an early moment in the recent film *Nightcrawler* (dir. Dan Gilroy, 2014), the main character, Lou Bloom, encounters a fiery, late-night car crash on an LA freeway.[1] Already on the scene is a rogue videographer, Joe Loder, intent on being the first to capture footage of the accident so he can sell it to the local TV news. Bloom—desperate to get a foot in the door anywhere he can make a dime—asks whether he might apprentice himself to Loder. Although he is quickly turned down, Bloom is a fast learner and decides to teach himself. That is, at the moment of collision, he is inspired to pick up a camera. For the remainder of the film, we watch Bloom learn the tricks of his new trade—driving the streets late at night tuned into a police radio, racing to the scene of reported crimes in affluent neighborhoods, learning how to get better access to his material, and observing and eventually sabotaging his competition.

After producing a particularly raw video of a carjacking victim, Bloom lands his first payday at KWLA, confirming the old adage, "If it bleeds it leads." From there we see him become more aggressive in the pursuit of his images. Not only does he get uncomfortably close to his subjects, but he begins to cross both legal and ultimately moral boundaries. At first he trespasses behind the barricade of a crime scene, then he moves a body in order to make a better composition, and finally he sets the stage for an actual crime, all so he can be the first to get it on camera. As Bloom, the autodidact, recounts to Nina Romina, the KWLA station manager: "I'm focusing on framing. A proper frame not only draws the eye into a picture, but keeps it there longer, dissolving the barrier between the subject and the outside of the frame." She responds: "Is that blood on your shirt?"

1.
Nightcrawler, directed by Dan Gilroy (2014; Amazon Instant Video).

239

As *Nightcrawler* suggests, bodily violence is a symptom not just of the freeway, but of the production of the technologized image within late capitalism and the circuits of power in which it ensnares its mediated subjects. But as much as contemporary images are inscribed within systems of representation, as a tale in which the line between observation and participation is breached, *Nightcrawler* also reveals those systems' constructedness and the capacity of the individual to intervene in and even retaliate against them. This desire to rupture and make visible the conditions that underwrite contemporary images and their circulation can be observed in the work of artist Shannon Ebner. Occupying a space between the imaging of language and the language of the image, Ebner's photographs, sculptures, and videos suggest the incongruities and lapses within signs and systems that make them at once legible and vulnerable.

In her most recent work, *Auto Body Collision*, Ebner elaborates an autopoetics in which the alphabet and the automobile come together to form both a linguistic structure to be punctured (or perhaps just dented) and a physical form to be remobilized—an attempt to locate, if not to situate, a body politic amid the rampant sprawl of the Los Angeles freeway system. For Ebner, a kind of automatic writing of the machine and a found language of the hand coexist amid the exhaust fumes, on LED display boards and in the vernacular signage on the façades of auto repair shops. If the "violence of the letter" thus takes on a new valence within Ebner's (auto)poetic project, in *Auto Body Collision* the alphabet itself is likewise subject to an artistic recoding.

[A]

In this, Ebner's project draws on and at times runs counter to a lineage of postwar artistic practice that has attempted to reorient the very way we learn our ABCs. Chief among these precedents is the work of Martha Rosler, who has consistently challenged the status of the photographic document and the coding of the body. For Rosler, learning how to read the limitations of both visual and linguistic lexicons is central to unmasking the construction of representation and its consumptive powers. For example, in *House Beautiful: Bringing the War Home* (1967–72) graphic images of the Vietnam

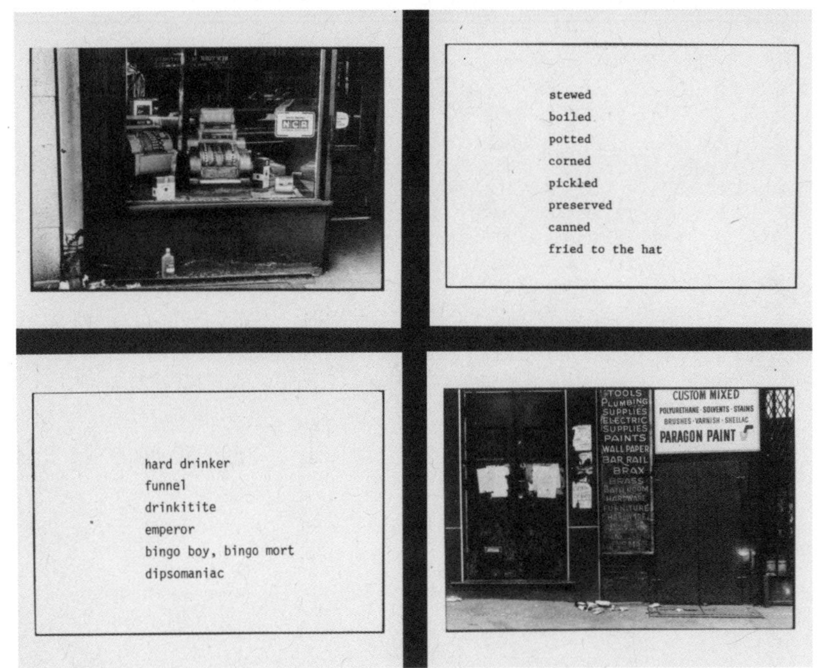

Fig. 1. Martha Rosler, Detail of *The Bowery in two inadequate descriptive systems*, 1974–75
Forty-five gelatin silver prints of text and image mounted on twenty-four backing boards,
dimension variable. Whitney Museum of American Art, New York,
Purchase, with funds from John L. Steffens, 93.4a-x

War are collaged onto found scenes of bourgeois living rooms and kitchens culled from the pages of *Life* magazine. Although advertising images are staged to divert our attention away from the world "out there," Rosler's manipulated photographs make visible the horrors that they obscure, underscoring the fact that the domestic sphere is itself a battlefield.

Likewise, in her seminal work *The Bowery in two inadequate descriptive systems* (1974–75, fig. 1) Rosler points to the slippage between language and image and the failure of representation. Using the image of the Bowery as a symbol of social and physical disenfranchisement, Rosler's grid of forty-five photographs shows a series of empty, seemingly banal black-and-white street scenes accompanied by lists of adjectives for drunkenness. The words, which read as nonsensical captions or poetry ("stewed, boiled, potted, corned, pickled, preserved, canned, fried to the hat," and so on), tell us as much about the people they purport to describe as do the missing bodies in the photographs. In this way, Rosler responds to a history of documentary photography that has both aestheticized and

241

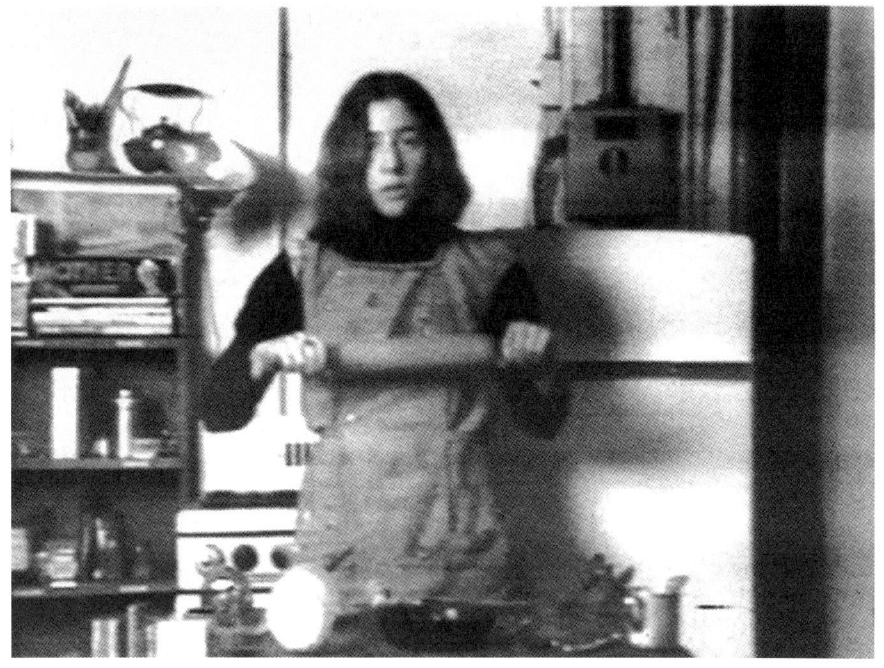

Fig. 2. Still from Martha Rosler, *Semiotics of the Kitchen*, 1975
Video, black-and-white, sound, 6:09 min.
Courtesy of Electronic Arts Intermix (EAI), New York

anesthetized its subjects, suggesting that both language and image have the capacity to simultaneously describe, detain, and distract.

If language falls flat on the Bowery, Rosler's letters perhaps come closest to Ebner in her 1975 video *Semiotics of the Kitchen* (fig. 2) in which the alphabet becomes a literal instrument of rage. Staged in the manner of a television cooking show, Rosler enacts a deadpan recitation of the alphabet using the implements of the kitchen. She begins by tying on her "apron," mixing her "bowl" assertively, and driving down the blade of her "chopper." Her manipulations proceed with increasing determination and focused aggression—"egg beater." "fork." "ice pick." "juicer." By the word "knife," Rosler wields her blade toward the screen. The alphabetic sequence of kitchen utensils progresses until she enacts the final letters with her body, knife and fork in hand—U, V, W, X, Y—Z becoming a final, Zorroesque slash. Here, language becomes both object and weapon as domestic tools and technologies are turned back on themselves through a logic of alphabetic substitution. In its use of

photography and video, Rosler's work thus proposes
a kind of *technics* of the alphabet, in which the body
becomes both the subject and agent of an alternately
oppressive and retributive violence.

[B]

Created against the backdrop of the Vietnam War and
its aftermath, Rosler's signature early works engage a
newly technologized—and embodied—viewing subject.
Although differently inflected, this dialectic resonates
with the eccentric polymath, poet, and physicist Bern
Porter's (fig. 3) prophetic observations about technology. Appropriately, with regard to the mediation of
violence, Porter also helped to develop both the cathode
ray tube, instrumental in the invention of the modern
television, and worked on the separation of uranium
in the labs of the Manhattan Project.[2] (He is said to
have abruptly quit the day after the first atomic bomb
was dropped in Hiroshima upon realizing the actual
purpose of his team's experiments.) The trauma of this
ultimate "collision" would prompt Porter to spend the
remainder of his life in an unfulfilled quest to marry
the utopian aims of art and science for the good of
humanity, a project he dubbed "Sciart."

One way in which Porter began to emerge from his
depression after the bomb was through his experimentation with photography. In his photograms and
"photopoems," Porter seems to literally bend energy
to his will as he employs his knowledge of physics to
make images in which light ripples in fantastical ways,
creating in effect a vision of aftershock or fallout.
Simultaneously, he began to further explore his concept
of the "Found" through photo-documentation of his
sculptures. Although similar in some respects to the
Surrealist "objet trouvé" or the Dada readymade—in
which preexisting materials are recast or repositioned—
Porter's "Founds" were distinct in that they were
reacting specifically to the militaristic and paranoiac
conditions of the atomic age and the rise of an acceler-
ated, globalized mass media (fig. 4).[3] Indeed, Porter's
"Founds" extended beyond the space of sculpture and
material to words, sound, images, and even subject
positions. In 1937 Porter had made a pilgrimage to
Gertrude Stein's salon in Paris where he was captivated
by the way that Stein spoke in a steady poetic stream

2.
It is also interest-
ing to observe that
Porter deemed
the automobile
"the single most
destructive force
in our enlightened
culture." James
Schevill, *Where
to Go, What to
Do, When You Are
Bern Porter: A
Personal Biography*
(Gardiner, ME:
Tilbury House
Publishers, 1992),
174.

3.
Ibid.

243

that seemed to disregard traditional notions of syntax or grammatical propriety: "The carved sculptural flow of her language dazed me…Certainly from her talk developed the whole contemporary movement of the so-called language poets."[4]

If Stein's delivery helped to further concretize and expand Porter's understanding of poetics, her rhythmic flow and performativity also left a marked impression. In his "autobiographical manifesto," *I've Left* (1971), Porter depicts a delirious future in which poetry and technology merge and disperse language in ways heretofore unimaginable. He describes a new form of publishing and distribution in which text, sound, image, and energy come together in a manic, expanded cinematic synesthesia:

> *In its place arose dots and dashes in full color, cinescope projected with mail-slot screens, intermittent spurts of chemically-dyed ether, alpha-radiated Geiger recordings emanated from my diaphragm with every third vowel crystallized. Textual poetry was at last off the typed ms, off the printed page and jet soaring… In transit to the point from which it should never have departed I touched poetry with all of these means… Fusillades of streaking arrows fused from the dots and dashes of the new expression. I spread them in waves, sheets and buckets full. I imparted density, opacity, heat, fear temperature, tenacity and anger. The lights, the dots, the dashes, the equivalents of words became meanings, tones of meaning and the image of meaning.*[5]

Although suggestive of a kind of psychedelic, neo-Futurist cacophony, here Porter's vision is informed by the very real and devastating effects of war. Rather than fetishize the industrialization of modern life, he proposes infusing the poetic into the technological in an effort to change society for the better. On the printed page, the momentum in Porter's poetry often takes the form of lists in which words are repeated, extracted, and reformulated. These repetitive strands suggest the mechanistic order of capital, but they are also evocative of the kind of verbal stutter that might be likened to the revving of an engine, or the put-put-putter of an old car's exhaust.

4.
Ibid., 48–49.

5.
Ibid.,167–68. The text was begun in 1954 and is quoted from Bern Porter, *I've Left: A Manifesto and a Testament of SCIence and ART (SCIART)* (New York: Something Else Press, 1971).

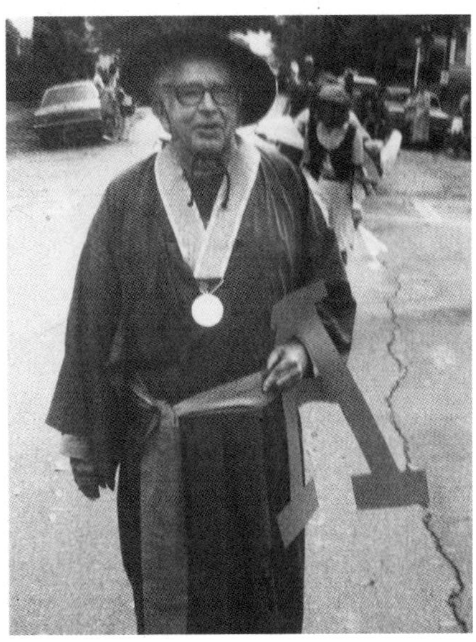

Fig. 3. Bern Porter in his poet's costume

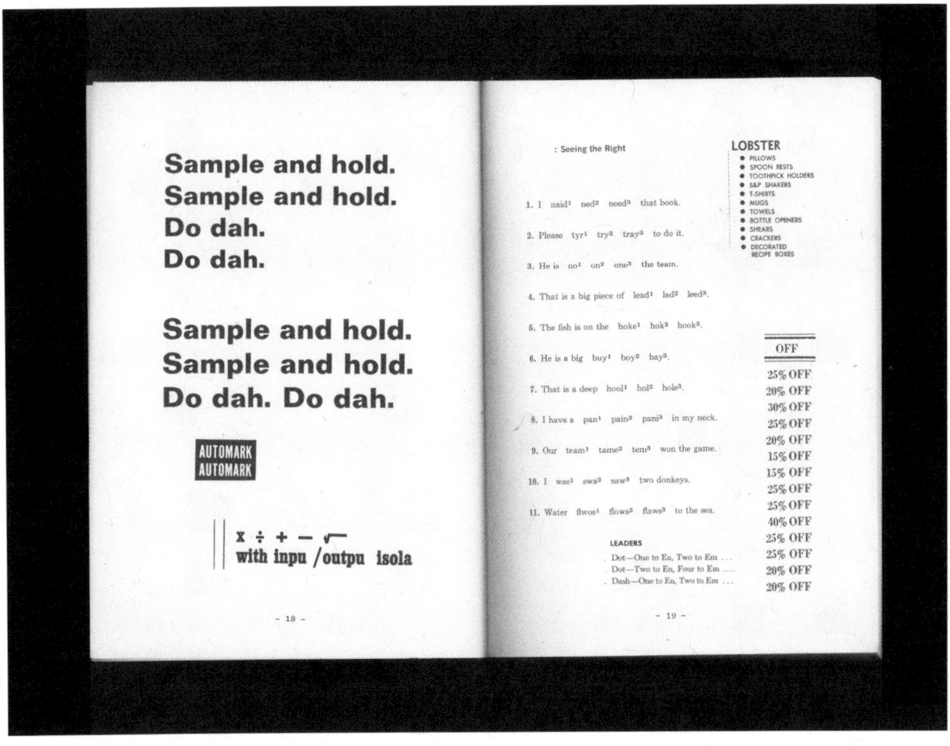

Fig. 4. Spread from Bern Porter, *Found Poems*
(Millerton, NY: Something Else Press, 1972)

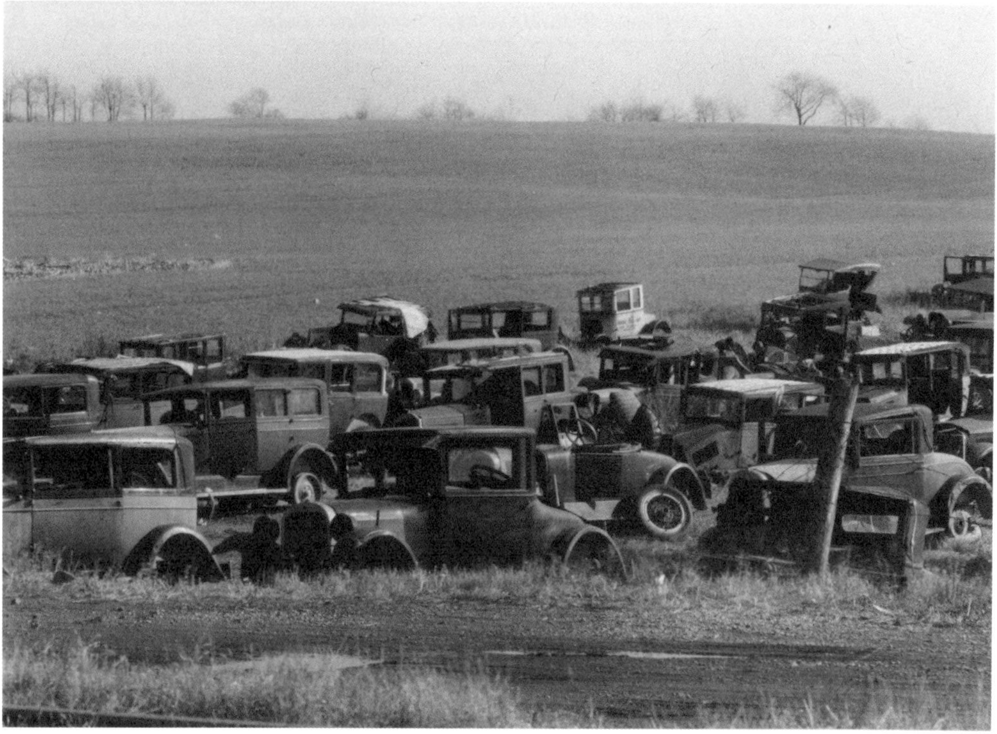

Fig. 6. Walker Evans, *Joe's Auto Graveyard, Near Bethlehem, Pennsylvania*, 1936, printed 1971, gelatin silver print, 4 ¾ × 6 ⅝ in. (12 × 16.9 cm), The Metropolitan Museum of Art, The Elisha Wittelsey Collection, The Elisha Whittelsey Fund, 1972, 1972.555.1

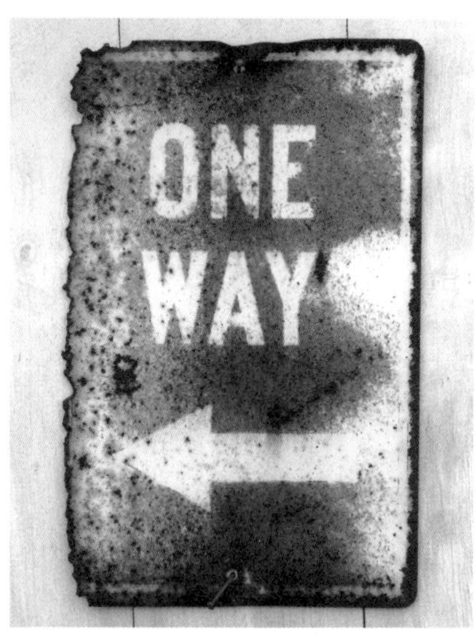

Fig. 5. Walker Evans, found
street sign, c. 1974

7.
Thompson (ibid., 99–100) makes a similar connection between Evans's speech patterns and visual poetry: "In these new pictures Walker went far beyond the role of selecting, which had occupied him during his recent period of collecting signs and making his odd home photographs of them. This new aggressive approach to his subject did not ignore or deny the simple beauty of these signs, but Walker was no longer content merely to copy and present this beauty. His intervention adds an extra layer of meaning to that already displayed in the sign itself and pushes his work with this subject-matter into new territory. Pieces of words form new words not imagined by the signs' makers, and pieces of letters play with other whole and partial letters in an orgy of semantic exuberance, clearly related to the wordplay and joking that sprinkled Walker's conversation and letters."

This play between the aural and the visual also extends to the work of Walker Evans. As his former student Jerry L. Thompson recounts, in his chronicle of the photographer's last years, Evans had a distinctive way of speaking that was part accent, part preference, and part wit. In conversation Evans would modify the syllables at the end of names so that they would be more pleasing to his own ear, or bestow nicknames that played off of a person's origin, proper name, or biography: "This rechristening was not a semiconscious slip of the brain but a deliberate, arch, linguistic construction, a bon mot."[6] Evans's interest in visual word play is evident in some of his earliest photographs that depict vernacular signage as markers of place, economy, and as vehicles for social commentary.[7] As curator Jeff Rosenheim has observed, "His continuing interest in quoting the written language of the roadside (and translating abbreviated graphic forms into witty, self-contained pictures) was fueled by his literary ambitions and by his understanding that the essential 'stuff' of the contemporary world was to be found in these often unconscious symbols of modern life."[8] This fascination with the "stuff' of the contemporary world resides not only in Evans's photographs, but in the rusted signs, twisted metal from roadside accidents, and pieces of driftwood that he continuously scavenged (fig. 5). On at least one occasion actual found signs were even displayed in an exhibition alongside Evans's iconic, framed photographs, literally testing the bounds between object and image.

Evans's lifelong investigation into the impoverished cast-offs and debris of contemporary consumer culture is evident early on in photographs such as *Joe's Auto Graveyard, Near Bethlehem, Pennsylvania* (1936, fig. 6). This is a vision of an American landscape that once held Edenic promise, but is now populated by the ruins of the assembly-line.[9] In these earlier works, signs, signage, and material goods are in dialogue with larger, historically specific conditions that are understood through the framework of documentary composition. Evans later shifts his focus to an in-depth investigation in which he singles out the signs and markings themselves. Often made with an SX-70 Polaroid camera, with its square format and relentless proximity, Evans's

6.
Jerry L. Thompson, *The Last Years of Walker Evans: A First-hand Account* (New York: Thames & Hudson, 1997), 18.

8.
Jeff L. Rosenheim, *Walker Evans: Polaroids* (Zurich: Scalo, 2002), 8.

9.
As Thompson writes (ibid., 74), "Its low-key ironic grayness skewers landscape photography (as it was understood and praised in 1935) into the bargain: a gesture not of simple negation, but of critical purification, a refusal to accept shoddy goods passed off as culture, or jingoistic slogans paraded as truth."

later pictorial language of signs becomes abbreviated and formally abstracted. This coincided with a moment when the artist's body was becoming increasingly frail. Thus, the new camera became a kind of prosthetic device that both facilitated his formal explorations and allowed him to see and physically experience his material anew.

Reenergized by this new way of working, Evans became preoccupied with the creation of what he described as an "alphabet book."[10] Although it is possible that Evans had a rather straightforward publication in mind, one can't help but wonder what this unfinished project might have looked like. The hundreds of Polaroids that he began taking in 1973, just two years before his death, not only depicted signs and crops of individual letters, but also close-ups of people's faces, lines, and arrows (fig. 7). It was as if he were mapping out a new way of relating to the world, and in turn a new visual-linguistic order made possible by the immediacy of the automatic technology of Polaroid with its mechanical whir and hum as the camera discharged the image and developed itself in plain view. One imagines that these other symbols, markings, and even bodies might have found their way into Evans's understanding of the letterform, providing an alternative to the limitations and inadequacies not just of proper names and words, but of the twenty-six letter alphabet itself.

[D]

The unfulfilled potential of Evans's alphabet book, which would have undoubtedly spun readers in symbolic circles, bears an affinity with filmmaker Hollis Frampton's groundbreaking opus, *Zorns Lemma* (1970). Frampton recounted how he was prompted to embark on the project through the tension he observed between the flat graphicness of the letterform when photographed and the three-dimensionality of the world.[11] In an effort to reduce the cognizance of a photographic illusion Frampton decided to switch from a static image to the time of cinema. The film, which is divided into three parts, introduces itself as a kind of educational tool. In the first scene, which Frampton describes as a "lesson," we hear a woman's voice reading couplets from the *Bay State Primer*, a colonial text used to teach children their ABCs. The second section of the film

10.
"He had an idea for an alphabet book: It was to be 9 × 12 inches in size and present a good picture of each letter. To help this project along we taped his letter pictures up on the walls of his bedroom in a line. A picture I made, probably in October, of that wall shows gaps and some duplications. There are lots of E's and W's." Ibid., 113.

11.
Hollis Frampton, Remarks, *The Hollis Frampton Odyssey* (2012; Criterion Collection, DVD).

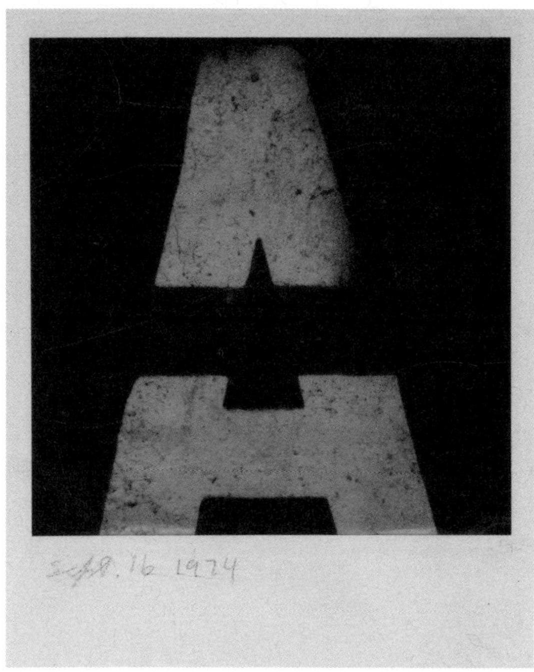

Fig. 7. Walker Evans, [Detail of Street Lettering], September 16, 1974, instant color print, 3 ⅛ × 3 ⅛ in. (7.9 × 7.9 cm), The Metropolitan Museum of Art, Purchase, Samuel J. Wagstaff Jr. Bequest and Lila Acheson Wallace Gift, 1994, 1994.245.23

begins with a quick parade of the twenty-four-letter Roman alphabet (lacking "J" and "U") and takes partial inspiration from a poem by the sculptor Carl Andre that lists words correlating to different letters.

However, for Frampton, the aim was not poetry, but instead a kind of systematic investigation. As a result, he decided that his footage of letters and words should be seen in a random order, which he surprisingly discovered in the most traditional of places: within the alphabet. Intent on divorcing himself from any subjective position or personal imprint, Frampton invited other filmmakers to provide footage that focused on words that began with each letter of the alphabet. These letters and words were most often recorded on the streets from found signage in locations that were not disclosed to Frampton, to avoid any possibility of the content informing his decisions. Scrolling silently in alphabetical order, this collapsed English alphabet reverberates back to the length of time that each image appears on the screen, twenty-four frames per second. Thus, the logic of the letter is enmeshed with the structure of celluloid.

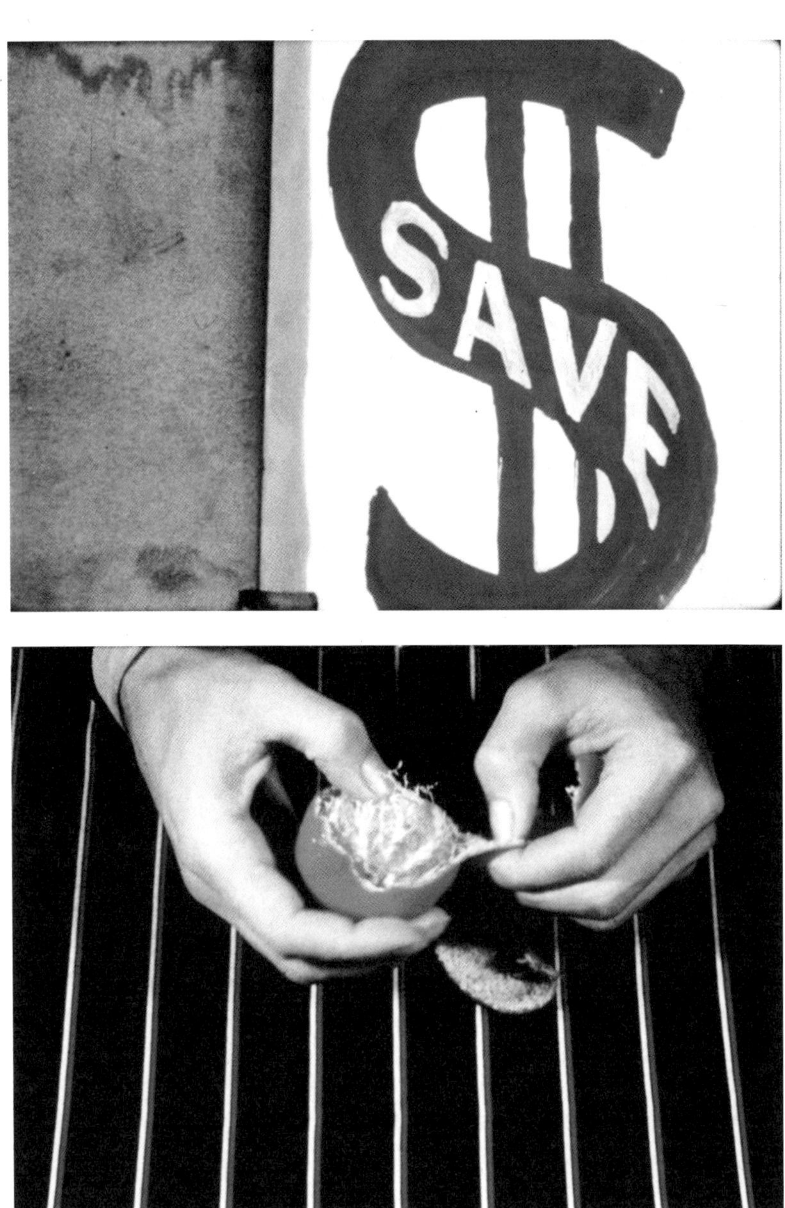

Fig. 8. Stills from Hollis Frampton, *Zorns Lemma*, 1970
16mm film, color, sound, 60 min.
Anthology Film Archives, New York

Bruce Jenkins has remarked how Frampton's work provokes in the viewer a simultaneous act of reading and seeing.[12] For, Frampton seems to be asking what happens when reading is divorced from literacy and it becomes something else altogether. In *Zorns Lemma* (fig. 8) the alphabet at first appears as a straightforward series of letters, which, in primer fashion, become words that start with those letters. However, as soon as we become accustomed to this rhythm, Frampton begins to replace individual letters with actions and scenes: the ocean at sunset, a man painting a wall, a crackling fire, hands flipping through a book, and so on. We begin to realize that we are now learning a new system, a different way to read. Before we know it, these other actions and images come to temporarily replace the letterforms, suggesting in a sense that the alphabet can be understood as a "found" piece of material as much as any old sign or piece of stock footage. As Frampton remarked, making small incisions can in a Borgesian sense have the effect of implying a whole new universe.[13]

[E]

Rosler, Porter, Evans, and Frampton each invite us to think how the alphabetic "interface" might begin to offer up new modes of being and relating, mobilizing divergent energies and remappings that, I suggest, might also help us unpack Shannon Ebner's artistic project. Since 2007 Ebner has embarked on a series of publications of her photographic letterforms as images, poems, grids, landscapes, and test patterns. Spread across time and differing in format, these books may be read together or as individual "stanzas" extracted from a larger body of text. Yet because of the extended periods of time between production, publication, and distribution, they also sit outside of a linear experience of the written word. Rather than provide a continuous experience of reading, they are instead traversed by a sense of delay and feedback. In this, her latest book, *Auto Body Collision*, words move rhythmically across the page and then suddenly accelerate to an up-and-down motion until a reader is thrust into the abstracted forms of Ebner's visual lexicon. On the page, the camera collides with the matter of the world, but it also reorients the way we read it. In Ebner's photographs and sculptures, "signs" inevitably play with and loop back to the role of signification, but they also disrupt

12.
See Bruce Jenkins, *Zorns Lemma*, liner notes to *The Hollis Frampton Odyssey* (2012; Criterion Collection, DVD), 20–22.

13.
Hollis Frampton, Remarks, *The Hollis Frampton Odyssey* (2012; Criterion Collection, DVD).

it, simultaneously giving us direction—as in *Traffic Control Device* (2014, pp. 4–5)—and in an absurd gesture, pointing us nowhere in particular. In *Service Club Signs Verso* (2014), for example, we see a cluster of geometric forms, the back side of signs, whose shapes seem familiar, but we can't say for sure (pp. 222–23). Mounted on the twisted wire of a chain-link fence that allows the viewer to see the trees beyond, the signs construct a scene of nature glimpsed through the gridded precision of the machine and the societal structures that are meant to keep us in check.

One key to this linguistic reordering might be located in a photograph from 2006 in which Ebner installed a box in the desert filled with letters made from cardboard and at bodily scale, which were initially produced for her *Dead Democracy Letters* series as a form of protest (fig. 9). The lid to the box is propped open, and in rough-hewn graffiti is scrawled "SCULPTURES INVOLUNTAIRES," a reference to Brassaï's involuntary sculptures in which he took everyday objects and made them strange through the act of photography. Here, Ebner not only displays her sculptural letterforms as a kit of parts to be stacked, hung, rearranged, and composed, but she proposes them as a new kind of found material. The letters form an alphabet of resistance, but they are also functional (fig. 10). As Ebner has noted, there are several multiples in her letter set, and the initial group included more vowels than consonants due to the necessity of the language used in her outdoor setups. Additional letters were produced as old ones were used and retired.[14] Although the alphabetic set was eventually completed and stored away in its container, the potential remains for the individual characters to be endlessly reconfigured and put in motion through the act of photography.

For Ebner, the conventional letterforms—even when made heavy and rough using the cinderblocks she has favored in other alphabetic experiments—are as important as the stops, starts, dots, and dashes that punctuate her work. As Ebner has previously remarked about her interest in the asterisk, "You could easily say that I have become obsessed with this graphic symbol, not only because of the beauty of its form but also because it is the symbol for elsewhere. It literally redirects you, and as a reader it continually repositions or

14.
Ebner, in e-mail exchange with the author, May 28, 2015.

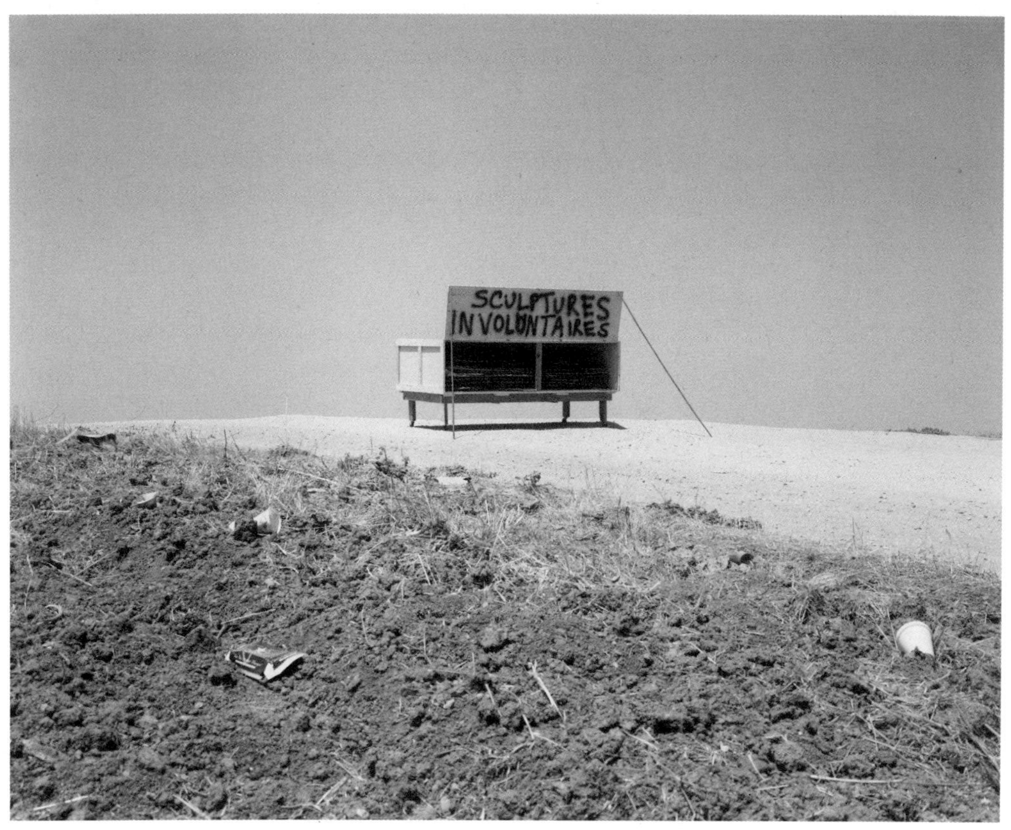

Fig. 9. Shannon Ebner, *Sculptures Involuntaires*, 2006
Chromogenic print mounted on cintra, 53 × 66 ¾ in. (134.6 × 169.5 cm)
Courtesy of the artist and Wallspace Gallery, New York

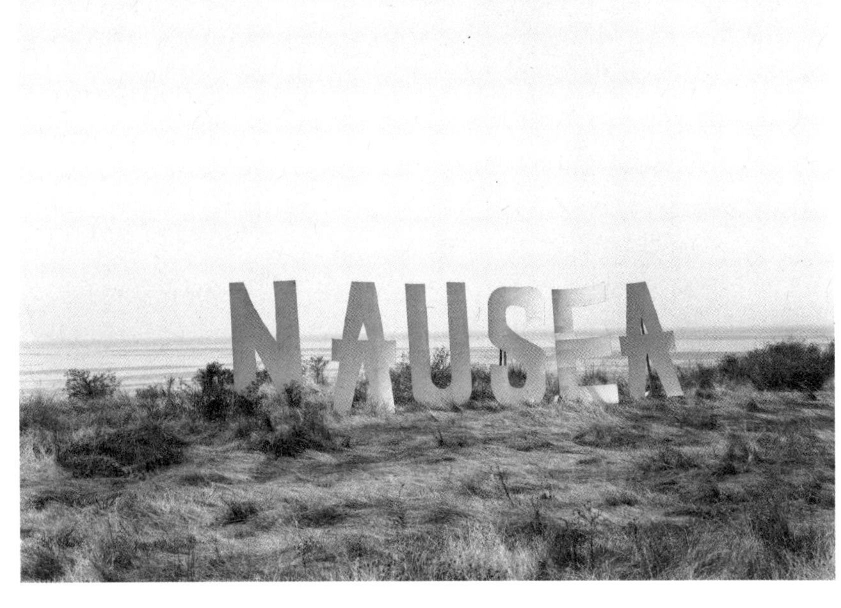

Fig. 10. Shannon Ebner, *USA*, 2004
Chromogenic print, 32 × 40 ½ in. (81.3 × 102.9 cm)
Courtesy of the artist and Wallspace Gallery, New York

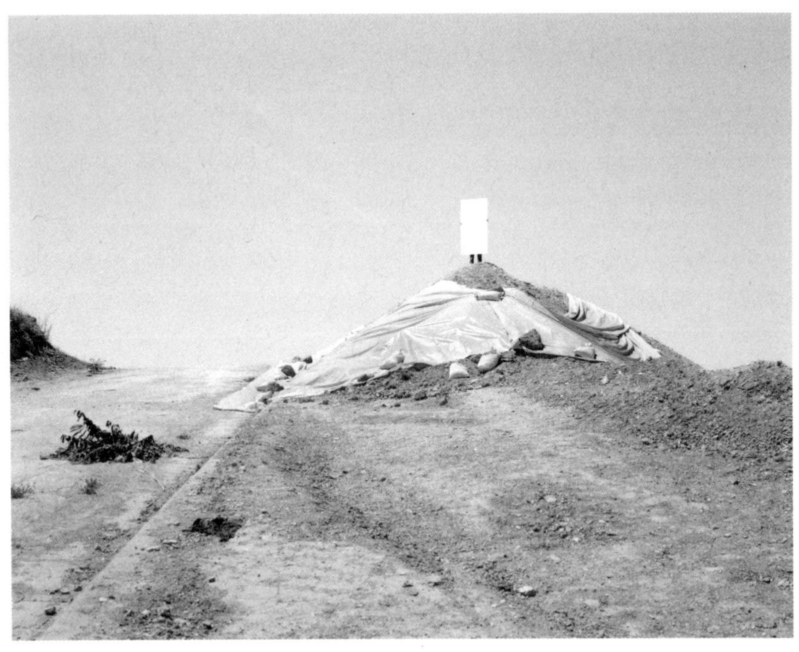

Fig. 11. Shannon Ebner, *Untitled Blank No. 1*, 2008
Chromogenic print, 31 × 40 in. (78.74 × 101.6 cm)
Courtesy of the artist and Wallspace Gallery, New York

reorients you."[15] This "elsewhere" also manifests itself
in Ebner's occasional refusal of language, such as in
Untitled Blank No. 1 (2008, fig. 11), in which the box of
letters in the landscape has been replaced by a literal
blank—potentially the backside of a sign or an empty
screen—with a body barely visible, holding it aloft.
These negatives or pauses also correspond to the sculptural counterforms Ebner produces from the interior
spaces of letters. One imagines them as cast-offs, or the
leftovers from when the artist first produced her original
letter sculptures. Also made from the same poor material, these recycled forms are not readable in the same
way as their alphabetic siblings. Instead, they more
closely resemble the black outlines of instruments and
tools on the pegboard seen in Ebner's 2013 photograph
Instrumentals (pp. 88–89), as shadows and holes, even as
a strange kind of punctuation or proto-alphabet.

In Ebner's "instruments" we see an alphabet, even in
its absence, as a form and material that has the power to
provoke, if not disrupt, the system of signs determined
by the hegemonic conditions inscribed in everyday
language. For Bern Porter, this system was emblem-
atized by the atomic weapons that he himself helped
to create, sparking a lifelong quest to infuse the poetic
into the technological and to liberate the very basis of
language from the mechanisms of consumerism and
warfare. For Evans, as his own body was becoming less
reliable, his classic compositions turned instead into a
kind of poetic stutter that is both manifest in his speech
and in his "prosthetic" Polaroids, which take on the
letter as a material thing—an abstraction of the break-
down of both syntax and the physical body. Left unresolved, its energy is seen again in the work of Hollis
Frampton, for whom the ultimate system and structure
of the letter pointed back to a notion of the found, the
filmic, and of bodily experience. Yet if in these prev-
ious examples language was reshuffled and reframed,
for Rosler the alphabet is employed—and embodied—
above all as a tool to expose not only the space of
domestic oppression, but the exploitative potential of
any syntactic descriptive system.

To begin to think of the synergy between Ebner's
mature work—which we might trace back to her own
disgust with the onset of the Iraq War in 2003—
as tapping into the unfulfilled potential that still

15.
Shannon Ebner,
"500 Words," March
5, 2009, artforum.
com, http://artfo-
rum.com/words/
id=22213.

resides in these artistic projects is to imagine how one might merge the syncopation of linguistic punctuation with the precise, and pernicious, cut of Roland Barthes's photographic *punctum*. In Ebner's video *Dear Reader* (2013), she addresses her viewers/readers directly by describing an image of an "electric comma" that will disrupt the cohesion of what Vilém Flusser called the "photographic universe."[16] Rather than depict a closed graphical system, in Ebner's work the alphabet is reclaimed as a tangible, physical thing whose material and linguistic potential are made legible and possible through the very confrontation of the camera with the found material of the letterform. This is indeed an alternative alphabet and a "counter" form to be used; it is an ABCs in which the letter and the body is recast—to recall Rosler—as a semiotics of collision.

16.
Vilém Flusser, *Towards a Philosophy of Photography*, trans. Anthony Mathews (London: Reaktion, 2000).

Mark Owens

A Note on the Type

J. G. Ballard's 1974 novel *Concrete Island* culminates in a scene of writing. Speeding along the M4 outside London, architect Robert Maitland crashes his Jaguar through a guardrail and into a vast triangle of waste ground beneath an intersection of overpasses, finding himself injured and unable to climb the steep embankments to rescue. As night falls he manages to ignite the engine of the mangled Jag with the car's cigarette lighter, but the brief, intense blaze fails to halt the rush of traffic overhead. Left to sleep in the charred hulk of the automobile, Maitland awakens to notice a retaining wall across the island: "The rain-washed concrete shone brightly in the sunlight like an empty notice-board. A message scrawled across it in three-feet-high letters would be legible to drivers on the motorway."[1] Desperately in need of writing instruments, he harvests the blackened, burnt rubber terminals from the engine's distributor caps, using them to mark out "in wavering letters" on the concrete: "HELP INJURED DRIVER CALL POLICE."

Soon, storm clouds gather and it begins to pour, and Maitland is forced to take cover, fashioning a crude shelter in the crumbling remnants of a basement doorway. Bruised and feverish, he gazes down:

A small printing shop had once been here, and a few copper-backed letterpress blocks lay around his feet. Maitland picked one up and examined the cloudy figures of a dark-suited man and a white-haired woman. As he listened to the rain he thought of his parents' divorce; the uncertainties of this period, when he was eight years old, seemed to be replicated in the negative image on the letterpress plate, in the reverse tones of this unknown man and woman.[2]

It is a brief, reflective moment, and when Maitland emerges following the storm he notices that the letters of his hand-scrawled message have been "reduced to black smudges." Delirious with fever, he finds that "the rounded smears were exactly those of a wind-shield wiper," and wonders: "Was he still trapped inside his car? Was the entire island an extension of the Jaguar, its windshield and windows transformed by his delirium into these embankments? Perhaps the windshield wipers had jammed... and were tracing some incoherent message on the steaming glass."[3]

This scene of writing and erasure, interrupted by the interlude in the basement print shop, traces the contours of western typographic history—from the marks made by the human hand and the mechanical reproduction of text and image made possible by the printing press, to a vision of an automated, machinic writing that exceeds both human agency and comprehension. So too, the contraction of the island in Maitland's mind to the space of the crashed Jaguar is mirrored by its expansion in Ballard's narrative to encompass the recent history of Great Britain: as he explores the overgrown rubble Maitland discovers the remains of a churchyard, Edwardian houses, an air-raid shelter, and a postwar cinema. Similarly, the shattered body of the Jaguar echoes Maitland's own, just as the inhabitants he soon encounters—a radical hippie dropout named Jane Sheppard and a brutish former acrobat known only as Proctor—double his riven psyche. The scene itself is doubled, too, when Maitland attempts to trick a reluctant Proctor into spelling out a rescue message on the retaining wall under the pretense of teaching him to write his own name: "Already the wavering letters of his first alphabet had become strong and well-formed. Using both hands he

struck at the concrete slope, slashing his A's and X's side by side." Maitland traces out words for Proctor to copy, but soon enthusiasm gets the best of him and he begins to mix up the letters "into an indecipherable mass," eventually rubbing out the message and refusing to go on.[4]

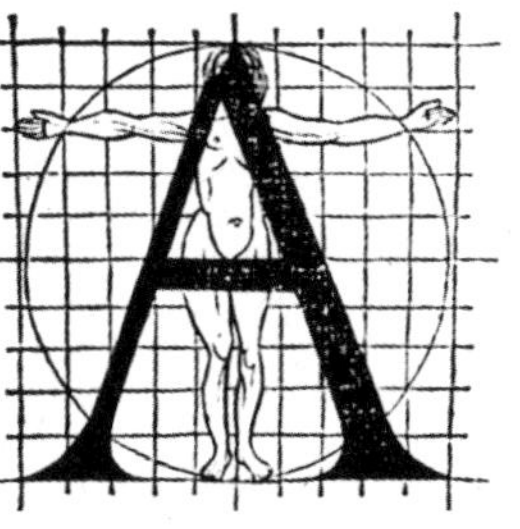

From Geoffroy Tory, *Champ Fleury*, 1529

The failure of Maitland's writing lesson, read off against the earlier episode in the ruins of the printshop, foregrounds what remains "uncertain" and "indecipherable" in the mechanization of human language. For, the writing lesson is the lynchpin of all western typography. Beginning in the fifteenth century, humanist handwriting, secured through a pedagogy of imitation and a disciplining of the body, transformed the hand into a writing machine.[5] While lowercase roman letters emerged from this prosthetic pen-in-hand imitating the "litterae antiquae" of Carolingian manuscripts, capitals traced their origins to the letters engraved on classical roman monuments, the work of stone carvers wielding the simple machines of hammer and chisel. Geoffroy Tory's 1529 *Champ Fleury* was one of a

259

number of Renaissance treatises that subsequently sought to delineate the proportions of the ideal Roman capital "according to the human body and face," thus submitting both typography and the body to the logic of geometry and the instrumentality of the grid, compass, and rule. With the invention of the printing press the humanist's bicameral script was further adapted to mechanical reproduction through the cutting of punches and the casting of molds, a process that largely remained unchanged until the end of the nineteenth century, giving rise to the digitized roman fonts we use today.

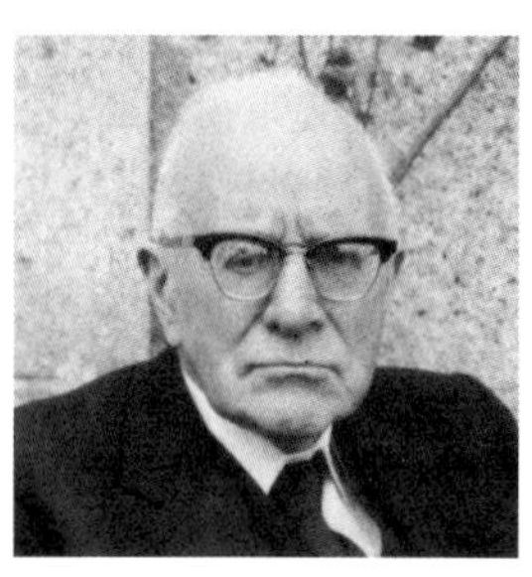

In what follows I thus want to use Ballard's narrative to reflect on one of the more curious episodes in recent typographic history—the controversy surrounding the creation of Times New Roman, perhaps the most ubiquitous of all typefaces. So the story goes, in 1929 an advertising request by *The Times* of London prompted a tirade against the paper's outdated typography by Stanley Morison, imminent British typographer, type historian, and advisor to the Monotype Corporation, leading to his appointment as "typographical advisor" to William Lints-Smith, the manager of *The Times*.[6] A series of trials followed in which sample pages of the paper were set in a variety of existing faces, but Morison was dissatisfied and decided that a new, supremely legible, economical, modern, and decidedly English typeface was needed. A special committee was convened, and at a meeting on January 28, 1931, two approaches were approved: a thickened version of Eric Gill's Perpetua, and a "modernized Plantin."

Focusing his energies on this second option, according to Morison he "excogitated" the design of Times New Roman, "pencilled the original set of drawings, and handed them to Victor Lardent, a draughtsman in the publicity department of Printing House Square [where *The Times* was located] whom he considered capable of producing an unusually firm and lean line."[7] It was from these finished drawings that the final metal punches, in both text and titling sizes, were cut by Monotype after a large number of revisions and refinements. In the interim the matter of the change of the paper's masthead to an all-caps roman was resolved, and thus, on October 3, 1932, Times New Roman debuted in the pages of *The Times* to universal acclaim. Released for general use the following year, it has become in subsequent decades one of the most recognizable typefaces of all time.

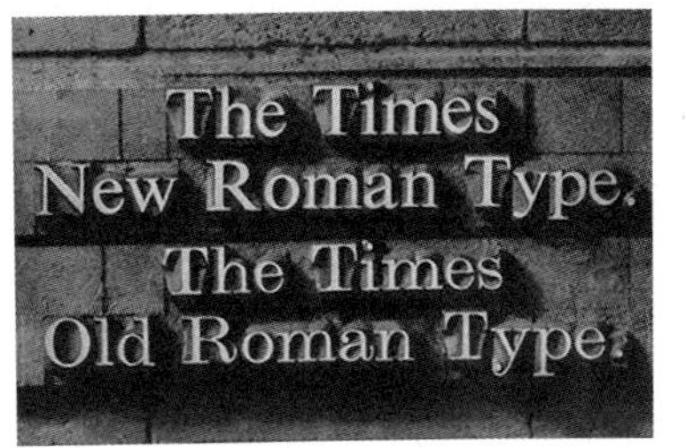

However, with Morison's death in 1967 his biographers almost immediately began to identify inconsistencies in the official account of his role in the design of Times New Roman.[8] Although he could render hand-drawn "comps" for the creation of layouts, Morison was not a draftsman, and it was unlikely that he had "pencilled" the forms and given them to Lardent to redraw. Later, in *Printing The Times* (1954), Morison recounted a decision "to modify the normal Plantin," suggesting that existing metal types had been used as a starting point. When questioned in January 1968 Victor Lardent was unable to recall specifics, but did tell biographer James Moran unequivocally that Morison had *not* given him any drawings, but instead had "handed him a photographic copy of a page from a book printed by Plantin to use as a basis."[9]

The precise nature of this "photographic copy" has subsequently become the source of considerable speculation. Was it merely a type specimen of Monotype Plantin? Or perhaps it was a photographic reproduction of a much older, original page of Robert Granjon's Gros Cicero type, first cut in the sixteenth century, or a later impression of it, as typographer Walter Tracy has argued?[10] Measurements from the first metal types for Times New Roman bear a close mathematical resemblance to those for Monotype Plantin, and the speed with which the initial designs were completed would suggest some form of preexisting model, since Renaissance print samples provide only rough outlines to work from, requiring considerable, time-consuming refinement and recasting.[11]

Detail from *The Monotype Recorder* 21 (1932)

n fait à Granjon
ie grande lettre f
de matrices, deux
Augustín italique

Sample impression of Robert Granjon's Gros Cicero type

Still, this ur-form of Times New Roman—and who was really responsible for it— has remained elusive, and Morison's own remarks in a 1937 letter to the American type historian D. B. Updike only served to cloud the issue: "It is my one effort at designing a fount. I wish it could be redesigned, but it seems to be doing its job day by day in *The Times*. It has the merit of looking as if it had not been

261

designed by anyone in particular."[12] Who designed Times
New Roman, then? Morison
himself does not seem entirely
sure, and the doublings that
trouble the accounts of its
creation would seem to require
a lost original of uncertain
agency, a "photographic copy"
whose adaptation would
appear to be designed by no
one in particular. Indeed,
Tracy, in his summary assess-
ment of Times New Roman
concludes that its "chief
defect" lies in that it "lacks
the insignia of true creation,"
precisely what Morison finds
to recommend it.[13]

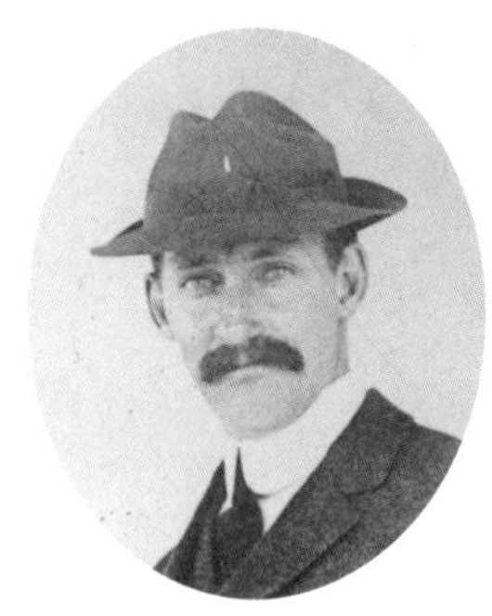

William
Starling
Burgess,
1878–1947,
in an
undated
portrait

Fast-forward to 1994, when
the question of the origin of
Times New Roman gained
new traction thanks to Mike
Parker, a former director at
Linotype and co-founder of
Bitstream, one of the first
digital type foundries. In his
article "W. Starling Burgess:
Type Designer?" in the journal
Printing History Parker made
the radical suggestion that the
original drawings for the font
were in fact created in the early
1900s by the American yacht
designer, aviation pioneer,
and engineer William Starling

Burgess.[14] Parker described
the "discovery of an ancient
set of pattern letters" among
"the remnants of the Lanston
Monotype Machine Company
of Philadelphia," which
had been purchased by the
Canadian printer and typographer Gerald Giampa, and
documentation tying the
designs, designated Series 54,
to Burgess.

Although Giampa, citing
a vague "bond of confi-
dentiality," had withdrawn
access to the archive, Parker
explained that he had uncov-
ered evidence to corroborate
a rumor that had circulated
in the "drawing office at
Mergenthaler Linotype in the
1960s and '70s" that "Times
Roman had been designed by a
naval architect in Philadelphia
who had committed suicide."[15]
What followed was a highly
detailed set of speculations
relying heavily on Burgess's
biography and second-hand
information suggesting that
in 1904 Burgess had drawn
and commissioned Series 54
from Lanston Monotype, the
American counterpart to the
British Monotype Corporation
for use by his design firm.
Although work on the face
had already begun, Burgess,
in Parker's account, was soon
distracted by a new-found
interest in aviation and, following a 1918 fire in his Boston
offices, found himself unable
to pay for the completion of
the project, and Series 54
was shelved.

According to Parker, in 1923 Lanston then attempted to sell Series 54 to a fledgling *Time* magazine under the name Time 54, even going so far as to create a trial setting and masthead design, but its development was also never completed.

TIME
TIME

And so it only remained for the drawings and pattern letters to make their way, in 1931, from Philadelphia to the Monotype Works in Salfords outside London and into the hands of Stanley Morison, then out of his depth and struggling with the design of a "modernized Plantin" for *The Times*.

Parker provides neither reproductions of the original drawings he claims to have seen, nor any independent evidence. Instead, he relies on an elaborate set of formal comparisons using digitized versions of Monotype Plantin, Lanston Series 54, the Lardent drawings, and Monotype Times New Roman alongside photographs of what he claims are original brass Lanston pattern letters, a capital "B" and lowercase "f" stamped twice in their lower left corners with the numerals 54 and 362, Monotype's series numbers for both Lanston 54 and Times New Roman.

It was a bold claim, made on the scantest of evidence, which occasioned a reply in the pages of *Printing History* by four respected figures in the field: attorney and printer Harold Berliner, Morison biographer Nicolas Barker, type designer Jim Rimmer, and president of the Printing Historical Society John Dreyfus.[16]

In a measured, if rather blistering, rebuttal the four respondents dismantled Parker's argument, sweeping aside its fog of irrelevant details, remaining careful to avoid attributing "dubious motives" to Parker himself. Berliner finds no trace of the "bond of confidentiality" that Giampa cited as the reason for his withdrawal of the archive, nor any drawings marked Series 54 in the Lanston holdings at the Smithsonian Institution in Washington, DC.

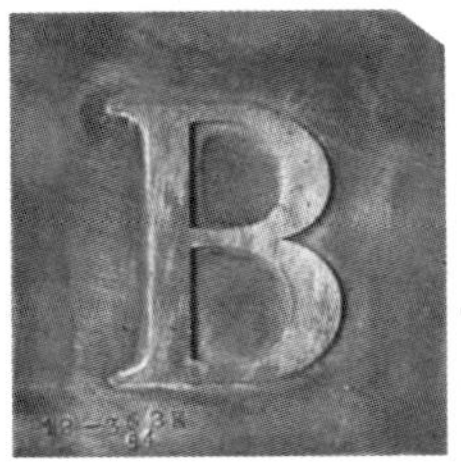

Double-stamped Lanston Series 54 pattern letter reproduced by Parker

Barker, in turn, questions Parker's appeal to digitized versions of typefaces and, after close scrutiny of the test setting of Time 54 and the trial *Time* masthead reproduced in Parker's essay, shows that neither could have been produced as early as he claims.

263

Reviewing the accepted pre-history of Times New Roman and citing extant memos from the Monotype type drawing office in 1931, Barker concludes that the "photographic copy" handed to Lardent by Morison must have been an image of a later printing of Granjon's Gros Cicero type, likely Max Roose's *Index Characterum Architypographiae* of 1905.[17] The proof, he argues, is the appearance of the lowercase "a" in the final design, a remnant of the substitution of an "a" from another font when Granjon's original types were acquired by the Plantin-Moretus Museum in Antwerp and used to print Roose's *Index*, which then served as the model for Times New Roman.[18]

Roman
Roman
Roman

Perhaps most damning, Barker further suggests that the photographs of the double-stamped pattern letters in fact depict patterns for Times New Roman from 1961, onto which the numerals "54" had been added after the fact.[19] Rimmer, quoted at length in a letter to Dreyfus, reveals that the fragmentary "Burgess Italic" that Parker also reproduced in his essay was in fact drawn by *him* at Giampa's

request to accompany a 1993 revival of Time 54, for which a "cloudy outline" and digital files were supplied. Moreover, Rimmer states that Giampa had also given him a set of punches identical to the "54" that appears on the double-stamped pattern letters.

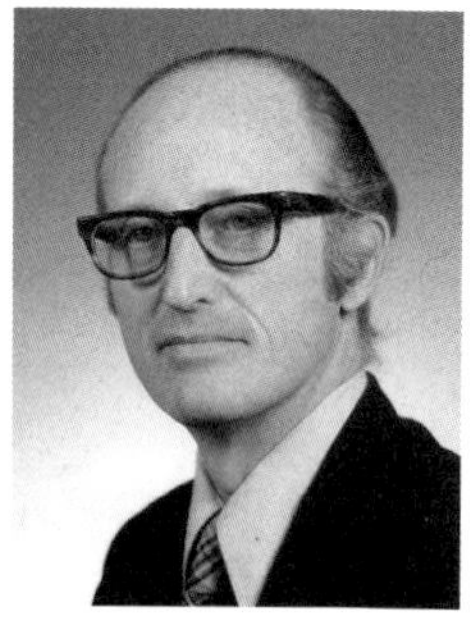

One might assume that these detailed counterarguments would have finally put Parker's claims to rest, but to the end of his life he never wavered. Instead, he proceeded to develop Giampa's "Burgess" into a full-fledged typeface in six weights, renamed Starling, which was commercially released in 2009. To accompany the release Parker's tale regarding the "true" origin of Times New Roman was largely taken as fact, and a number of press outlets picked up the story, including the *Financial Times*.[20] With Parker's death in 2014 his theory circulated once again, and today, no less an authority than Wikipedia includes a mention of Burgess in its entry on Times New Roman.[21] Nevertheless, a comprehensive biography of Burgess published in 2015 cites no "reference whatever in extant Burgess letters, note-books, autobiographical writings, or in his surviving library to typography or to the art and craft of type design." "Nor, finally," the author adds, "was Burgess, despite taking basic courses in mechanical drawing at Harvard, a proficient draftsman."[22]

So the question remains, who designed Times New Roman? Parker, a typographic expert and respected industry veteran, could hardly be described as a crank or a dupe. Giampa, meanwhile, who died in 2009, is a shadowy figure whose motives remain obscure—financial gain? character assassination? legitimate historical recovery? As recounted in the *Financial Times*, a 2000 flood destroyed any remaining evidence in the Lanston Monotype archive that Giampa had purchased, and supposed original documents reviewed by Parker in the Smithsonian in 1996 are reportedly contaminated and no longer accessible. A 1941 bomb blast near Monotype's London offices had also destroyed many of the original records concerning Morison's work on Times New Roman.[23] Still, surely an authority like Parker must have seem *something* that convinced him, and the persistence of the Burgess story and its grudging acceptance within design history points, at the very least, to an unresolved need to come to terms with its creation.

This detour into the gentlemanly world of typographic controversy is traversed by a complex series of doublings that locate the development of Times New Roman firmly within the "body machine complex" of the early twentieth century.[24] Naval architect, aviation pioneer, and later co-designer of the Dymaxion car with Buckminster Fuller, Burgess doubles Morison, authority on the mechanization of typography and a railroad enthusiast who rode on the footplate of a Gresley A1 Pacific locomotive all the way to Edinburgh and enthusiastically attended the departure of the high-speed Flying Scotsman on its first non-stop trip along the London and North Eastern Railway.[25]

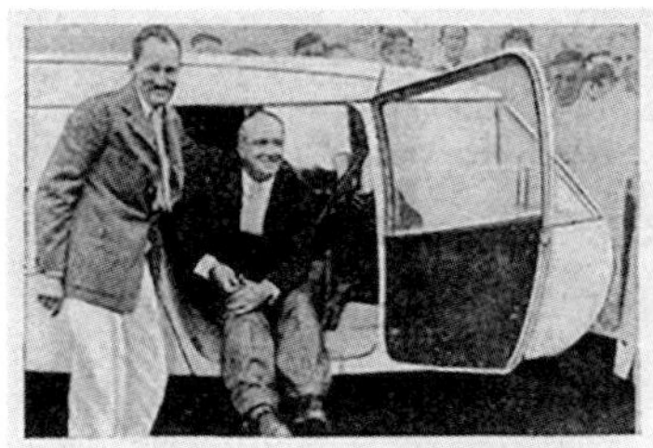

Burgess and Fuller in *Modern Mechanix Magazine*, October 1933

Like J. G. Ballard's Maitland behind the wheel of his Jaguar, both were men whose "intimacy with machines" is of a piece with a culture of locomotion in which agency is uncertain, and the human body, no less than the type body, is submitted to new disciplinary regimes—the timetable, machine work, and the grid—that are shadowed by the spectre of the automaton.[26]

In fact, in a promotional pamphlet published by *The Times* in conjunction with the debut of the new redesign of the paper Morison explained that the need for the new typeface was a respose to the dramatic changes in reading habits occasioned by the acceleration of human transport:

It is evident that there must be changes in typography as long as our social habits are open to variation. When it was founded, The Times was largely read in coffeehouses; in the nineteenth century it came to be read in trains; to-day it is largely read in cars and airliners. Reading habits, dependent on social habits, will not remain constant. Neither must newspaper typography remain constant.[27]

Who better, then, to have designed Times New Roman than an architect-engineer and future car designer? Or perhaps "Burgess" might simply stand for the uncertainties that obtain in the collision of bodies and technologies whose contours the writing scenes in Ballard's *Concrete Island* circumscribe, and which lie at the very heart of typographic history, from the humanist pen and the printing press straight through to the TextEdit software that this essay is being written in—the "no one in particular" whose authorship Morison takes as "the chief merit" of Times New Roman.

By way of conclusion this question of agency suggests one more doubling, and a silence that thus far marks a glaring absence from any account of Stanley Morison: the figure of Beatrice Warde.[28]

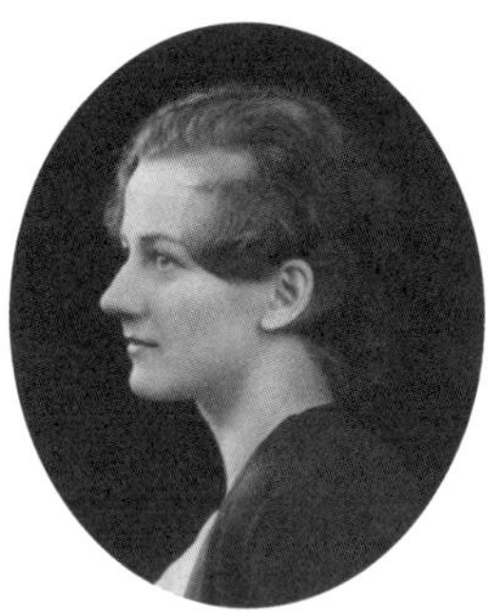

Former librarian for ATC, the American Type Founders Company, and ex-wife of Frederic Warde, director of printing at Princeton University, Beatrice Warde joined the Monotype Corporation in London in 1927 as editor of its house journal, *The Monotype Recorder*, and was soon promoted to head of publicity, a position she held until her retirement in 1960. Warde's initial appointment had come thanks to an article she had written for the typographic journal that Morison edited, *The Fleuron*, in which she had unraveled the question of the origins of the typeface Garamond, having tracked down the original sixteenth-century punches in Europe. It was an impressive piece of typographic detective work, published by Warde anonymously under the pseudonym Paul Beaujon. Monotype, it was said, had been shocked when a woman arrived to take the job.

Warde and Morison would become lifelong friends and close colleagues, and it was to her that he sent a cable announcing the committee's approval of the decision to change the masthead of *The Times*, the final element in the paper's conversion to Times New Roman: "DIRECTORS AND ALL EDITORIAL EMINENTISSIMI UNANIMOUS ROMAN HEADING."[29] Morison, who famously disdained the use of first names, addressed his letters to Warde at this time "Dear P," and it was thus as Paul Beaujon—a male moniker that seems to have been something between an open secret, an inside joke, and a mark of respect—that Beatrice Warde came to join the fraternity of men who led the typographic renaissance that began after World War I, although she was still unable to attend meetings of the Double Crown Club.

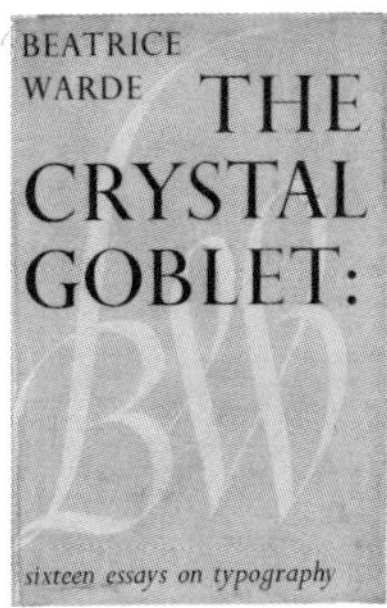

Warde's other great contribution to the theory of typography is the essay "The Crystal Goblet, or Printing Should be Invisible," first delivered as a lecture in 1930 and still read by every undergraduate design student, in which she advocates for the transparent quality of good typography. The essay could easily serve as a brief for Times New Roman, now so commonplace that one contemporary commentator has stated that, "To look at Times New Roman is to gaze into the void."[30]

Recalling the "negative image" of the "unknown man and woman" that occasions Robert Maitland's reverie in the ruined printshop in *Concrete Island*, it is tempting to imagine what Beatrice Warde's role in the development of Times New Roman might have been, and the status of the still-elusive "photographic copy" that Lardent claims to have been handed by Morison. As an accomplished type scholar and researcher Warde most certainly knew her way around an archive, and as an American and former librarian at ATC she had industry connections in the States. Her ex-husband, Frederic, we know, attended the Lanston Monotype School in Philadelphia to learn how to work the machinery.[31] As a publicist at Monotype, Warde would also, no doubt, have had regular dealings with the publicity department at *The Times*, and could have recommended Victor Lardent—whose primary occupation was the drafting of advertisements—for his "unusually firm and lean line."

Beatrice Warde, *The Crystal Goblet: Sixteen Essays on Typography*, 1955

Could "Paul Beaujon"—that doubly-gendered vanishing mediator—have been the source of the "photographic copy" that served as the model for Times New Roman? That, we cannot know. After all, invisibility, Warde insisted, is the sign of good typography, just as every type designer knows that the spaces between letters—the counterforms— are just as important as the marks on the page. So too, the questions and doublings that persist around the design of Times New Roman point to the collision of bodies and technologies that shape the development of modern letter- forms—and the lapses and failures that attend them.

Auto Body Collision is typeset in Helvetica Autospaced and Monotype Times New Roman Seven. The work reproduced incorporates letterforms includ- ing Times New Roman and Arial Condensed Light.

1 J. G. Ballard, *Concrete Island* (New York: Farrar, Straus and Giroux, 1974), 62.

2 Ibid., 65.

3 Ibid., 67.

4 Ibid., 151–52.

5 See Jonathan Goldberg, *Writing Matter: From the Hands of the English Renaissance* (Stanford: Stanford University Press, 1990).

6 For the account that follows see James Moran, *Stanley Morison: His Typographic Achievement* (New York: Hastings House Publishers, 1971), 123–38; Nicolas Barker, *Stanley Morison* (London: Macmillan, 1972), 268–71, 283–302; and Stanley Morison, *A Tally of Types* (Boston: David R. Godine, 1999), 105–9.

7 Morison, *A Tally of Types*, 105.

8 The uncertainties regarding Morison's version of events described here relies on the discussion in Walter Tracy, *Letters of Credit: A View of Type Design* (Boston: David R. Godine, 2003), 194–210.

9 Moran, *Stanley Morison*, 128. Here, Moran is paraphrasing Lardent.

10 Tracy, *Letters of Credit*, 196–202.

11 Ibid., 196–97.

12 David McKitterick, ed., *Stanley Morison and D. B. Updike: Selected Correspondence* (New York: The Moretus Press, 1979), 185.

13 Tracy, *Letters of Credit*, 210.

14 Mike Parker, "W. Starling Burgess: Type Designer?," *Printing History* 16, nos. 1–2 (1994): 52–87.

15 Ibid., 52.

16 Harold Berliner, Nicolas Barker, Jim Rimmer, and John Dreyfus, "Starling Burgess, No Type Designer," *Printing History* 19, no. 1 (1998): 3–22.

17 Ibid., 15.

18 See http://typophile.com/node/53050 and Hendrik D. L. Vervliet, *The Paleotypography of the French Renaissance: Selected Papers in Sixteenth-Century Typefaces* (Leiden and Boston: Brill, 2008), 226–27.

19 Berliner et al., "Starling Burgess, No Type Designer," 18.

20 Joel Alas, "The History of the Times New Roman Typeface," *The Financial Times*, August 1, 2009, http://www.ft.com/cms/s/0/a2fa033e-7ca1-11de-a7bf-00144feabdc0.html#axzz3XJ4b-KQdT.

21 Wikipedia, http://en.wikipedia.org/wiki/Times_New_Roman.

22 Llewelllyn Howland III, *No Ordinary Being: W. Starling Burgess: Inventor, Naval Architect, Poet, Aviation Pioneer, and Master of American Design* (Jaffrey, NH: David R. Godine, 2015), 65.

23 Alas, "The History of Times New Roman Typeface."

24 See Mark Seltzer, *Bodies and Machines* (New York: Routledge, 1992).

25 Barker, *Stanley Morison*, 268, 295.

26 Seltzer, *Bodies and Machines*, 17–18.

27 Stanley Morison, *Printing The Times: A Record of the Changes Introduced in the Issue for October 3, 1932* (London: The Times of London, 1932).

28 The historical account that follows relies on Simon Loxley, "The Doves and the Serpent: Stanley Morison and the Wardes," in *Type: The Secret History of Letters* (London and New York: I. B. Tauris & Co. Ltd, 2004), 123–35.

29 Barker, *Stanley Morison*, 296.

30 Matthew Butterick, *Typography for Lawyers* (Houston: Jones McClure Publishing, 2010).

31 Loxley, "The Doves and the Serpent," 126.

Special Note of Thanks

Shannon Ebner: Auto Body Collision is produced
under the auspices of Carnegie Museum of Art's
Hillman Photography Initiative, a living laboratory
for exploring the rapidly shifting field of photography and its impact in the world. This important
experimental program would not have been possible
without the generosity of the William T. Hillman
and Henry L. Hillman Foundations. We are especially grateful to Bill Hillman, who has championed
our efforts to establish the Initiative as a center for
innovative thinking about the photographic image.
His dedication and support have been indispensable.

The success of the Initiative thus far is due in no
small part to projects such as this book, which
makes a significant contribution to the field. Our
sincere thanks go to the artist, Shannon Ebner,
without whom there would be no publication. It is
a privilege to share her work with the world. We are
also very grateful to the project co-curators Tina
Kukielski and Alex Klein for their insightful essays,
and to Mark Owens for his text and thoughtful
design. At CMOA, thanks to Katie Reilly, director
of publications, graphics, and photographic services;
Divya Rao Heffley, program manager of the
Hillman Photography Initiative; Matthew Newton,
associate editor; and Laurel Mitchell, manager of
rights and reproductions and photographic services.

Lynn Zelevansky
The Henry J. Heinz II Director
Carnegie Museum of Art

Illustration Credits

Unless otherwise noted, all images are © Shannon Ebner, Courtesy of the artist and Wallspace Gallery, New York.

The following credits apply to all images for which separate acknowledgment is due. Many of the images in this publication are protected by copyright and may not be available for further reproduction without permission of the copyright holder. Every reasonable attempt has been made to identify owners of copyright. Errors or omissions will be corrected in subsequent editions.

Kukielski
Fig. 1: Claude E. Shannon, "A Mathematical Theory of Communication," originally printed in *The Bell System Technical Journal* 27 (July 1948): 379–423, and (October 1948): 623–56; Fig. 2: Images courtesy of the artist and Murray Guy, New York; Fig. 6: Augusto de Campos, "sem um numero," in *Noigandres* 4 (1958); Fig. 8: From *Tom Tit Tot* © 2014 by Susan Howe, reproduced courtesy of the poet and the Grenfell Press; Fig. 9: © The Warburg Institute, London.

Klein
Fig. 1: Digital Image © Whitney Museum of American Art, N. Y.; Fig. 2: Courtesy of Electronic Arts Intermix (EAI), New York; Fig. 3: From Bern Porter, *I've Left: A Manifesto and a Testament of SCIence and ART(SCIART)* (New York: Something Else Press, 1971), Courtesy of Bern Porter Estate; Fig. 4: Courtesy of Bern Porter Estate; Fig. 5: Image courtesy of Jerry L. Thompson; Fig. 6: Image copyright © The Metropolitan Museum of Art. Image source: Art Resource, NY; Fig. 7: Image copyright © The Metropolitan Museum of Art. Image source: Art Resource, NY; Fig. 8: Courtesy of the Estate of Hollis Frampton and Anthology Film Archives, New York.

Owens
p. 260: From *Stanley Morison, 1889–1967: A Radio Portrait*, compiled by Nicolas Barker and Douglas Celverdon (Ipswich: W. S. Cowell Ltd, 1969); p. 261 left: *The Monotype Recorder* 21 (1932); p. 262: George Grantham Bain Collection, Library of Congress Prints and Photographs Division, LC-DIG-ggbain-15458; p. 263: From Mike Parker, "W. Starling Burgess: Type Designer?" *Printing History* 16, no. 1–2 (1994); p. 264 right: Courtesy of FontBureau; p. 265: *Modern Mechanix Magazine*, October 1933; p. 266: From Simon Loxley, "The Doves and the Serpent: Stanley Morison and the Wardes," in *Type: The Secret History of Letters* (London and New York: I. B. Tauris, 2004); p. 267: Cover of Beatrice Warde, *The Crystal Goblet: Sixteen Essays on Typography* (London: Sylvan, 1955).

Auto Body Collision
Shannon Ebner

Texts by Alex Klein, Tina Kukielski, and Mark Owens

Published by Carnegie Museum of Art
4400 Forbes Avenue
Pittsburgh, Pennsylvania
15213–4080
www.cmoa.org

Available through D.A.P./ Distributed Art Publishers
155 Sixth Avenue, 2nd Floor
New York, New York 10013
Tel.: (212) 627–1999
Fax.: (212) 627–9484
www.artbook.com

©2015 Carnegie Museum of Art, Carnegie Institute and Shannon Ebner

All rights reserved under pan-American copyright conventions. No part of this book may be reproduced, stored in a retrieval system, or transmitted in any form or by any means, electronic, mechanical, photocopying, recording, or otherwise, without permission in writing from Carnegie Museum of Art.

ISBN 978-0-88039-057-6

Library of Congress Cataloging-in-Publication Data

Auto body collision : Shannon Ebner / Texts by Alex Klein, Tina Kukielski, and Mark Owens.
    pages cm — (Orphaned Images)
  Includes bibliographical references and index.
   ISBN 978-0-88039-057-6 (pbk. : alk. paper) 1. Photography, Artistic. 2. Ebner, Shannon. I. Klein, Alex (Alex P.), 1978- II. Kukielski, Tina. III. Owens, Mark, 1971- IV. Ebner, Shannon. Photographs. Selections.
   TR655.A89 2015
   770–dc23

2015024028

This publication is a commission of *Orphaned Images*, a project within Carnegie Museum of Art's Hillman Photography Initiative, curated by Tina Kukielski and Alex Klein. *Orphaned Images* addresses questions raised within art practice by the increasingly widespread digital dissemination of photographs. As images are shared, manipulated, recirculated, and reused, they lose authorship, and become itinerant. Attentive to the shifting role of the photographic image in society, *Orphaned Images* explores the intersections and collisions of humans and technology in the contemporary world.

Designed by Mark Owens with Nilas Andersen

Edited by Katie Reilly and Matt Newton

Photo research by Laurel Mitchell

Printed by The Avery Group at Shapco Printing, Minneapolis

Support for the Hillman Photography Initiative is provided by the William T. Hillman Foundation and the Henry L. Hillman Foundation. General operating support for Carnegie Museum of Art is provided by The Heinz Endowments and Allegheny Regional Asset District. Carnegie Museum of Art receives state arts funding support through a grant from the Pennsylvania Council on the Arts, a state agency funded by the Commonwealth of Pennsylvania.

HILLMAN**PHOTOGRAPHY**INITIATIVE
CARNEGIE MUSEUM OF **ART**

www.nowseethis.org

The artist wishes to sincerely thank Lynn Zelevansky at Carnegie Museum of Art as well as Katie Reilly and the entire publications staff at the museum for their support of this artist book project.

Special thanks to Tina Kukielski and Alex Klein as well as Mark Owens and Nilas Anderson.

Thanks also to Math Bass, Victoria Brooks, Cameron Crone, Moyra Davey, Marten Elder, Chris McElrath and Alexandra Pacheco Garcia at Contact Lab, Anna Helm, Mackenzie Hoffman, Arthur Ou, Adam Putnam, Andrea Rossetti for the installation images from Rome and Milan, Erika Vogt, and Evan Calder Williams.

This book is the result of the following projects and excursions:

Auto Body Collision
March 18–June 27, 2014
Foundation Memmo
Palazzo Ruspoli, Rome

Black Box Collision A: Gasoline & Auto Electric
May 22–August 8, 2014
kaufmann repetto, Milan

Los Angeles Auto Show and Connected Car Expo
November 17–19, 2014
Los Angeles Convention Center

Thank you to Matt Mullican for permission to publish the photographs of his public artwork (pages 9, 77, 190) from the Los Angeles Convention Center Art Program, 1993 (Concourse Level 1).

Thank you to "text mechanic" Enrique Romero at Hopefully Reliable Restorations for the cover image.

Thanks to Cornel Windlin at lineto.com for permission to use his "A" typography on pages 12–23.

Special thanks to the creators and supporters of the Hillman Photography Initiative for their commitment to artistic freedom and experimentation.